Brief Therapy Inside Out
—Cognitive Therapy for Depression
Judith Beck, Ph.D.

Cognitive Therapy of Depression: Interview #1
—Patient with Hopelessness Problem
Demonstration of the Cognitive Therapy of Depression: Interview #1
—Patient with a Family Problem
Aaron T. Beck, M.D.

Beck & Beckの
認知行動療法ライブセッション
［解説］

日本語版監修・解説　古川壽亮
京都大学大学院医学研究科教授　健康増進・行動学分野

日本語字幕作成協力　伊藤実里
南山大学英語非常勤講師

医学書院

Disc 1
Authorized translation of the original English language edition, "Brief Therapy Inside Out —Cognitive Therapy for Depression" first published in the United States by Zeig, Tucker & Theisen, Inc., Phoenix
DVD Copyright © exactly as it appears in the original English language edition by arrangement with Paterson Marsh Ltd.
First Japanese edition 2008 by Igaku-Shoin Ltd., Tokyo
Disc 2
Authorized translation of the original English language edition, "Cognitive Therapy of Depression: Interview #1 — Patient with Hopelessness Problem" and "Demonstration of the Cognitive Therapy of Depression: Interview #1 — Patient with a Family Problem" first published in the United States by Beck Institute
DVD Copyright © Aaron T. Beck, M. D., 1977, 1979. All rights reserved.
First Japanese edition 2008 by Igaku-Shoin Ltd., Tokyo

DVD ＋ BOOK
Beck&Beckの認知行動療法ライブセッション

発　行	2008年9月15日　第1版第1刷©	
	2021年8月15日　第1版第3刷	

日本語版監修・解説　　古川壽亮
　　　　　　　　　　　ふるかわとしあき
発行者　　株式会社　医学書院
　　　　　代表取締役　金原　俊
　　　　　〒113-8719　東京都文京区本郷1-28-23
　　　　　電話　03-3817-5600（社内案内）

印刷・製本　アイワード

本書の複製権・翻訳権・上映権・譲渡権・貸与権・公衆送信権（送信可能化権を含む）は株式会社医学書院が保有します．

ISBN 978-4-260-00650-7

本書を無断で複製する行為（複写，スキャン，デジタルデータ化など）は，「私的使用のための複製」など著作権法上の限られた例外を除き禁じられています．大学，病院，診療所，企業などにおいて，業務上使用する目的（診療，研究活動を含む）で上記の行為を行うことは，その使用範囲が内部的であっても，私的使用には該当せず，違法です．また私的使用に該当する場合であっても，代行業者等の第三者に依頼して上記の行為を行うことは違法となります．

|JCOPY|〈出版者著作権管理機構　委託出版物〉
本書の無断複製は著作権法上での例外を除き禁じられています．複製される場合は，そのつど事前に，出版者著作権管理機構（電話 03-5244-5088，FAX 03-5244-5089，info@jcopy.or.jp）の許諾を得てください．

はじめに

　本DVDは，認知療法の創始者Aaron T. Beck，およびその実娘にして認知療法のメッカBeck Instituteの所長であるJudith Beckによって，実際の患者を対象に行われた初回セッションを含む貴重な映像である．

　Judith Beckによるセッションは，約50分にわたり本当の患者に対して行われた認知行動療法の典型的なセッションのデモンストレーションであるが，加えてその前後にJudith Beck本人による詳しい解説が録画されている(Disc 1)．Aaron T. Beckによって行われた2つの症例(1人は現実の患者で，もう1人は模擬患者であるらしいが，ほとんど区別がつかない)の初回セッションは，1970年代の非常に貴重な映像で，若き日のAaron T. Beckが30年の月日を経ても変わらぬ認知行動療法の本質を鮮やかにデモンストレートしてくれている(Disc 2)．

　21世紀に入り，ようやく日本でも認知行動療法がメンタルヘルス関連の広い場面で熱い注目を集めるようになってきた．今や認知行動療法の入門書が翻訳物や書き下ろしを含めて多く出版されている．これらを利用すれば，たとえば認知再構成，段階的暴露，アサーション訓練，問題解決技法などの個別の認知行動技法を学ぶことができる．そのためであろうか，時に認知行動療法がこういう個別の技法に矮小化されることがある．個別の技法のデモンストレーションを見れば，技法だけではない認知行動療法の雰囲気をうかがうことができるが，それでもまだ技法に偏った着眼になりがちである．

　今回ここに収載した3編の映像は，日本で現在入手できる教科書

やDVDとは異なり，認知療法の超大家2人による3回分のセッションの始めから終わりまでを録画したものである．そこでは，

① 最も基本的な態度として「今，ここで」の問題の解決を志向すること（これを**問題解決モード**と呼ぶ）．
② 1回のセッションを，さらに治療全体をどのように組み立ててゆくか（これを**セッションおよび治療の構造化**という）．
③ 面接の中でどのようにして患者を認知行動モデルに沿って理解してゆくか（これを**認知行動モデル**による症例の**フォーミュレーション**，あるいは認知的概念化という）．
④ セッションの中で具体的にどのような患者に対応するか（**ソクラテス的問答**，あるいは**発見的質問**と呼ばれる）．

という，認知行動療法の基本中の基本の要諦が，余すところなく，デモンストレートされている．

　さらにDVDの中では①〜④の基本を踏まえて，自動思考の同定，自動思考への反論，行動活性化，イメージ書き換え，行動実験，ロールプレイ，宿題設定などなどの具体的な認知行動療法の技法がちりばめられている．治療の自然な流れの中で1つひとつの技法をどのように施行するか，患者が技法になじむにはどのような細かい工夫を凝らせばよいか，これらのDVDは認知行動療法家にとっては明日の臨床のヒントが満載の宝箱といえるであろう．

　お恥ずかしい話だが私もこれらのセッション映像を見て初めて，認知行動療法の教科書に書いてあることの意味がわかるようになった．これらのセッション映像でデモンストレートされている基本は，振り返ってみれば，確かに多くの教科書に書かれているのである．しかし，本物を知らずに本だけを読んでもそれを読みとることができないでいた．これらの基本中の基本を知らずに認知療法を行うこ

とは本末転倒であるはずであるのに，この基本を見聞する機会が今までなかったのである．

　考えてみれば，外科医が手術を学ぶのに，教師が授業法を学ぶのに，それぞれの先輩が実際に当の技術を施行している様子を見学せずに習得することなど，ありうるであろうか．しかし，振り返ってみれば，精神療法を学ぶのに，先達が行う精神療法セッションの全体を見学する機会は精神医学あるいは臨床心理学の教育の現場で今日，どれくらい保証されているであろうか．

　Aaron T. Beck と Judith Beck という大家が本物の患者に対して行ったセッションは，いやがおうにも DVD の臨場感を高め，見る者に感銘を与えてくれる．本物のみが与えうるエッセンスを体感できる．認知行動療法の習得・実践を目指す臨床家にとって，この DVD は自分の臨床を磨くために不可欠の教材のひとつであると言ってよいと思う．解説文では，DVD に沿って上記の認知行動療法の基本がどのようにデモンストレートされているかを注釈しているので，あわせて読んでいただくとさらに学習効果が上がることを期待している．

2008 年 8 月

古川壽亮

目次

はじめに III

第 1 部
Beck & Beck に学ぶ認知行動療法の基本原理

3つの面接の概要 3
- Judith Beck 『うつ病』 3
- Aaron T. Beck 1 『絶望感―初回面接』 4
- Aaron T. Beck 2 『家族の問題―初回面接』 5

3つの面接でデモンストレートされている認知行動療法の基本原則 6
- ①問題解決モード 6
- ②セッションおよび治療全体の構造化 8
- ③認知行動モデルによる症例のフォーミュレーション 15
- ④質問による発見 (ソクラテス的問答, 協力的実証主義) 22

その他の認知行動療法の大原則 28
- ⑤心理教育と学習の重視 28
- ⑥宿題の重視：おさらいと設定 31
- ⑦セッション中のホットな認知を見逃さないこと 33

- ⑧症例の認知行動的理解に沿った認知的技法, 行動的技法の応用 35
  - a) 自動思考の同定 35
  - b) 自動思考への反論 (認知再構成) 37
  - c) イメージ書き換え (イメージ再構成) 38
  - d) 中核信念の修正 38
  - e) 行動実験 38
  - f) メリット・デメリット分析 39
  - g) 活動モニタリング 40

- h) 行動活性化 40
- i) アサーション訓練 41
- j) 問題解決技法 41
- k) 段階的課題設定 43
- l) ロールプレイ 43
- m) 行動用語で記述 44
- n) 相対化(数量化, 命名) 45
- o) カードやノートに書き留める 45

第2部
3つの面接のやりとりの英語原文, 日本語訳, 註釈

Judith Beck 『うつ病』 49
Aaron T. Beck 1 『絶望感―初回面接』 123
Aaron T. Beck 2 『家族の問題―初回面接』 149

付録 177
- 1. 認知療法尺度　Cognitive Therapy Rating Scale (CTRS) 178
- 2. 認知行動療法についてよくある質問 186

終わりに 191
索引 193

DVD 2枚組み

- Disc 1　**Judith Beck** 『うつ病』
- Disc 2　**Aaron T. Beck 1** 『絶望感―初回面接』
   　　　　Aaron T. Beck 2 『家族の問題―初回面接』

ユーザーサポートは行っておりません. ご了承ください.

装丁　糟谷 一穂

第 **1** 部

Beck & Beck に学ぶ認知行動療法の基本原理

3つの面接の概要

　ここに収載した3つのセッションの概要を最初に示す．なお，本解説では「認知療法」と「認知行動療法」という用語をほとんど区別せずに互換可能な呼称として使用する．なぜなら，「認知療法」という呼称で呼ばれている治療法の中におけるバリエーションが，「認知療法」と「認知行動療法」の間に理念的に存在しうるバリエーションよりもしばしば大きく，これらを区別することに実際的な意味がないからである．

● **Judith Beck『うつ病』**（Disc 1 収録）
　20歳代に見えるアフリカ系アメリカ人女性との初回セッション．被面接者は実際の患者である．セッションの前に記入されたベック抑うつ質問票のスコアは41点で重症うつ病と考えられるレベルであった．

　本DVDは，短期精神療法シリーズとして作成されたDVDシリーズのうち，認知療法に焦点を当てたものである．まず2人のロジャーズ派かと思われる臨床心理士によるインタビューを介し，Judith Beckが認知療法を概説する．2人の臨床心理士は認知療法についてほとんど無知であるかのように質問をしているので，ロジャーズ派あるいは精神分析的な精神療法がベースにある人にも非常にわかりやすいやりとりの解説になっている．またその一部ではJudith Beckが父からのアドバイスも含めた個人史を語る箇所もあり臨場感を盛り上げている．

続いて実際の症例との初回面接を見ることになるが，インタビュアーはこのあたりでも非常に上手で，面接を見る前に何に注意すべきでしょうと Beck 自身に問いかけ，語らせている．

面接自体は 48 分あり，その後さらに Judith Beck によるその解説が続く．インタビュアーが問いかけ，セッションのビデオの一部をリプレイし，Judith Beck が解説する．Judith Beck が何を考えながらそういう質問をしているかという解説が入るが，このような解説を聞けるのは稀有な機会といえよう．合計 115 分（カラー）．

面接では，問題解決モード，セッションの構造化，症例のフォーミュレーション，ソクラテス的問答という基本の中に，心理教育，イメージ書き換え（イメージ再構成），アサーション，行動実験，宿題設定などの技法が見事なまでに組み入れられている．面接の最初の頃は患者は今にも泣きだしそうであったが，終了時には笑顔も見られたことが印象的なセッションであった．

● Aaron T. Beck 1:『絶望感―初回面接』(Disc 2 収録)

症例は，絶望感を訴える 20 歳代のヨーロッパ系アメリカ人女性患者との初回セッション．実際の患者とされている．1979 年に撮影された，43 分間のセッションの録画（白黒）．

夫婦関係の問題をかかえ，抑うつ気分，気力低下，決断力低下，自尊心低下，希死念慮などの抑うつ状態の患者に対し，主訴および現症を傾聴した上で，扱うことのできる問題にアジェンダを設定し，ソクラテス的問答を含めていくつもの認知行動的手法を使いながら面接を進めてゆく．セッションの構造からいうと，23 分までが導入，そこから 38 分までがアジェンダ，最後の 5 分がまとめという構成になっている．初回セッションなので病歴聴取と心理教育を含めた導入部分が長くなっているのであろう．

ホットな認知の扱い方，上手なアジェンダの設定方法，行動活性化，行動実験，段階的課題設定，活動モニタリング，まとめのフィードバックを求めるという技法が印象的に使用されている．セッションの途中で何度もサマリーを入れ患者のフィードバックを求めている様子も，教科書的な技法とはいえ，実際に Aaron T. Beck が行っている様子は興味深い．認知療法の初回セッションとはこのように行うものだという例を，認知療法の創始者である Aaron T. Beck が実際に示したきわめて貴重な映像である．

● Aaron T. Beck 2:『家族の問題―初回面接』（Disc 2 収録）

　症例は夫および息子との問題を抱える，32 歳のヨーロッパ系アメリカ人女性のうつ病の患者で，模擬患者であるはずだが，ほとんどそのように感じさせない．電話での問い合わせの後の初回セッションという位置づけになっている．1977 年に撮影された 40 分のセッションの録画（白黒）．

　最初の 5 分で問題リストから当日のアジェンダを患者と協力しながら設定する．アジェンダの中では問題解決技法，認知行動モデルの心理教育，認知再構成法が試みられる．また，協力しながら行動実験を宿題に設定する中でアサーションのロールプレイを行っている．36 分からはまとめに入り，患者のフィードバックを，否定的な感想も含めて聞いている．認知行動療法の教科書では確かにこのようなネガティブなフィードバックまで求めることになっているが，実際にはなかなか聞けるものではなく，先達が実践しているところを見るのは啓発的であろう．

3つの面接でデモンストレートされている認知行動療法の基本原則

　認知行動療法の原則をいくつかの箇条書きにまとめることができるが，ここでは特にこのDVDを通してデモンストレートされている4箇条にまとめて見てゆこう．

①問題解決モード
　認知行動療法の第一原則は，「患者とともに，今ここで患者が抱えている問題の解決を目指す」ことである［図1］．これを**問題解決モード** problem-solving mode と呼ぶ．「患者とともに」の部分は，④(→ p.22)の協力的実証主義のことなので，④で説明する．

　残念ながら，そして当然ながら，患者は常に問題解決モードで治療者の前に現れるわけではない．患者が**なげき破局化モード** catastrophizing mode にある時，治療者の最初の仕事は患者を**問題解決モード**に持ってゆくことである［図2］．患者が治療の主人公であることを念頭に置きながら，患者が破局化モードから徐々に脱するのを待つしかないこともある．

　さて，問題解決モードになって，患者の抱えている問題を検討してみると，時として患者が考える問題が実際に存在し，現実上の困難となっていることがある．この場合，患者の認知がゆがんでいるわけではないので，治療者は患者とともに問題解決を図る．したがって，典型的には問題解決技法を用いる．

　一方，患者が考える問題が現実に即していない場合，それは患者

の考えがゆがんでいるということであるので,認知の修正を図ることになる.したがって,典型的には認知再構成を用いる.

問題解決を図るためにも,認知を修正するためにも,実際には様々な認知的技法および行動的技法が使用される(→ P.35)ので,[図2]はやや簡素化しすぎであろうが,この理解は,実際の認知行動療法の進むべき流れを考える時に,非常に有用である.Judith Beckも解説の中で「時には患者さんの考えが正しいことがあります.そういう場合は,変化に直結するような問題解決を行います.問題が,患者さんが状況をどうとらえているかということにより深く関わるならば,我々はその問題に対する認知の修正を具体的に教えます」と明瞭に述べている(→ P.53).

<blockquote>
Judith Beck は患者に対しても以下のような説明で明確に問題解決モードの重要性を説明している「そこで今からやりたいのは,あな
</blockquote>

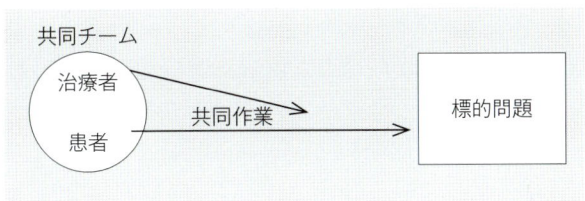

[図1] 協力的実証主義による問題解決モード

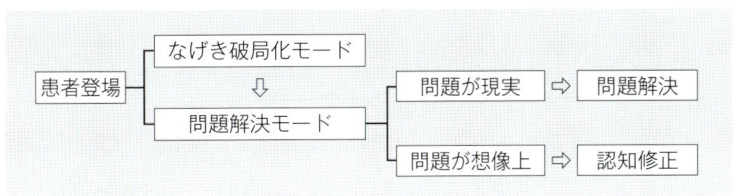

[図2] 問題解決モードの流れ

たが自分の考えを知り，その考えがどの程度事実なのかを自分で見つける方法です．もしもあなたの考えが事実であることがわかったら，あなたは問題解決に取り組まなければなりません．もしも考えが事実ではないことがわかったら，あなたは自分の考えを変えなければなりません」(→ P.77).

なげき破局化モードの患者を上手に問題解決モードに導入するスキルは，Aaron T. Beck 2『家族の問題─初回面接』で頻回にデモンストレートされている．たとえば，「先生がすべてをよくしてくれたらいいのに」という依存的・願望的な患者に対して，「ではいっしょに，何ができるか考えてみましょう．あなた自身が問題解決に向かうことができるのではないでしょうか．では，ご主人のお話をしますか，それとも息子さんの話がいいですか」と筋道をつけたり，学校の先生から子どもの素行について報告を受けて嘆くだけの患者に対し「あなたもご主人も動揺しています．確かに問題は存在します．そこでまず最初に，何が問題なのかを具体的に見てみましょう」と切り返したり，我が子は悪い子，不道徳な子と決めつける患者に「解決が必要な具体的な問題という観点から息子さんのことを整理できますか」と発見的質問を投げかけている(→ P.152).

実際，この DVD では，終わりのほうで Aaron T. Beck その人が，"problem-oriented" と "catastrophe-oriented" という用語を使用して，後者から前者への移行の重要性を患者に説明している(→ P.158).

②セッションおよび治療全体の構造化

セッションを問題解決モードで運用するために，最も大切なのが，セッションおよび治療全体の構造化である．Judith Beck も DVD の解説の中で認知療法の特徴を 4 回尋ねられているが，4 回とも筆頭

に構造化の重要性を挙げている.

　まずセッションの構造化 structuring of session であるが，ほとんどの患者のほとんどのセッションは，[表1]の要素から構成される.

　セッションの最初にはその週の患者の症状の変化をまずチェックする(**症状チェック** mood check)．ベック抑うつ質問票 Beck Depression Inventory などの自記式調査票を用いるのもよいだろう．この段階で，もし患者の希死念慮や絶望感が圧倒的であったり，あるいは患者が他者に危害を加える可能性が高い，すなわち患者がなげき破局化モードにあると判断されれば，その点についての危機介入が最優先される．危機介入に十分な時間をとれるように，症状チェックが最初に来るのである．

　2回目以降のセッションでは次に，前回セッションから今回セッションへの**橋渡し**を行う．典型的には，「先週のセッションについて何を覚えていらっしゃいますか．あらためてまとめるとどうなりますか．この1週間，何が役立ちましたか」のような質問を行うと

[表1] セッションの構造化

●導入部 (5～10分)	・症状チェック ・前回セッションからの橋渡し ・宿題の復習 ・協力してアジェンダを設定
●アジェンダ (30分)	・心理教育 ・認知技法，行動技法の学習 ・定期的にまとめをはさむこと
●まとめ (10分)	・フィードバック ・協力して新しい宿題を設定

よい．あるいは，「橋渡しワークシート」（J. Beck『認知療法実践ガイド・基礎から応用まで』p. 64）を利用するのもよいだろう．予想以上に患者は前回セッションのことを覚えていないが，毎回この質問をすると患者のほうできちんと復習するようになってゆくことが多い．

　また，2回目以降のセッションでは必ず**宿題の復習**（おさらい）を入れなくてはならない．宿題は認知行動療法の4大原則には入れなかったが，負けず劣らず，認知行動療法に必須の要素である（→ P.31）．出した宿題をその次に治療者がおさらいしなければ，治療者は暗に宿題など重要でないというメッセージを送っていることになる．したがって，必ずおさらいをしなくてはならない．ただし，導入部分には最大で5〜10分しかあてられないので，ここで宿題の詳しい検討を始めないほうがよいだろう．宿題をやってきたか，どの程度やってきたか，あるいはできなかったかという実施状況のみを確認し，宿題の検討はアジェンダの1つとして設定すればよい．

　このような検討から，患者が抱えている問題のいくつかが明らかになったら，いよいよそのセッションの**アジェンダ**の設定に入る．そのセッションで検討すべき課題，話題のことをアジェンダと呼ぶ．「○○，××，□□といった問題があるようですが，今日はどれを検討しましょうか」「今日は何を中心にやっていきましょうか」というような質問をしてあくまで患者と協力して設定する．実際にセッションで扱えるのは通常1つ，たかだか2つの課題になるので，課題の中で優先順位をつけることが非常に大切になる．「それでは○○をまずやって，時間があれば××も考えるということでよいですか」．このように協力しながら，具体的に，セッションで扱うべきアジェンダを設定していくことは，問題解決モードを維持するために不可欠といえよう．

今回のDVDに収録されたすべてのセッションで，アジェンダの設定が行われているのは当然のことであるが，中でもAaron T. Beck 1『絶望感―初回面接』のセッションでBeckが患者に「今あなたが話したいこと，決めたいことはありますか？」と質問した時，患者が離婚の問題を取り上げようとしたら，「それは大きな問題です．時間がかかるでしょう．ご主人について話をすることは重要ですが，ほかに，すぐにあなたの人生を左右しそうな，もっと小さい決めごとはありますか？」と問い返している様が，印象的であった (→ P.135)．

Aaron T. Beck 2『家族の問題―初回面接』のやり方が，より典型的なのであろう．患者から問題リストを聴取したあと，「最初にどのことを話したいですか．○○，××，□□，それから△△という問題があるようですが」と患者に問いかけている (→ P.151)．

Judith BeckのDVDでは「では，あなたが話してくれた問題を見て，どれについて話し合うか決めましょう」と前置きをした上で，最初に挙げたのは「まず最初に，家のことがありますね．でもこれについては，今ここで私にできることはあまりありません」とざっくりと切っている．その上で，2つ目，3つ目，4つ目の問題をリストアップし「では，今夜はどのことについて話し合いたいですか？」と患者に選択を任せている (→ P.69)．

　次に，セッションの中ほど，その日のアジェンダを扱っている時は，要所要所でまとめを入れることが重要である．また，理解が難しいこと，あるいは感情的な負荷が高いであろうことが出てきたら，その段階ですぐさま患者に「あなたはどう思われますか」というような質問をし，患者からのフィードバックを得る（治療者からみれ

ば，患者についてデータを収集する)のが重要である．

> これが一番上手にデモンストレーションされているのは，Aaron T. Beck 1『絶望感―初回面接』の DVD である．セッションの途中で，Beck は何度も患者の感情や思考についてのまとめを述べている．
> Judith Beck のセッションでも，Beck のとある提案に患者が，半納得の風で「はい」と肯んじた時に，すかさず Beck は「そう思いますか？」と問い返している(→ p.88).

　各セッションの最後の 10 分程度は，まとめに費やされる．まとめの部分も構造化されている．まず大切なのは，患者からのフィードバックをもらうことである．**フィードバック**は，セッションの内容についてと，セッションを行った治療者についてのものに分かれる．セッションの内容については，「残り 10 分になりました．今日やったことでわかりにくかったことはありましたか」と質問した上で，「今日やったことをまとめると，どうなりますか．今日は何を学びましたか，発見しましたか」と「今後役立ちそうな場面はありそうですか」の 2 点を確認するとよい．患者によっては非常に明快に理解してもらえる場合と，正反対に，治療者が意図したことを意外にも誤解している場合がある．後者の場合，補足説明するなり，宿題に組みこむなり，さらには次のセッションをもう一度同じトピックに費やすなりの対策を立てなくてはならない．

　次に治療者については，「何か気に障りましたか．言われて嫌だったことはありますか」を必ず聞くようにする．「もし私の理解で間違っていたところがあったり，またあなたにとって不快であったりしたことがあったら，ぜひ教えてください．治療にとってはそれが大切なのです．私が誤解したまま，あなたが不快なままでは治療が

進まないでしょう？」「何か気に障ることがあったら言いづらくてもぜひ言ってください．第一に治療の非常によい材料になるし，第二に私が修正する材料になります」と説明する．最初は何とも問いにくい質問であるが，この質問をすることだけで治療の主人公が患者であることを実地に証明することができる．また，実際に聞いてみると治療者にとってきわめて有用なコメントをもらえることが多い．

> Judith Beck は「では，今夜話したことをまとめてみてください．どんなことが重要だと思いますか？」「今夜の話の中で，私が誤解しているようなことはありますか？ あるいはお気に障ったことは？」「話の中であなたがいいなと思ったことは？」という質問を使っている（→ P.98）．

> Aaron T. Beck 1『絶望感―初回面接』では，時間がなかったためであろうか，「治療について，否定的な考えを持つ人もいます．もしあなたがそう感じたら，それはとても重要なことなので，書き留めておいてください」と宿題に回している（→ P.148）．

> Aaron T. Beck 2『家族の問題―初回面接』では，最後に「では，セッションを終える前に確認させてください．今日私が言ったこと，ここで起こったことで，あなたが嫌だったことはありますか？」と問うている（→ P.174）．

次に患者と協力して今週の宿題を設定するが，その詳細は⑥（→ P.31）へ．

本DVDに収録した3セッションはすべて初回セッションなので，治療全体の流れが見えにくいが，認知行動療法では治療全体も構造化されている(structuring of treatment)．パーソナリティ障害などの重症患者に対しては1年以上にわたる認知行動療法も行われるが，併存症のない不安障害や気分障害に対する認知行動療法は典型的には10〜20回の間で行われる．このように少ない回数で最大限の効果を上げるためには，治療全体が構造化されていなくてはならない[表2]．

　導入期(セッション1〜2)は，病歴聴取から患者の問題(困りごと)リストの作成，認知行動療法とは何かとか，患者が患っているのはどんな病気でどんな症状があるかの心理教育，週間記録や思考記録表も利用して患者の認知行動モデルの作成を目標に行われる．

　第一の，患者の困りごとリストの共有は，「どういうことでお困りですか」といった定番の質問だけではなく，「それがどうなったら，少しでも生活しやすくなりそうですか」あるいは「解決したい，達成したい目標は何でしょう．もし1年後に私があなたを見て，それが達成できたかどうかを見ただけで判断できるとしたら，何がどう変化していると目標を達成したと判断できそうでしょうか」などの発見的質問を用いながら，標的問題を患者と共有することが目標である．第二の心理教育については，⑤ P.28を参照．第3の認知行動モデルによるフォーミュレーションについては，③ P.15を参照．

　実践期の前半では，標的問題に合致した，具体的な認知行動スキルを教育し，練習してもらう．またその際の患者からのフィードバッ

[表2] 治療全体の構造化

| ◎導入期 | ◎実践期前半 | ◎実践期後半 | ◎まとめ |

クに応じて，患者の認知行動モデルが活発に書き換えられるのもこの時期である．実践期の後半では，ほぼ必要と思われるスキルの教育が終わり，患者はまさに「自分が運転席に座って」自分でスキルを血や肉とする時期である．もちろんこの時期でも認知行動モデルの改訂は続けられる．この時期は，1つひとつのセッションの真ん中でアジェンダを扱う部分に似て，治療の中核をなす部分であり，患者が実際にさまざまなスキルを実践してみないことには治療が前に進まないので，実践期と呼んだ．ここで実際に患者が学習する認知的スキル，行動的スキルの代表例は，⑧ p.35 に集めた．

　まとめは通常最後の1セッションを使い，今回の治療で学んだこと，変わったことを振り返り，どのスキルが一番自分に役に立ったか，役に立ったスキルを今後も継続するにはどうしたらよいだろうか，近い将来にどのような困難が予期されて，もしそうなった時には何ができるだろうか，などを話し合う．このような点をあらかじめ話し合っておくことにより，再発予防を目指す．最後のほうのセッションは毎週ではなく，患者が自分1人で習い覚えたスキルを実行できることを確かめられるように，少しセッションとセッションの間を置くことが通常である．

　導入期から実践期そしてまとめの段階での力点の推移を，[図3]に模式化した．

③認知行動モデルによる症例のフォーミュレーション

　認知行動療法の認知行動療法たるゆえんは，認知行動モデルによって患者を理解することにある．これを認知行動モデルによる症例の**フォーミュレーション** cognitive-behavioral case formulation，あるいは**認知行動的概念化** cognitive-behavioral conceptualization と呼ぶ．この認知行動モデルによる理解には，横断面のそれと，縦断面のそ

れとがある.

　横断的な認知行動モデルは，Judith Beck『認知療法実践ガイド 基礎から応用まで』(星和書店, 2004)の説明では，人の感情や行動は，できごとそのものではなくその人のできごとに対する理解の仕方によって影響を受けるとする仮説であるとされている．できごとに対して素早く，自動的に浮かび上がってくる評価的な思考を，自動思考 automatic thought と呼ぶ［図4］．できごとに対してどういう自動思考が生じるかに応じて，感情も行動も身体的反応も変わってくると説明する．

　私は認知行動モデルをもう少し広くとらえて次のように説明している．「人間は状況，状況に応じて，反応をします．人間の反応は，気持ち，体，考え，行動の4つの側面に分けることができます．特定の状況に応じて，特定の気持ちを抱き，体が特定の反応を起こし，ある考えを持ち，ある行動を起こすわけです．これらの4つの側面は互いが互いに影響を及ぼしあって，状況に対する反応を形成しています．あなたは認知行動療法を受けたいとお考えですから，ある悩ましい気持ち，もしくは体の反応を示しがちでいらっしゃるので

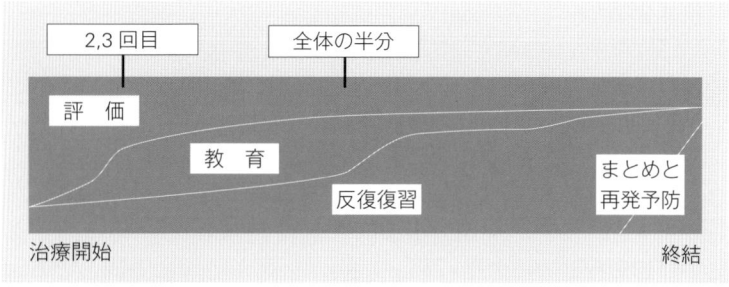

［図3］治療の構造化

しょう．例えば，ついつい不安になって，心臓がどきどきしやすい．あるいは，しばしば憂うつになって，体が重いし食欲もない，など．しかし，残念なことに，どのような感情を抱き，どのような体の反応が起こるかは，人間が自分で意識的に変えることはできません．しかし，幸いなことに，どのように考え，どのように行動するかは，ある程度，人間の意識の支配下にあります．そして，これら4つの側面は互いに密接に影響し合っていますから，考え（認知）や行動を変えることによって，感情や身体反応を変えてゆくことができます．これが認知行動療法です」［図5］．〔付録②「認知行動療法についてよくある質問」（→ p.186）〕

認知，行動，感情の3側面のみを取り上げるのか，これらプラス身体反応を含めた4側面まで取り上げるのか，また，認知のプライマシーを強調するのか3ないし4側面の相互作用を強調するのかは，おそらく，いずれが絶対の真理というわけではなく，患者に応じて説明しやすい図式を使用するのが実際的であろう．

横断的な認知行動モデルをさまざまな状況に即して積み重ねてゆ

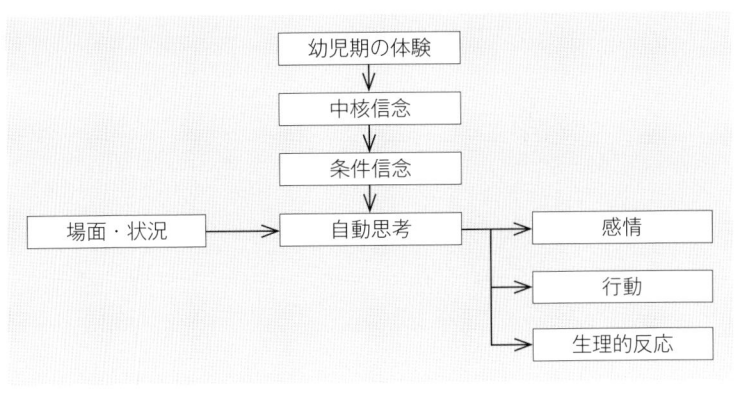

［図4］Judith Beck の認知モデル

くと，自動思考や行動には人それぞれの傾向・パターンがあることに気づかれる．自動思考のパターンは各人が幼少期のかなり早い時期から抱くようになった，自分について，他者について，また自分を取りまく世界についての**中核信念** core belief と，これに基づく**条件信念** conditional belief から影響を受け，行動パターンは中核信念や条件信念に見合った**代償行動** compensatory behavior のパターンになっている．［図 4, 5］にはこれらの要素も書き加えた．

　例を挙げよう．「私は無能だ」という中核信念を抱いた患者は，「常にベストを尽くさなければ，落ちこぼれる」という条件信念とそれに見合った代償行動（同僚の 2 倍の時間働き，土日も出勤する）を取っているかもしれない．代償行動が機能している限りは破綻をきたさなかった患者でも，たとえば会社および当人にとっては不可抗力であるはずの取引先の倒産が起これば，「こんな難局はもう私の手に負えない」という自動思考と，それに影響された引きこもり，そして抑うつ気分を発症するかもしれない．

　あるいは「私は人よりもみすぼらしい」という中核信念を持った社会不安障害の患者は，「教室で目立つ位置に座れば，みんなが私に注目し私のことを嘲笑するだろう」という条件信念と，これを補

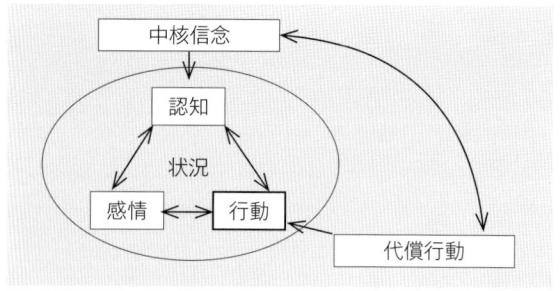

［図 5］より広い認知モデル

うような代償行動として「クラス会や会議では決して自分から話をすることはなく、いつも部屋の隅で下を向いておとなしく座っている」という行動に及んでいることがあるだろう。こういう人が、たとえば少人数ゼミのような状況を経験すると、「もし指名されたら、私はろくなことも言えず、恥をさらすだろう」という自動思考から、不安と恥ずかしさに耐えながら時間を過ごすであろう。

Aaron T. Beck(1979)はJudith Beckとは少し違った図式を発表しており、それは［図6］のようである。ここではできごとが中核信念（スキーマ）を活性化し、それが認知、行動、気分の3分野に現れることになる。

認知行動概念化は常に仮説である。上手に概念化を行う、つまり上手にフォーミュレーションを書き上げるためのこつは以下の5つ、
1. 治療のできるだけ早期から概念化を始める
2. まず包括的な問題リストを作る
3. 具体個別的な状況に即して、具体的・行動的な言葉で記述する
4. 実証された理論を概念化の基礎とする。これは病態ごとに異なると考えられる
5. そして、できてきたフォーミュレーションを患者と共有する

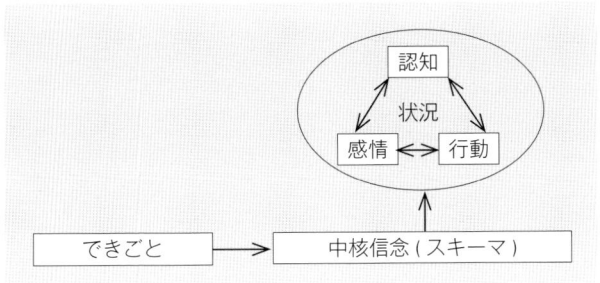

［図6］ Aaron T. Beckの認知モデル

のがよいとされる.

Judith Beck は認知行動モデルを図示するために,［図7］のような図式を推奨している．これは［図5］を複数の状況ごとの書きこみができるように開いて，幼児期の体験の項を加えたような図式といえる．3側面の相互作用を強調するために原図を改変した．上記②「治療の構造化」で説明したように，第1〜2回セッションを通じてひとまずこの図式を埋められるくらいの症例把握を目指そう．そして，このモデルは治療の進展に応じて毎回書き換えられてゆくものであることを忘れないように．

> DVD中の実際のセッションの患者とのやりとりの中では概念化の内容そのものは出てきていないが，Judith Beck は概念化が彼女の介入の方向性を決めている様を以下のように説明している．「彼女は

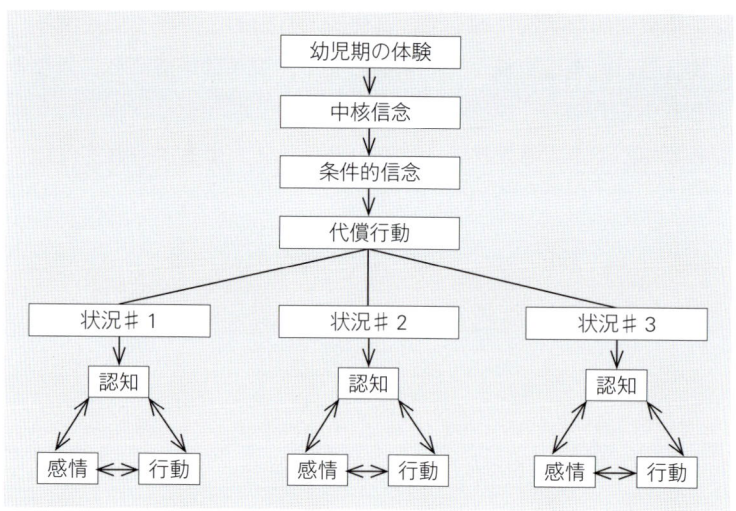

［図7］Judith Beck の認知的概念図

重度のうつ病患者であり，どうやって病気を治していけばいいのかわかっていません．彼女の問題に耳を傾けそこで起こっていることを概念化することにより，私にはどの方向に進めていくべきかがわかってきます．どの介入方法が成功するかなどということは前もってわかりません．しかし少なくとも私は，心の中に進め方の計画を用意します」(→ p.106)．

そして，「彼女はこの1週間，さまざまな考え，否定的でうまく機能しない考えを持ったでしょうが，セッションでは1つか2つ，あるいは3つくらいしか取り組む時間がありません．ですから私は，何らかの意味で明らかに歪んでいて，過去にしばしば出てきたし，今後も出てくるであろう，たくさんの否定的な感情を生みだす考えを探しています」と述べているが(→ p.109)，あらためてビデオを見てみると，この治療方針から Judith Beck が患者の認知再構成の題材として選んだ条件的信念が「もしお母さんがいなくなったら，私はやっていけない」であったことがよく見て取れる．

また，同じく Judith Beck は「患者さんが自分でできるスキルを持っている場合，最初は指示を与えないようにします．なぜならば，彼女は根底で非常にどうしようもなく能力不足だと感じているというのが私の概念化ですから，私はセッションの間，彼女がその信念を弱める機会を提供することを非常に意識しています」(→ p.113)「彼らは否定的なことしか見ないからです．うつ病のために，それ以外のことを排除してしまい，肯定的な情報を取りこもうとしません．ですから私は，うつ病の患者さんには，そこで起こっている肯定的なできごとを指摘するようにしています．患者さんの考えには正確でないものがあること，とくに自分自身をどう思うかということにつ

いては正確ではないということが患者さんにわかるように手助けをするために，率直な励まし，肯定的な励ましを与えます」とフォーミュレーションに従って介入している背景を説明している(→ p.117).

④質問による発見（ソクラテス的問答，協力的実証主義）

　認知行動療法は，ほかのすべての有効な精神療法と同様，暖かさ，共感，理解，誠実といった特性に基づく確固たる治療同盟を重視する．認知行動療法は，しかし，これらのほかの精神療法に比して，患者との共同作業を中心に据え，実際に試してみる実証を重視する．

　Beck ら(1979)は，認知行動療法における治療者患者関係を説明するのに，**協力的実証主義** collaborative empiricism[*1] という用語を使用した．患者と治療者が共同の研究チームとして協力しながら，さまざまな認知や行動が現実に即した適応的なものであるのかどうかを一緒に仮説を立てて，一緒に実際に試してみるからである．[図1]（→ p.7）は協同チームのありようを上手に図式化している．私は時々[図1]を患者の前で書いて説明するが，少なくとも一部の患者にとっては新しい発見であるようだ．

　この協力的実証主義を，治療の中で具体的に実現する質問形式を**ソクラテス的問答** Socratic questioning と呼ぶ．かつて古代ギリシャの哲学者ソクラテスは，弟子たちにできあがった真実を教えるのではなく，弟子たちと問答を重ねることで真実にたどりつこうとした．認知行動療法でも，治療者は患者みずから気づいたり発見できるところまで**質問による発見** guided discovery（直訳は「誘導による発見」

[*1] Collaborative empiricism は「協同的経験主義」や「協力的経験主義」とも訳されている．患者に説明をするのに「協同してやりましょう」というよりも「協力してやりましょう」と言うほうが日本語としてこなれていると思うので，「協力的」の訳語を採用した．次に，この empiricism が，哲学用語として「経験主義」に近いのか「実証主義」に近いのかという議論とは無関係に，やはり患者に説明する時の語感として「経験しましょう」と言ったのでは，認知行動療法をする前から患者は経験しているには違いがないので，それよりは「実際にそうかどうか試しましょう」と説明した方が認知行動療法の実際に近い．よって「実証主義」の用語を採用した．

であるが，それはしばしば実態を表していないと思う．なぜなら，質問によって患者が発見するだけでなく，治療者も発見するからであり，治療者はえてして誘導先を知らないからである）あるいは**発見的質問**を重ねていくのがよい．最善の認知行動療法に答えはない，よい質問しかない，とすら言われる．

> Judith Beck のビデオで解説者が Judith Beck のセッションに対して「あなたは彼女（＝患者）に自分の言ったことを考えさせ，彼女は時間をかけて考えていました．彼女は実際に同意しましたが，私はその時が彼女が初めて本当にそのことを考えた時だったと思います」という感想を述べている箇所がある．ソクラテス的問答は，初めて見る第三者から見ると，まさしくそのように見えるのであろう（→ p.116）．

　質問による発見は［表3］のような3レベルに分けて考えると，習得しやすい．レベル0，入門編は「患者が洞察を深めることができるように，適度に制約されたオープンクエスチョン」である．すべての良質の精神療法に，暖かさ，誠実さ，共感が必要なように，すべての良質の精神療法は開かれた質問 open question（はい／いいえで答えられる閉じられた質問 closed question に対して，はい／いいえだけでは答えられないような質問を開かれた質問という）を多用する．患者に患者の言葉で語ってもらい，治療者が患者の理解を深めるためである．認知行動療法では，同じオープンクエスチョンを使用するにも，適度に制約があって患者がふと考えこまなくてはならないような質問が向いている．［表4］の左側の純粋なオープンクエスチョンも悪くはないが，右側のように治療者のフォーカスが伝わるような質問を多用できるようになりたい．

　もう1つ，このレベルで忘れてはならない必須質問は，患者の固

有の言い回し(患者の idiosyncratic な言い回し)を許さないことである．許さないというのはきつい言い方であるが，患者が独特の言い方で表現することを早わかりしては決してならない．その意味を問い返すことは，具体的に問題を協力的に取り扱ってゆく時に不可欠である．

[表3] 質問による発見の3レベル

レベル0 適度に制約された，患者の考えるヒントになる，開かれた質問
レベル1 教えたくなったら，解釈を与えたくなったら，質問せよ
レベル2 目標に達するまで4つも5つも質問を重ねなくてはならない例

[表4] 適度に制約された質問の例

純粋なオープンクエスチョン	フォーカスが伝わる質問
趣味は何ですか	何をしている時が，楽しいですか
その時，何を考えていましたか	その時，あなたの頭にはどのような考えが浮かんでいましたか
もしそうだとすると，どうなりそうですか	そうだとすると，あなたの人間関係，経済状態，将来はどうなりそうですか
	もしそうだとすると，自分は，周りの人は，未来はどうなりそうですか
治療の目標は何でしょう どうなりたいですか	何ができるようになったら，あなたは病気を克服したことになるでしょう
その時，どんな気分になりましたか	そのように考えると，どのような気分になりますか
なぜそんなことをしたのですか	どうやって○○になったのか，私にもわかるように説明してください

一例がJudith Beckに出てくる．患者が「時々…ただ，あれさえもっとよければいいのに，いつかもっとよくなるように」と言った時，治療者は「あれ」を早わかりせず，「あれとは，何のことですか？」などと明確化を迫らなくてはならない(→ p.67)．

　レベル1，応用編は，"Ask when you want to teach or interpret"「教えたくなったら，質問せよ」というモットーに集約できるであろう．患者が陥っている疾病の性質や悪循環の勘所について，ついつい教えたくなるのは人情だが，人間が最も効率的に学習できるのは，自分で考え自分で発見した時であることを忘れてはならない．応用編はさまざまな切り口に基づいているが，「うまくいった時と，うまくいかなかった時の対比」「治療場面での治療者と患者との関係と，治療の外での人々と患者との関係の対比」「今学んだことと，予測される近い将来の対比」「患者からの正直なフィードバックを求める」というような心がけが，よい発見的質問を生むようである．［表5］にそれらのいくつかの，ついつい教えたくなって言いそうな言葉と，それをソクラテス的に変形した質問を列挙してみた．

学校の先生から我が子の問題行動の連絡を受けて「だめな子だ，だから私はだめな母親だ」と思いこんでいる患者に対して，Aaron T. Beckは発見的質問を連発している（『家族の問題―初回面接』）．患者が実は子どもが何をしたかの詳細を把握していないことが明らかになると「では，それについて知るためには，あなたに何ができると思いますか？」と返し，その子のよい点を挙げさせた上で「そのことと，彼が悪い子だという考えとを，どう折り合いをつけますか」と患者自身に考えさせている(→ p.156)．
また同じセッションであるが，夫がいなくなれば自分は死んでしま

うだろうと悲嘆に暮れる患者に対し，夫と出会う前の様子を問い，「21歳の時，あなたはデビッドを知っていましたか？ その時，あなたは人生は生きている価値がないと感じていましたか？」「いいえ，違います．その頃私は，人生はもっとオープンだと感じていま

[表5] 教える代わりの質問

教える言い回し	発見的質問
× ○○すると，気分がよくなるようですねえ．○○しましょう．	○ ○○すると落ちこんでいた気分が少し楽になったということですね．このことから，どんなことがわかりますか．
× 結婚の問題は今日ここで扱うには大きすぎます．	○ 結婚したいという希望をお持ちであることはわかりました．これはここでの治療の目標にできることでしょうか．
× いつもいつも落ちこんでばかりいるわけではないでしょう．だって，○○の時は	○ 同じような状況だけど，落ちこまなかった時はありましたか？ 何が違うのでしょう？ 何を学ぶことができますか．
× みんながみんな怒りを爆発させるわけではありません．	○ 怒りに対して，あなたが尊敬できる対応をしている人を誰かご存じですか．何が違いますか．
× △△は○○です．わかりましたか．	○ （ながながと説明した時，難しそうなことを言った時）どう思われましたか？ これを見て，何か気がつかれますか．
× 宿題は必ずやりましょう．	○ 宿題はできそうですか？できる自信は何％ありますか． ○ できないかなと思う20％には何がありますか． ○ 何か困難が予想されますか？なるほど，もしそうなったら，どうしましょう？

(つづく)

した」「そうすると矛盾しますね？ デビッドがいなかったその時点で，あなたは人生には生きる価値があると思っていた．今のあな

[表5] 教える代わりの質問（続き）

教える言い回し	発見的質問
× 今日は○○について学びました．何かご質問はありますか．	○ 今日学んだことをまとめるとどうなりますか．
× 来週○○があるというお話でしたよね．今日学んだ方法をぜひ試みましょう．	○ 似たような状況は近々ありそうですか． ○ その時は，あなたはどうしますか． ○ もし次に同じことが起こったら，どうしますか．
× あなたと私の間で起こっていることは，あなたとお母さんの間で起こったことと，似ていますね．	○ あなたが○○した時，お母さんは△△と反応されたんですね． ○ 一方，同じあなたに対して，私はどのように反応しましたか． ○ 何が違いますか．何が似ていますか．これらを比較すると，何がわかりますか．
× それはそれとして，○○してみるのがよいと思いますよ．	○ この状況下で，せめてできることは，建設的に考えて何があるでしょうか．
× （たとえば患者の思考記録表が何枚かたまってくると）これらを見ていると，どうも○○の状況をあなたは苦手なようですね．	○ これらを見て，何か気がつきますか． ○ 何が目立ちますか． ○ ほかに何か気がつきますか．

たは完璧ではなくてもデビッドといっしょにいるのに，生きる価値がないと思っている．この矛盾をどうやって説明しますか？」という，レベル2のソクラテス的問答をしている（→ p.166）．

セッションでも発見的質問がふんだんに使用されている．対訳の右欄に注記をつけたので，どのような発見的質問が使用されているかを見てみよう．

その他の認知行動療法の大原則

①から④以外に，認知行動療法の大原則を挙げるとしたら，さらに以下の4原則を取り上げてもよいかもしれない．私の理解ではこれら⑤〜⑧は，①〜④の大原則とも，またお互いにも，重なるところが多いように思う．当然であろう．3つのセッションはこれらの追加の原則も雄弁にデモンストレートしているので，そのような目でDVDを鑑賞し学習していただくのもよいだろう．

⑤心理教育と学習の重視

認知行動療法の重要な要素は，適応的な思考や行動パターンの学習である．この学習が最も効率的に行われるようにする手段の1つが，セッションおよび治療の構造化である（②→ p.8）が，もう1つの手段が心理教育 psychoeducation である．

治療導入期の心理教育では，まず最初に，**疾病そのものの教育**（原因，メカニズム，症状など）を行わなければならない．やや荒っぽい言い方だが，患者が抑うつに打ちひしがれ不安におののいている

のは，実は抑うつや不安の正体がわからないからである．「幽霊の正体見たり枯れ尾花」ではないが，相手がどのような存在であるかを知ることは，それ自体が安心を生むし，また本当の相手がどのような相手であるかを知らずにこれを克服することは不可能であろう．

> Judith Beck はセッションのあちこちで，患者が経験している種々の症状が実は（患者自身の価値のなさに由来するものではなく）うつ病の症状であり，したがって治癒を期待できることを説明している．たとえば，記憶力の低下という症状について「あなたはうつ病という病気にかかっていて，そのためにこのような症状があるのだということを知っておくことは大切です」と説明を加え，さらに「うつ病が治ればこれらの症状も軽くなります」と希望を与えることも怠っていない（→ p.75）．

　もう1つ，セッション初期の心理教育で大切なのは，**認知行動療法そのものについての心理教育**である．認知行動療法とは何か，治療はどのような予定になっているか，認知行動療法を受ける際にはどういう心がけが必要か，についての説明である．私たちは認知行動療法を通じて，患者に彼らが抱えている問題に対する新しい見方，新しい行動を見いだしてもらうことになる．新しい見方，新しい行動には，当然，新しい名前が付いているのが普通であろう．古い名前，患者が慣れ親しんだ名前で新しい概念を教えるか，新しい名前で新しい概念を教えるかは，どちらがよいとも限らないかもしれないが，私は後者を好んでいる．

> Judith Beck は，患者と協力して問題解決にあたるためにセッションの構造化について心理教育することが非常に重要であることを強

調している．心理教育が，原則①から④のベースにあるというわけである．

DVDは初回セッションであるので，Judith Beckは「セッションの初めに，今夜話し合うアジェンダをあなたと一緒に決めたいと思います」と宣言してから，そのタスクに患者と取りかかるようにしている．これは認知行動療法の進め方についての心理教育の例である（→ p.64）．

一方，認知行動モデルについての説明も，初回セッションから行われている．「あなたが悲しくて怖いと感じていたのは，その時頭の中で考えていたことのためだということはわかりますか？ もしその時に違うことを考えていたら，違う気持ちを感じていたでしょう．たとえば，『お母さん，よくもそんなことを言うものだわ』と思っていたら，あなたは怒りを感じたかもしれません．あるいは，『またお母さんが八つ当たりしている，そんなことに耳を貸す必要はないわ』と思っていたら，平気だったかもしれません．そうですね？」「つまり，その状況であなたの考えていることがあなたの気持ちに影響しているということがわかりますか？」「もう1つ，うつ病についてあなたに知っておいてもらいたいのは，うつ病の人はみんなこういう気持ちを感じているということです．落ちこんだ考えがあり，怖いという考えもありますが，そういう考えは，事実ではない，あるいはすべてが事実ではないということです」「でも今のところ，あなたはそう考えています．絶対に事実だと思っていて，そうじゃないかもしれない，うつ病だから考えるだけのことかもしれない，とは考えません．そこで今からやりたいのは，あなたが自分の考えを知り，その考えがどの程度事実なのかを自分で見つける方法です」かなり単刀直入な説明である（→ p.76）．

> Aaron T. Beck 2『家族の問題—初回面接』でも,「夫の帰りが遅いので,悲しくなる」ととらえている患者に,かなりの手間暇をかけて,状況と感情の間には認知が来るということを説明している(→ p.149).

 しかし,いずれの方法をとるにしても,新しい概念について丁寧に患者に伝えなくてはならないことは,大原則である.そこで,私たちは,付録②(p.186)に示す「認知行動療法についてよくある質問」を第1回セッション(あるいは第1回セッションの前)に患者に渡し,新しい言葉を説明するようにしている.また,患者用マニュアルあるいは患者用練習帳などと称したワークブックを疾患ごとにできるだけ用意して患者に手渡すようにしている.
 治療の中盤では,具体的に患者の問題に即した認知スキルあるいは行動スキルについての,心理教育が行われなくてはならないことはもちろんであるが,それらの例は以下の⑧(p.35)に示す.

⑥宿題の重視:おさらいと設定

 宿題 homework(ホームワーク,課題などとも呼ばれる)は,認知行動療法の必須アイテムである.認知行動療法において宿題が果たす役割は複数ある.
 第一は,もちろん,患者がセッション中に学んだ認知スキルや行動スキルを練習して身につけるためのものである.練習なしに身につくスキルは地上に存在しない.Judith Beck の DVD 中の解説の言葉を借りれば,「我々は患者さんが最初に治療に来た時に,週1回の45分か50分のセッションに来るだけでは十分ではないこと,そして治療で学んだことをその後の1週間,できればその後の人生でずっと活用する必要があるということを伝えます」(→ p.118).

第二は，セッション内の時間と，セッション外の時間をつなぐためのものである．たとえば，セッション内でロールプレイでアサーションを練習した患者は，次回のセッションまでにそれを応用する機会を持つのがよいであろう．これを繰り返すことにより，新しく学んだスキルを実生活に生かすという姿勢が涵養される．DVDの解説の中で Judith Beck はこの意義を次のような言葉で雄弁に説明している「私は心の中で，どうすればセッションの外で彼女にとって役に立つことができるだろうか，と考えていました」(→ p.115).

　第三は，宿題ができたならできたものが，できなかったならできなかったことが，次のセッションのアジェンダとなりうる．つまりアジェンダ→宿題→アジェンダ…という形で，宿題がセッションの主要な題材を提供してくれるように，治療全体の流れが構造化されていることが多い．また，このことが意味することは，宿題はできた時はもちろんすばらしいが，できなかった時も同じくらい大切な素材となるということである．

> セッションの内容に対応しながら，患者と一緒に宿題を設定することはあまりに当然のことであり，ここに収載した3つのセッションすべてで見事に治療の流れの中で扱われているので，よく味わっていただきたい．

　このように重要な宿題であるので，上記②で触れたように，毎回セッションの最初に前回に出された宿題の成果をチェックすることを，決して忘れてはならない．また，そのチェックにおいて，患者がきちんとやってきたのならば，心から（つまりわざとではなく），少し大げさと思われるくらいに，肯定的なコメントをしてあげよう．

きっと次の宿題へのモチベーションを高めてくれるであろう．

また，その週の宿題は，まとめの時間に患者と治療者が協力しながら設定する．治療全体の流れの中で，当初はどうしても治療者が主導権を握るが，途中からは患者が自ら目標を設定できるくらいに患者を動機づけできていれば，すばらしい．

宿題の不遵守に対してどのように対応するかは，成書に譲りたい（Judith Beck『認知療法実践ガイド　基礎から応用まで』（星和書店 pp.331-350, 2007），Judith Beck『認知療法実践ガイド：困難事例編』（星和書店，pp.291-348, 2007），Jessie H. Wright『認知行動療法トレーニングブック』（医学書院，pp. 243-246, 2007）．

⑦セッション中のホットな認知を見逃さないこと

ホットな認知 hot cognition とは，強い情動を伴う認知のことである．とりわけ，治療セッション中に，治療者との間でホットな認知が生じた時こそ，治療展開のビッグチャンスである．

したがって，有能な認知行動療法家は，セッション中の患者の感情の動きを示唆する，言語的および非言語的兆候に敏感でなくてはならない．Aaron T. Beck は「感情は認知へ至る王道である」と書いた．Judith Beck も「感情負荷の高い思考は，治療で扱うべき最も重要な思考である」と指摘している．

> Judith Beck のセッションでは，当初非常に落ちこみ泣きだしそうであった患者が，突然明るくなった．Judith Beck はこの感情の変化，そしてそれに伴う認知の変化をハイライトしている．たとえば，下記⑧-c を使い，繰り返し浮かんでくるネガティブなイメージを書き換えたあと Beck は患者に「（修正したイメージを思い浮かべた時），どんな気持ちになりますか」とすでに表情の明るくなった患者に自

己確認を促している(→ p.82).
 一方，自動思考への反論を患者に書き留めてもらっている中で，患者の反応が変化したことを決して見逃さず「さきほどよりも確信がないようですね？」とすかさず明確化している(→ p.95).

Aaron T. Beck 1『絶望感―初回面接』のDVDでは，セッション中のホットな認知の扱い方が見事に示されている．治療への期待を問われて患者が「これは私の最後の望みで…」と述べた時，Beckは『今しがた，あなたが「これは私の最後の望み」とおっしゃった時，ずいぶん悲しそうでした』と感情を指摘した上で，すぐさま「これは最後の望みだと言った時，あなたの頭の中にはどんなことが浮かんでいましたか？ 心の中に何か絵が浮かびましたか？」と自動思考の同定に見事につなげている(→ p.130).
 また，宿題として活動記録表の説明をした時には，患者が表面的には同意したが表情が伴っていないことも見逃さず「否定的な考えが浮かびましたか？」と言語化している．患者は自分が本当にケアされている，理解しようとされていることを感じたであろう(→ p.145).

やはり同じセッションであるが，セッションに来る前からセッションの前半まで「とても絶望的に感じて問題に圧倒されていた」患者がセッションを通じて変化していることを，Beckは「今もまだ，問題に対して絶望的だと感じていますか？」という質問によって明確化し自覚させている．セッションの中で感情が動くこと，そしてそれが治療者とのやりとり（たとえば問題解決技法，認知再構成など）によって変わることを患者に実感させることができれば，認知行動技法の有効性を患者はまさに体感できるであろう(→ p.146).
 また，最近の感情の動きに話題が及ぶと，Beckは「今もそのよう

に感じていますか」「今はどうですか？」と何度も聞いている．そしてその感情の原因となった思考の同定へとつなげているのも見事で，なかなか実際にできることではないと感じるのは私だけであろうか．

　Judith Beck は DVD の中で解説者から「あなたが彼女に対し，言語的，非言語的フィードバックの両方を使っている様子に感銘を受けました．非言語的行動を解釈するというのは，認知療法家の特徴ですか？」と問われ，「もちろんです．それは非常に重要です」と即答している．

⑧症例の認知行動的理解に沿った認知的技法，行動的技法の応用

　認知行動療法の範疇でとらえられるスキルにはかなりの幅がある．以下に，この DVD でデモンストレートされている主なスキルの名前と，その簡単な解説を加えた．DVD のやりとりの対訳の右欄に，上記の①から⑦までの主な原則と並んで，以下の a から o の 15 のスキルを該当箇所に記したので，DVD を見る時に参照していただくとよいだろう．

a）自動思考の同定

　自動思考はできごとに対して瞬時にかつ自動的に浮かび上がるので，通常我々自身それに気付いていることは少ない．そこで，認知行動療法では自動思考に気付くことが治療の第一歩になる．この間の事情を，Judith Beck は DVD の解説中で以下のように述べている．「我々は患者に対し，その考えを変えなさいと言うのではなく，自分の考えを自分で評価することを教えます」と．

　この DVD に収載されたすべてのセッションで，もちろん，自動

思考の同定が行われているが，例をいくつか挙げよう．

　Judith Beck のセッションでは，患者が取り上げたいと選んだ問題について最近の具体的な状況を患者から聴取する中で，まず患者の感情を問うたところ，悲しみと恐怖の両方があったので，それぞれに応じた自動思考を問うことになった「とくに悲しいという思いはありましたか？」それから「怖いとか，心細いという気持ちとつながっているのは，どのような考えですか？」(→ P.71).

　Aaron T. Beck 1『絶望感―初回面接』のDVDでは，ホットな認知に着目してAaron T. Beck は次のように自動思考の同定につなげている．Beck が「あなたがどうしてそう考えるようになったのでしょう？　私たちにはあなたの考え方を手助けすることができるかもしれない，と？」と問うた時，患者が「私を助けることはできない，ということですか？」と聞いてきたら，すかさず「それは興味深い考えですね．私は，私たちにはあなたを助けることはできるだろうと言ったのです」と指摘し，患者が「どうも否定的な考えでしたね」と気付いたら，「そうです．重要なこと，大切な発見です．もしこの先も否定的な考えが浮かんだら，私に話してくれますか？」と誘導している(→ P.134).

　Aaron T. Beck 2『家族の問題―初回面接』では，なかなか自動思考を同定できない患者に，「その状況にいっしょに身をおいて，あなたの考えを捕まえることができるかどうか，あなたの頭の中に否定的な考えが浮かぶかどうか見てみましょう．では想像してみましょう．自分が家にいる様子を思い浮かべてください．できますか？」と誘導している(→ P.161).

b) 自動思考への反論（認知再構成）cognitive restructuring

　ここでは認知再構成のための細かい技法を詳説することはしないが，DVDの中ではネガティブな自動思考に反論するための方法がいくつか実演されている．

> 成書にあるように，自動思考に反論するための質問はたくさんあるが，Judith Beck が最初に用いているのは「○○というのは，どの程度現実にありそうですか？」「○○という根拠があるのですか？」「逆に，○○ではないだろうという根拠はありますか？」，次に「この先5年間のうちに○○の可能性はどれくらいありますか？」を用いている（→ p.77）．

> 30年前の Aaron T. Beck はこのあたりではもっと理知的であったようだ．『家族の問題―初回面接』では「からかっているのではありませんよ．あなたの考えの中に間違いはないのか，実際の問題以上に悪い問題をあなたが創ってしまっているのではないか，見ようとしているだけです．何らかの問題があることは確かです．彼は夕食の時間に帰ってこない．しかし私には，その問題は究極の結論にまで至り，あなたは彼なしでは存在できない，死んだほうがまし，と信じてしまっているように思えます」というような反論をしたり（→ p.166），「あなたは心の中で最悪の解釈をする傾向がありますよね．起こりうる最悪のことは何ですか」（→ p.169）また「今日おわかりのように，あなたの考えの多くは，実は正確ではないように思えるからです．そういう否定的な考えのほとんどは正確ではなく，間違っているところを正すことができれば，あなたはもっと楽になるはずです」とかなり単刀直入に指摘している（→ p.174）．

その他の認知行動療法の大原則

c）イメージ書き換え（イメージ再構成）imagery rescripting

　認知行動モデルにおける「認知」はしばしば自動思考と等値されるが，実際には多くの患者においては脳裏に浮かぶイメージ，映像，絵であることが多い．

> Judith Beck の患者では，「どうしようもなく無力だ」という感情に伴うイメージ（自分が育ったシカゴのアパートが，今は空っぽになって，そこで自分1人が窓から外を見ている）を同定し，それを書き換えるという作業を見事に実現していて，きわめて印象深い（→ p.80）．

d）中核信念の修正 schema work

　③認知行動モデルで述べたように，複数の状況に対する自動思考には一定の傾向，パターンが見られる．このように現実の如何に関わらず一定であるところの，すなわち現実には，えてしてそぐわない自動思考が生み出される基になっているのが，中核信念，スキーマである．中核信念そのものに働きかけ，これを修正することは可能である．

> Aaron T. Beck 1『絶望感―初回面接』は第1回セッションではあるが，はやくも，「自分はダメだ」という中核信念にかなり近い思考について，そうだと思える理由とそうではないと思える理由を問い，中核信念の修正を図っている（→ p.139）．

e）行動実験 behavioral experiment

　自動思考やさらにはそのベースにある条件信念，中核信念が現実にそぐっているか否かを直接に試すことができるような行動を試み

ることを行動実験という．30年前のAaron T. Beckがすでに DVD の中で行動実験を勧めていたのは新鮮であった．

> Aaron T. Beck 1『絶望感―初回面接』の DVD では Beck が宿題設定で「今日から水曜日までの間に第一歩を踏み出したら，二歩目について話し合いましょう．そして最初よりも簡単になるかどうかみてみましょう」と述べるところがある(→ p.141)．また，行動活性化の1つとしてブラックジャックについての本を患者が見てみようと設定するところがあるが，それに対して Beck は「わかったら私にも教えてください」と動機づけしている．行動実験という用語は使っていないが，行動実験の精神であろう(→ p.144)．

> Aaron T. Beck 2『家族の問題―初回面接』で，夫がいないと生きていけないと述べる患者に，夫と出会う前のことを思いださせて，当時と比較することを提案している．これを"test out some of these beliefs"（あなたの考えが本当にそうかどうか試してみてみましょうよ）と述べ，実験的態度を強調している(→ p.168)．

f) メリット・デメリット分析 merits-demerits analysis

下記の問題解決技法の中でも使われるが，広く，行動の選択肢の中から意思決定をする際の援助として使われる．自動思考への反論の1つの方法として，そのように信じることのメリットとデメリットを列記してみるという方法もある．

> Judith Beck は自立するためには母の家から出るのが最初か，とどまって車を買うのが最初かと迷う患者に，それぞれのメリット・デメリットをあげてもらった上で，判断を求めている．この方法は

DVD 中の患者にとって特に気に入ったようで，セッションのまとめで感想を問うた時に一番よかったこととして挙げていた（→ P.99）.

g）活動モニタリング activity monitoring

　典型的には，1週間の各曜日について1時間ごとに区切った表を用意し，1時間ごとに何をしたかを患者に記入してもらうことをいう．患者の活動や生活についてのデータ収集に役立つ．診察室で聞いていた以上に乱れた生活パターンが浮かび上がってくることも多い．さらに，活動ごとに喜び pleasure や達成感 accomplishment を各10段階で記入してもらうと，患者にとって喜びまたは達成感が高い活動や，逆に低い活動を一緒に探求することができる．

　Aaron T. Beck 1『絶望感―初回面接』の DVD では活動モニタリングが宿題として出されている（→ P.145）.

h）行動活性化 behavioral activation

　喜びをもたらしそうな活動リストの中から，あるいは上記の活動モニタリングで患者にとって喜びや達成感が高い活動の中から，現実に患者にとってやれそうでかつやりがいがありそうな課題を選んでもらって，それを行うことによる気分の変化を見てもらう．

　Aaron T. Beck 1『絶望感―初回面接』の DVD では具体的事例がみられる．その部分の最初の Beck の問いかけは「リストアップしてどうなるか，見てみましょうか．興味があってやってみたいと思っていることには，何がありますか？」（→ P.136）であったり，「では，何もしない時間が長いとは言えなくするために，今から水曜日までに，あなたにできることは何でしょう？」（→ P.142）で始まっている．

i) アサーション訓練 assertion training

　自己主張訓練とも訳されるが，日本語としてはニュアンスが強すぎる．アサーションとは，相手の気持ちをおもんばかりながら，自分の気持ちや考えを上手に伝えることをいう．

> Judith Beck は宿題の1つとして，セッション中にメリット・デメリット分析から患者が出した結論を，お姉さんに対してアサーションしてみることを取り上げている (→ p.90).

> Aaron T. Beck も Aaron T. Beck 2『家族の問題─初回面接』で，「もし彼が，『お母さんはぼくを愛してくれていない，家では愛されていない』と言うなら，あなたは，『お母さんはこのところずっと落ちこんでいて，うつ病の人は気持ちをうまく表現できないの』と言えばいいのです」と，アサーションの方法を具体的に示して推奨している (→ p.159).

j) 問題解決技法 problem-solving technique

　問題解決モード（上記①参照）で治療上取り扱うべき問題を検討した時，もしその問題が現実のものであれば，患者側の認知を修正することに意味はなく，現実にその問題を取り扱わなくてはならない．現実の問題には(i)大切でない問題─あなたの人生の重要な目的には関係がない問題，(ii)大切で解決できる問題，(iii)大切だが解決できない問題があり，これらを区別することを患者にまず教えないといけない．そうしたら，問題解決技法で扱うのは間違いなく(ii)であり，これを，1)扱える大きさの問題に分解し，2)可能な解決方法をブレーンストーミングし，3)各解決策の案のメリットとデメリットを列挙し，4)最終的に最もメリットとデメリットのバランスのよい解決策

を選んでその具体的施行方法を検討し，5)実行する，という順番で解決しようとするとよい．

> ここに収載した3つのセッションでは，構造化した問題解決技法は行われていないが，Aaron T. Beck 1『絶望感―初回面接』では「問題を小さく砕いたら，（あなた自身が）それほど強くなくてもいいかもしれないと思いますか？」と問題解決技法のステップ1を行っている(→ p.139)．
>
> Aaron T. Beck 2『家庭の問題―初回面接』では「私に伝わってくるのは，これがとても悪い大問題で，あまりにも圧倒的で広範囲すぎて，誰にも何もできないということです．あなたは，この問題を細かい要素に砕いて，問題がなんなのかを正確に見ようとしたことがあるのでしょうか」と問いかけている(→ p.154)．

問題解決モードを維持する上で覚えておかなくてはならないことは，常に問題を具体的に，細やかになぞることである．たとえば，Judith Beck の患者が，アジェンダ設定で「母の悲しみとどうつきあうか」という問題を選んだ時，Beck が次に聞いている質問は「この問題はこの1週間に起こりましたか？」である．そして「それはいつでしたか？」「どんなことがあったのか話してください」と具体的な状況を扱うのであって，一般的な問題を扱ってはいない(→ p.70)．

このあたりの機微を彼女自身，DVDのあとの解説で「普通，患者さんは，私の人生はめちゃくちゃだ，とても不幸だ，どうすればいいのかわからない，といった大きな問題を抱えてやってきます．でもそれは取り組むには大きすぎるので，我々はそういう大きな問題を具体的なものにしていきます．話ができるように問題を絞っていき，

そのセッションで問題解決に取り組みます」と説明している(→ p.104).

　問題全般を解決することはできない．私たちが解決できるのは，常に，個別具体的な問題である．

k) 段階的課題設定 graded task assignment
　行動活性化，アサーション訓練，問題解決技法などの行動スキルにそった課題設定の際には，一挙に目標を目指すのではなく，小さな達成可能な数段階に分けて設定するとよい．達成できない大きなステップよりも，達成できた小さなステップのほうがはるかに治療のモチベーションを高めてくれるであろう．

> Aaron T. Beck 1『絶望感──初回面接』は，このあたりをかなり強調している．たとえば，行動活性化の課題の1つとしてボーリングを取り上げているが，ついつい患者が「ボーリングに行く」と述べるのに対し，「情報を得る，することはそれだけです」「私はあなたに行きなさいと言いませんでしたよ」「ボーリングについては，情報を得るだけでいいのですよ」と何度も押しとどめている(→ p.138)．そして，セッションの最後のまとめでは「すぐにできてしまえばいいのにと思いますよ．そうすればあなたもすぐに気持ちが楽になります．しかし時間をかけてください．そうすれば大きな問題も小さくなり，小さくなった問題に取り組んでいるうちに，大きな問題もすでに解決しているということがわかるでしょう」と解説している(→ p.147).

l) ロールプレイ role play
　行動活性化，アサーション訓練，問題解決技法，あるいは段階的課題設定のような行動スキルの宿題のアドヒアランスをよくする1

つのこつは，セッション内ですでに一度リハーサルをしておくことである．セッション内という，患者にとって治療者に保護された環境下で行うことは，セッション外で初めて試みるよりも通常はるかに容易であろう．治療者が相手役となってロールプレイをしたり，時には治療者が患者役をやる逆ロールプレイの形で，試行するとよい．

> Aaron T. Beck 2『家族の問題─初回面接』では，夫の帰りが遅い理由を尋ねる質問文を実際に患者に言わせて，適不適を検討している（→ p.169）．3つの DVD 中には，残念ながら，典型的なロールプレイは含まれていなかった．

m）行動用語で記述

以下の3項目は認知行動療法の「技法」と呼ぶにはおこがましいが，しかし，実際の認知行動療法の施行において，キーとなる要素であるので，あえて列挙したい．

行動用語 behavioral terms で記述するとは，端で見ている第三者にもそのことが起こったかどうかが見るだけで判定できるように記述することを言う．目標を行動用語で記述することによって，目標は患者と治療者が共有可能なものとなり，「できたけどできなかった」というような患者の認知のゆがみに左右されない目標となる．

> Aaron T. Beck 1『絶望感─初回面接』の DVD で行動活性化を図る時，「～します」（たとえば，ボーリングをします）と患者が言うところで止めずに，どのようにして探しますか，そこへ行ったら何ができますかなどと，具体的な行動で想像・記述させている．このようにすることで，実際に患者が行動活性化に取り組む可能性は高まるであろうし，また，次週復習をする時にそれができたかどうかを患者も

治療者も知ることができる(→ p.136).

n) 相対化(数量化, 命名)

　生じた感情を10段階あるいは100点満点で数量化することは，認知行動療法で常に行われる．通常 Subjective Units of Distress (SUD)と称されるが，患者が「つらい，つらい」としか認識できない状態を，たとえば8/10つらい状態と6/10つらい状態で弁別できるようになると，改善のための方策を見つけやすくなる．

　　Judith Beck は自動思考に反論を考えたあと，患者に「あなたはどのくらい信じますか？」「心のどこかで信じていないところはありますか？」と，数量化までは求めていないが，心の中に両面があること，ネガティブな部分には何があるかを明確化しようとしている (→ p.91).
　　また「○○することは大変だろうが，不可能ではない」という反論を何度か使っているが，これも数量化の一例であろう．

o) カードやノートに書き留める

　これも認知行動療法の1つの技法である．セッションのまとめや宿題を患者自らがカードやノートに書き留め，さらにセッション外でもレビューできるようにする．認知行動療法は学習であるという原点に立ち戻れば，果たして，授業でノートを取らないで学ぶことが可能かどうかを自問すれば，この技法の重要性は明らかであろう．

　同様に，治療者のほうも，ホワイトボードやフリップチャートを積極的に利用し，患者と過程を共有しながら認知再構成を行ったり，段階的課題を設定したりすると，より大きな効果を望めるであろう．

Judith Beck のセッションでは，アジェンダが進み結論が見えてきた段階で，治療者が「紙に書いてみましょうよ．覚えておけるように」と促している(→ p.88)．セッションを振り返った解説の中で，Beck が「患者さんは診察室の中でのことをほとんど全部忘れてしまうということが研究からわかっています．ですから経験則に従い，患者さんに覚えておいてもらいたいことは何らかの形で記録する必要があるのです」(→ p.114)と理由付けしているが，実際，私自身もセッションの橋渡しで患者に前回治療の内容を聞くと驚くほど覚えていないものであることには今更ながら驚きがある．

Aaron T. Beck 1『絶望感─初回面接』の DVD では，宿題のリストは Beck 自身がメモした上でその紙を患者に手渡している(→ p.146)．また，次回への橋渡しとして，治療について否定的な考えを持ったら書き留めてくるように求めている(→ p.148)．

第2部
3つの面接のやりとりの英語原文, 日本語訳, 注釈

英語とその翻訳を対訳でつけた．さらに右端にどのような原則が反映されているか，あるいはどのような認知的技法，行動的技法が使われているか，を示した．
読者はセッションを見ながら，そうかこれが教科書にあった○○だなどとわかっていただけると嬉しい．

Judith Beck『うつ病』(Disc 1)

登場人物　Judith Beck(以下 JB)
　　　　　Jon Carlson 心理学博士，教育学博士(以下 JC)
　　　　　心理学及びカウンセリング教授，ガバナーズステート大学
　　　　　Diane Kjos，博士(以下 DK)
　　　　　心理学及びカウンセリング教授，ガバナーズステート大学
　　　　　患者(以下 C)

> この DVD は，① JC と DK による Judith Beck のインタビュー，② Judith Beck による患者の面接，③そして再び JC と DK による Judith Beck のインタビューの3部構成になっている．③では②を 10 個のセグメントに分けて再録し，そのつど検討を加えている．そこでこれらの 10 セグメントを§1〜10 と表し，②の発言に「§1 ここから」「§1 ここまで」などと記入する．

JC	All therapy attempts to be brief. Brief therapy clearly attempts to identify a therapeutic focus and then strives to reach that goal in a time-limited, efficient and systematic fashion. This series brings together the leading strategies in the area of brief therapy. Each will demonstrate their therapy with real people with real life problems.	治療はどれもできるだけ短期であろうとしますが，短期精神療法は治療目的を明確にした上で，限られた時間内に組織的にその目的に到達することを目指します．このシリーズでは短期精神療法分野における主要な方法をご紹介します．それぞれの DVD では実際の患者と現実の問題をお示しします．
	Hi, I'm Jon Carlson. Welcome to "Brief Therapy Inside Out."	ジョン・カールソンです．「短期精神療法に親しむ」にようこそ．
DK	And I'm Diane Kjos. This is our guest, Judith Beck, who's going to talk with us today about cognitive brief therapy. Judith, I'm interested in... what is your idea of brief therapy? How long is it? How do we define brief therapy?	ダイアン・クジョスです．こちらはジュディス・ベックさんです．認知療法についてお話ししてくださいます．ジュディス，あなたがお考えになる短期精神療法とは何ですか？　長さはどれくらいですか？　短期精神療法をどう定義づけますか？
JB	I think cognitive therapy actually tries to be time-sensitive, and that is, we try to help patients overcome disorders and stay better in as brief a time as we can.	認知療法は時間を考慮に入れており，できるだけ短期間に患者さんが障害を克服し，よりよい状態でいられるように手助けをすることを目指します．

JB	For easy patients like the one we will be watching in a few minutes, you might see the patient for some place between 12 to 14 sessions. For more difficult patients, particularly one who might have a comorbid Axis II type diagnosis, we might see the patient for a year or even a little bit more.	後ほどこのDVDでお見せするような軽症の患者さんには12回から14回ほどのセッション、Ⅱ軸タイプの診断が並存するような難しい患者さんの場合は1年、あるいはそれ以上必要なこともあります．
JC	Just what is your therapy approach or strategies that you use?	あなたの治療アプローチや戦略とはどんなものですか？
JB	There're several components that are really important for cognitive therapy. One is that cognitive therapy tends to be very structured. They tend to follow the same kind of format for most sessions and most patients because we find that's how we get most done and most efficient use of the time. The second important component is that we have a cognitive conceptualization of the patient. We're always thinking to ourselves, "How is it that the patient got to that point? What are the patient's most basic beliefs about herself?"	認知療法には重要な要素がいくつかあります．その1つは非常に構造化されているということです．ほとんどの患者さんに対して同一の形式を用います．それが一番効果があり，時間的にも効率がよいことがわかっているからです．次に重要な要素は，患者さんの認知的概念図を我々が持つということです．その患者さんがどのようにしてそういう状態になったのか，自分についてのもっとも基本的な信念はどうなっているかを，我々は常に考えています． ②構造化 ③認知行動モデル
JC	Is it how the thinking of this is?	基本的な考え方？
JB	Very strong thinking this is. Both in understanding the underlying beliefs the patient has, and also the thinking of the specific situations today that are causing her problems.	非常に強力な考え方です．患者さんが持つ根本的な信念を理解することにおいても，患者さんが現在の問題を持つ原因となった具体的な状況を考えることにおいても．
JC	Just how does this structure work? Give us kind of a thumbnail sketch of the process.	その構造とはどういうものですか？　そのプロセスの概要を教えてください．

JB	Sure. First we usually do a mood check so we have a sense of whether the patient has made progress since we started the therapy, get a sense of how the past week was. Then we usually set an agenda and we ask the patient, "What problem do you want to work on today?" So we get the patient to be very specific about something that she wants help with.	まず最初に気分をチェックします．患者さんが前回のセッションから進歩があったかどうかを見ます．そしてアジェンダを決めます．今日は何について相談したいのかを特定してもらいます．患者さんには相談したいことを非常に具体的にしてもらいます．	②セッションの構造化 ①問題解決モード ⑥宿題のおさらい
JC	OK.		
JB	Then we usually make a bridge from the previous session to this current session. We might ask the patient what she remembers from the previous session that was important, what happened during the week that the therapist needs to know, what kind of homework did she get done. And this is very important. If we suspect the patient might have had a negative reaction from the previous session, we might ask what did you think of the last session, was there anything that bothered you, did it bother you particularly when I did so and so.	次に，前回のセッションから今回のセッションへの橋渡しをします．前回どんな重要なことを学んだか，この1週間にどんなことがあったか，宿題をやったかを尋ねます．そして重要なことは，もし患者さんが前回のセッションについて否定的な思いを持っていると感じたら，前回のセッションをどう思ったか，困惑したか，治療者が言ったことで嫌なことがあったか，と尋ねます．	
JC	So, there's a lot of feedback you solicit from the client.	患者さんから多くのフィードバックを得るのですね．	④協力的実証主義
JB	There is, throughout the session. The beginning part of the session has these kinds of components. Then the middle part of the session, usually we start with one problem, and do a combination of some problem-solving and also then teaching the patient some skills that she needs in order to solve this problem and hopefully skills that she'll use for the rest of her life.	それはセッション中ずっとです．それらがセッションの最初の部分の要素です．次に，セッションの中では，1つの問題に取り組み，問題解決とそのために必要なスキルを教えます．患者さんがその問題を解決し，また将来もずっと用いることのできるようなスキルです．	①問題解決モード ⑤心理教育：認知的スキル，行動的スキル
JC	So it's directive then.	つまり指示的なわけですね？	
JB	It is.	はい，ですが協力的でもあります．	②セッションの構造化 ④協力的実証主義

Judith Beck『うつ病』

JC	As well as collaborative, it's directive?	協力的であると同時に指示的でもある？	
JB	In the last part of the session we try to have the patient summarize what she got out of the session and then give the therapist some feedback. And we try to figure out what the patient needs to do this current week, this coming week I should say, in order to move ahead with her problems.	セッションの最後では，患者さんに学んだことをまとめてもらい，フィードバックしてもらいます．我々は患者さんが問題に取り組むためにそれからの1週間に必要なことを考えます．	⑥宿題の設定 ①問題解決モード
JC	So, then there's a homework assignment that's given, very directive homework assignment?	指示的な宿題を出すのですね．	
JB	It's usually collaboratively set. So one of the things I might say to the patient is, "OK, we've just discussed this problem you're having with being more independent. What kind of things would you like to try this week?" Or if I had some ideas where she'd stuck, I might suggest, "What do you think about doing this or doing that?"	患者さんと協力しながら考えます．「もっと自立したいというあなたの問題について話し合いましたが，今週はどのようなことを試みたいですか」と尋ねたり，患者さんがどこで行き詰まるかがわかっている時は，「こうしてはどうですか」と提案します．	
JC	You don't do this in an embedded hidden message kind of approach to these suggestions? Are they forthright, straight forward?	そういう提案を埋めこんだ隠れたメッセージとしては伝えない？ ずばりと言うストレートな表現なのですか？	
JB	Yes, very straight forward. Usually they have something to do with solving a specific problem or helping the patient practice something, some skill that she's learned during the therapy.	非常にストレートに言います．そのような提案は，患者さんの抱える問題を解決するためのことであったり，セッションで学んだスキルを練習する助けになるようなことですから．	⑤心理教育：認知的スキル，行動的スキル
DK	That sounds like you're both following the client and somewhat leading at the same time, or directing.	患者さんにまかせることと，指示を与えることを同時にしているように思えますが？	

JB	That's right. There's always coming tension in a session between having the patient talk on and on so you can get enough data about a problem and conceptualize it, and then stopping the patient and making an intervention. So the art of therapy I think is being able to resolve this tension and do as much work in as efficient manners as possible, but also in as effective manners as possible.	そうです．セッションでは，問題についてのデータを得て概念化するには患者さんにどんどん話してもらうということと，話を止めて介入するということの間に対立があります．この対立を解消し，できる限り効果的な方法で治療を行うことが治療のコツだと思います．	③認知行動モデル ④協力的実証主義 ⑤心理教育
JC	Maybe you can help me understand. Just how does this change occur in this model? That's the process that goes through but...	もう少し説明していただけますか．その変化は，このモデルではどのように生じるのですか？	
JB	I think the change occurs very directly. So one of the things we do is to help the patient learn a system for evaluating her thoughts because we know that when people are psychologically distressed they often have thoughts that are quite distorted. Now, rather than telling them how they need to change the thoughts, what we try to do is to teach them how to evaluate their thoughts themselves. Sometimes the thoughts, however, turn out to be true and in that case we need to do some straight problem solving which involves change. Sometimes the problem has more to do with their perception of the situation, in which case then we teach them the very specific cognitive change.	変化は非常に直接的に生じると思います．我々が行うことの1つは，患者さんに自分の考えを評価するシステムを学んでもらうことです．ストレス下では人の考えは歪んでいるからです．我々は患者さんに対し，その考えを変えなさいと言うのではなく，自分の考えを自分で評価することを教えます． 時には患者さんの考えが正しいことがあります．そういう場合は，変化に直結するような問題解決を行います．問題が，患者さんが状況をどうとらえているかということにより深く関わるならば，我々はその問題に対する認知の修正を具体的に教えます．	③認知行動モデル ⑧-a 自動思考の同定：セルフモニタリング ①問題解決モード
JC	So then, the change takes place by teaching them how to assess their thinking?	自分の考えを知り，自分の考え方をどうすればわかるかを教えることで変化が生じるわけですか？	
JB	Uh.	．	

Judith Beck『うつ病』

JC	And then how to change the way they think?	（字幕なし）
JB	That's right. And also in changing their behavior, oftentimes we find that the patients are very deficient in the problem solving skills or social skills or work-related skills. Then we very directly teach them how to be different.	そうです．行動を変える過程では，患者さんは問題解決スキルやソーシャルスキル，仕事に関わるスキルが不十分だとわかることが多いので，我々はそれらを直接的に教えます．
JC	So there's a behavioral component.	つまり行動的な要素もあるのですね．
JB	Oh, yes.	はい．
JC	I see.	
DK	What influence do you have to be a cognitive therapist? Can you tell me a little bit of a background of...	認知療法家として，あなたはどのような影響を受けてこられたのでしょうか？
JC	Give me what, or do you mean who?	何から，ということ？　誰から，ということ？
DK	Well, let her tell us that.	彼女の話を聞きましょうよ．
JB	I never thought that I'd be a psychologist. I started off as a teacher. I've wanted to be a teacher ever since probably I was five years old. Never had a thought about going into psychology at all. And didn't really have a thought about it until I was in graduate school in education. Actually, both of my parents suggested that I should give therapy a try, give cognitive therapy specifically a try. As you know, my father was Aaron Beck who developed this form of therapy. And I decided to listen to them, thank god, happily so, give it a try. I think one of the reasons I never thought about being a psychologist was that I was always a very good intuitive teacher. It's became very natural to me about how to teach kids, how to teach other people. And I didn't realize that... it's kind of an idea looking back at it... that one could learn how to be a psychologist and a therapist. You didn't have to be born with an intuitive knowledge of that, but there are actually steps you could learn.	私は自分が心理学者になるとは思ってもいませんでした．仕事のスタートは教師でした．子どもの頃から先生になりたかったのです．心理学をやろうと考えたことはありませんでした．でも大学院で教育学を学んでいる時に，両親から認知行動療法もやってみなさいと言われました．ご存知のように父はこの治療法を確立したアーロン・ベックです．私は言われたようにやってみようと思いました． 私が心理学者になることを考えてもいなかったのは，私が生まれつきの教師だったからだと思います．私にとって子どもを教えるということはとても自然なことだったので，心理学者や治療者になることを学ぶことができる，とは思っていなかったのです．生まれつきの素質ではなくて，学ぶことができる，ということをです．
JC	Certainly you're doing a lot of intuitive work. We talked about being an intuitive teacher.	あなたは多くの直感力のあるお仕事をなさっていますよ．

JB	That's right. Well, interestingly enough, I think the intuitiveness came later. First I had to spend, as most people do, enormous amount of time learning how to conceptualize patients, learning how to structure sessions, learning how to do different interventions. And I think I probably didn't realize, when I was first doing therapy, how important it is to be in tune with affective experience of the patient as she's sitting across from you. Once I realized that, then I became much more intuitive and I began using her non-verbal cues and her tone of voice and so forth as a guide to what I should do next in therapy.	そうですが，面白いことにその直観の鋭さは後から生じたと思います．最初私は誰もがするように，患者さんの概念化やセッションの構造化やさまざまな介入方法を時間をかけて学びました． 治療をするようになった当初は，自分の前に座っている患者さんの感情的体験を洞察することがいかに重要か気づいていませんでした．ですがいったん気づいてからは，私はより直観的になり，治療で次に何をすべきかを考える上で，患者さんの非言語的手がかりや声の調子などを活用するようになりました．	⑦ホットな認知： 感情の重視
JC	Is this approach, I mean when you talked about what you had to learn it, is there a research base to the work that you do?	この治療には研究の裏打ちはありますか？	
JB	Oh, yes. There's been over a hundred and fifty clinical trials, controlled trials, that show that cognitive therapy is effective for a whole range of disorders from depression to substance abuse to eating disorders, personality disorders, even schizophrenia we're finding as an add-on to medication.	もちろんです．150以上の臨床試験があり，認知療法はうつ病から薬物乱用，摂食障害，パーソナリティ障害にまで効果があることが示されています．統合失調症にも，薬物療法に認知療法を加えると効果があることがわかってきています．	

Judith Beck『うつ病』

JC	So there's outcome data that supports the work with specific clients. And is there process research that's done to indicate that you should do this particular kind of cognitive therapy technique or procedure in a certain essence?	つまり特定の患者さんに対する治療を支持するアウトカムデータはあるのですね. 個々のアプローチ方法を支持するようなプロセス研究についてはどうですか？
JB	There's been much less research on that. There have been some studies but they've tried to dismantle cognitive therapy to see what are the prime components.	これに関しては研究の数はずっと少ないです. 認知療法を分解して有効な要素を検討しようとした研究もあります.
JC	That's what I was wondering.	（字幕なし）
JB	But the bulk of research has really on its efficacy. And in fact, I think that the intuitive part of cognitive therapy would be understanding what the patient's experiencing as she's sitting across from you. It is the incredibly important part of the therapy itself. It's really the art of cognitive therapy, which is why the dismantling studies, to me, I think, do a little bit of disservice. You lose that very important part.	しかし大半の研究は認知療法全体としての有効性に関するものです. 私は, 認知療法における直感的な部分とは, 目の前に座っている患者さんの体験を理解することだと思います. それは治療そのもののきわめて重要な要素です. それこそが認知療法のアートです. だから認知療法を要素に分解するような研究は, いささか害があると思います. きわめて重要な部分を失ってしまいます.
DK	How does this compare with other brief therapies? Is it like some or different? Where would you put it?	この治療法は, ほかの短期精神療法と比べてどうですか？ 似ているものもありますか？ それとも異なりますか？

JB I think it's different in several really important ways. One is that it's very structured. And I think being structured is, of course, very important if you only have a few sessions with the patient.
The second thing is that it's very problem-solving-oriented. So in every session, we try to take a problem or part of a problem and then start solving them.
The third is that we try to use what the patient brings up right in the therapy session, the problems she's had in the past week or the problems she's going to have in the next week as important targets to focus on. And then, do this combination of both problem-solving and helping patients learn skills of evaluating their thoughts and learning behavioral skills and so forth. We do it in a very direct way that most patients really like. Just make sense to them to do it in this way. We also are very collaborative with patients. So together we make the important decisions in therapy such as what to talk about during the session, what homework to assign if there is not an externally imposing them on a number of sessions, how long we should meet, when we should go from once a week to once every two weeks or so forth.

いくつか非常に重要な点で異なっていると思います．まず第1に，この方法は非常に構造化されているということです．患者さんとのセッション回数が限られている時には構造化されていることは重要です．
第2に，問題解決を目指すということです．各セッションにおいて，1つの問題または問題の一部分を取り上げて解決を試みます．
第3に，患者さんがそのセッションで取り上げたいことを取り上げるということです．過去1週間に起きたこと，あるいはその先の1週間に起きそうなことを対象とします．そして問題解決と，患者さんが自分の考えを評価し行動的技法を学ぶ手助けの両方を行います．我々はきわめて直接的なやり方をするので，患者さんは喜びます．我々は協力的でもあり，何について話すか，何を宿題にするか，治療回数をどれくらいにするか，何分間話すか，いつ頃週1回から2週間に1回に変えるか，などを患者さんと一緒に決めます．

②セッションの構造化
①問題解決モード
④協力的実証主義

DK Are there clients that it doesn't work with? Are there particular clients?

不向きな患者さんはいますか？

Judith Beck『うつ病』

JB It's interesting. When my father first developed this therapy in the 1960s, he developed it for patients with major depression. And he says at that time he really had no idea whether or not it would apply to other disorders. He just assumed that it was made for depression. After it worked so well with the depression and there was a very important outcome to show it was actually more effective than medication for depressed patients, he and his colleagues applied it to anxiety disorders. And then new generation of people including I came along and now we've applied it to a whole range of both outpatient and inpatient disorders including endogenous depression, and as I mentioned before, schizophrenia. So we don't know the limits of therapy. One of the things we do know is that the therapy has to have a different focus on a different orientation for each disorder. So the way I've treated depressed patients might be quite different from the way I treat a panic disorder patient. What remains the same is the cognitive conceptualization, how I think about patients.

③認知行動モデル

1960年代に父がこの治療法を始めた時は大うつ病の患者さん用でした．当時父は，それ以外の障害にも用いることができるかどうかなど考えてもみず，うつ病向けということだけ考えていたそうです．やがてうつ病に対して非常に効果的で，時には薬物療法以上であることもわかり，父たちは不安障害に対してもこれを行いました．その後私を含めた次の世代がこの治療法をさまざまな障害に対して実施してきました．内因性うつ病，統合失調症にもです．可能性がどこまでなのか我々にもわかりません．わかっているのは，障害によって，異なった目標，異なった焦点を持つべきであるということです．うつ病の患者さんに対するやり方と，パニック障害の患者さんに対するやり方とでは異なります．同じなのは，私がその患者さんをどうとらえるかという認知行動モデルに則った概念化です．

JC Can we talk about the cognitive conceptualization a little bit? What's the basic formula that makes this approach work?

認知的概念化について少しお話をうかがえますか？ この治療法の基本的なやり方はどのようなものですか？

JB	The formulation has two important parts. One is looking at the patient's present life and seeing what are the typical situations that cause her a lot of distress. And then we do a kind of cross sectional analysis. We look for the thoughts the patients have in those situations, and the resulting reaction, emotional reaction, behavioral reaction and physiological reaction if there is one. So that's kind of looking at the current. Then, now this is especially important with axis II patients, we want to go back to see...	重要なことが2つあります．1つは，患者さんの現在の生活を見て，ストレスを生じさせる典型的な状況は何かを知ることです．それから横断的な分析をします．患者さんがそういった状況で抱く考え，その結果生じる情緒的反応や行動的反応や場合によっては生理的反応を探します．つまり現在を見るわけです．そしてⅡ軸の患者さんでは過去にさかのぼることがとくに重要で…．	③認知行動モデル：認知的概念化
JC	You mean the personality disorder.	パーソナリティ障害のことですね．	
JB	Personality disorder patients, right. We want to go back and see what are the patients' most basic beliefs about herself, her world and other people.	そうです．そしてさかのぼって，患者さんが自分自身や自分の周りの世界や他の人々について持っている基本的な信念を見ます．	
JC	Corebelief, or what we might call, lifestyle beliefs?	中核信念，つまり我々が言うところの生活信念ですね？	
JB	Exactly. And it's these beliefs that make it evident why it is the patient is having this kind of thoughts and reactions to current situations. We might go back and look at what kind of things happened in the patient's childhood that caused this belief to start and what kinds of events or traumas happened that helped maintain that belief. And then we say how did the patient cope with these beliefs all her life, what kind of behavioral strategies did she develop.	その通りです．そういう信念が，患者さんが現在の状況に関して特定の考えや反応を持つようにさせているものです．患者さんの子ども時代に起こったどんなことがこの信念をスタートさせ，どんなできごとやトラウマがそれを維持させてきたのか考えます．そして患者さんがこれらの信念にどう対処してきたか，どんな行動戦略を持つようになったか考えます．	
JC	They go back to one of those mistaken or faulty behaviors. What would be an example of that?	患者さんは間違った行動へ戻ってゆくわけですね．たとえば？	
JB	I think you'll see in a patient that'll come up in a few minutes. I think she probably has a belief that she's helpless and inadequate.	このDVDの患者さんに見ることができると思います．この患者さんは，自分がどうしようもなく能力不足だという信念を持っています．	
JC	That'll be the core of the belief.	それは中核信念ですね．	
JB	Core belief about herself, that's right.	自分自身についての中核信念です．	

JC	And how does that come out? What's the automatic thinking or automatic response you might have?	そのことはどのように現われますか？　どのような自動思考がありますか？
JB	When she's in a particular situation such as thinking about whether or not her mother is going to be with her for a long time or die soon, she has the thought that if I don't get independent before my mother dies then I might not make it. So there's really a sense that she doesn't feel as if she's a strong, independent, effective person. Rather the opposite. Oftentimes she sees herself as ineffective, incapable and helpless.	たとえば，この患者さんは母親が長生きするかすぐに死んでしまうか考える時に，お母さんが死ぬ前に自分が自立しないとだめだ，と考えます．自分が強く，自立した，有能な人間だとは感じていません．むしろその反対です．自分のことを何もできなくて役に立たないと思っています．
JC	Then she acts that way.	そうなるとその人はそういうふうに行動しますね．
JB	That's right. And then oftentimes what happens is she relies too much on her mother or her sister or other people instead of going ahead and doing things that she knows kind of in her heart that she needs to do.	そうです．そして彼女は母親や兄弟姉妹やほかの人たちに頼り過ぎ，心の底ではやらなくてはいけないとわかっているようなことをしなくなります．
JC	So how do you change those deeper core beliefs? I can see how you change some of the more beliefs in the present, but how do you deal with the deeper ones?	それであなたは，そのような奥底にある中核信念をどうやって変えるのですか？　現在の状況にある考えを変えることができるのはわかりますが，奥のほうにあるものは？

JB	Usually we tackle the deeper ones after the patients have learned the skills of evaluating their automatic thoughts in and around current situations. Then we have them apply some of the same techniques, the same kind of questions, to see to what degree this core belief is accurate or not. Oftentimes we find that the patients will then begin to change this belief at the intellectual level, but not necessarily at the gut level. They'll say you know I know intellectually I'm not really helpless or inadequate, but in my gut I still feet that way. And that's when we sometimes use more experiential kind of techniques, perhaps having the patient recall some early childhood memories when she felt very helpless or inadequate and then use various interventions to help her change the meaning of those memories and perhaps help her see that the reality was that she was not completely helpless and inadequate at that point. Maybe she was just acting like a normal kid but who was thrown into some difficult circumstances.	まず患者さんに現在の状況で持つ自動思考を評価するスキルを学んでもらった後で，奥のほうにあるものに取り組みます．学んだスキルを適用して中核信念がどの程度正確かを考えてもらいます．すると患者さんは知的レベルではその考えを変え始めることが多いのですが，腹の底のレベルではそうとは限りません．患者さんは，自分はそんなにどうしようもなく能力不足なわけでもないと理性ではわかるのだけれど心の底では相変わらずそう思ってしまう，と言います． そういう時我々は，より経験的な方法を使います．患者さんに子ども時代にどうしようもなく能力不足だと感じた時のことを思い出してもらい，さまざまな介入を行ってその記憶の意味を変える手助けをし，実際にはそれほどどうしようもなく能力不足だったわけではなく，たぶんごく普通の子どもが困難な状況に置かれただけのことだったのだとわかってもらうようにします．	⑧-b 自動思考への反論 ⑧-d 中核信念の修正 ⑧-c イメージ書き換え
JC	And you need to do that, though, to change the core belief before you terminate treatment.	治療を終了する前に，そういう中核信念を変えなくてはならないわけですね？	

Judith Beck『うつ病』

JB	Ideally we do. With the straightforward access on depressed patients who do not have personality disorder, oftentimes that belief work can be fairly quick. And just by working at the automatic thought level, they can begin to see in current situations that the core belief is not true and then the core belief in itself flips back to where it was before the depression started which is usually a fairly healthy, more equal, more realistic belief.	それが理想です．パーソナリティ障害ではないうつ病の患者さんならば，自動思考レベルだけでかなり簡単に，中核信念が正確ではないということを現在の状況の中で見い出します．すると中核信念は，健全でより現実的な，うつ病発症前の段階に戻ります．
JC	So in some cases, this can be done quite quickly.	症例によってはかなり短期間で可能なのですね．
JB	That's right. It's in the more severely disordered cases of patients where the belief change takes longer.	そうです．重症なⅡ軸のある患者さんはもっと時間がかかります．
DK	What about cultural differences? Does that play a part in this?	文化的差異はどうですか？
JB	It's very important. Just as we have to change the therapy according to the patient's diagnosis, do we also have to alter therapy according to their cultural background and their degrees of comfort. Some patients really like to have a very structured session. Other patients get very uncomfortable with that. That doesn't necessarily mean that they're from a different culture, but sometimes that's why. And so the therapist has to really in tune to what's going on in the patient as she's sitting there. Sometimes her beliefs are more culturally-based beliefs so the patient might have a belief if I stand up to my parents it'll be a sign of disrespect, maybe something she learned in her culture. The therapist needs to be aware of the cultural belief and oftentimes just labeling that as a cultural belief and then it allows the patient to work at it more objectively.	非常に重要です．診断によって治療法を変えなくてはならないのと同じように，患者さんの文化的背景やどこまでを快適と感じるかによっても変える必要があります．非常に構造化されたセッションを好む患者さんもいれば，そうでない患者さんもいます．常にではありませんが，それは患者さんの文化的背景が原因のこともあります．だからこそ治療者は，目の前に座っている患者さんの体験を理解しなくてはなりません． たとえば，自分の親に立ち向かうことは親を尊敬していないことになると考える患者さんもいます．それはその患者さんが育ってくる中で学んだことです．治療者はそのような文化的背景を認識する必要があります．文化的信念であると知ることにより，患者さんはより客観的に考えることができることも多いのです．
JC	In a few minutes, we're going to watch you work with a young woman. Prior to the interview, what goes on inside?	皆さんにはこれからDVDをご覧いただくわけですが，あなたはセッションの前にはどんなことをお考えになるのですか？

		②セッションの構造化:セッションの前になすべきこと
JB	Well, not necessarily with this patient because this was just the first time that I had seen her but with an ongoing patient, I always take a few minutes before the patient walks in the door to preview what we have done in the previous session, how far the patient has come since she first came to therapy, what her overall goals are in the therapy, where I hope to get her to go in this specific session. And I also look if there's a time constrain, how many sessions we have left. And then I review my conceptualization. What are her most central beliefs and behavioral strategies that are causing her trouble? Remind myself of those so that if there's a choice she doesn't have a strong choice between one or two problems to bring up, I'd probably steer her towards the one that's more centrally connected.	このDVDの患者さんとはこれが初めてのセッションでしたのでちょっと違いますが,普通は患者さんが部屋に入ってくる前に,前回のセッションで何をしたか,患者さんが初めて治療に来た時からこれまでにどのくらい進歩したか,治療の最終目標は何か,今日のセッションではどこまでやろうとしているのか,そして時間的な制限,つまりあと何回セッションがあるかを考えます.それからその患者さんを苦しめている中心的な信念や行動戦術を概念化し,もし患者さんが選択に迷ったら,より核心に関係のある方向へ導くことを確認します.
DK	You gave her the Beck Depression Inventory. Would you talk a little about what that was about and what kind of thoughts that brought to you before start working with her?	ベック抑うつ質問票をなさいましたね.少しその説明をしていただけますか? そしてその結果を見てセッションの前にどのようなことをお考えになりましたか?
JB	We actually give our patients three forms before every single session; Beck Depression Inventory, Anxiety Inventory, and Hopelessness Scale. This collects a great deal of information for the therapist in a very short period of time. So by looking at the total score, I can see how the patient objectively has been doing compared to other weeks, especially compared to the one when she first came in. And then looking at some individual items are also very important. I can uncover some problems that we might need to address as the patient might not bring up directly unless I asked about them, most importantly about suicide. So we always look at the hopeless item and the suicide item as well.	我々は患者さんに毎回,ベック抑うつ質問票,ベック不安質問票,ベック絶望感尺度をやってもらいます.短時間に多くのデータがとれるからです.合計スコアを見れば,患者さんがその1週間,とくに治療を開始した週と比べてどのように過ごしていたかがわかります.個々のスコアを見ることも非常に重要です.患者さんが話題にしない場合に取り上げたい問題がわかります.とくに自殺についてです.絶望感の項目と希死念慮の項目はいつも見ます.

Judith Beck『うつ病』

JC So, prior to the interview, you re-school yourself or refresh just who this person is. You review the data that they've just given you to know where they are prior to the session. So you really begin therapy already running, already moving forward.

セッションの前にはその患者さんについてデータを見ておくわけですね．つまりもうすでにセッションは始まっていることになりますね．

JB That's the game plan. That might have to be adjusted, of course, for what the patient says when she first comes in, but at least I have an idea of where we're starting, where we want to get by the end of the session.

そうしたいと思っています．もちろん実際に患者さんが話すこと次第で修正しますが，少なくともどこから始めるのか，セッションが終わる時にはどうなっていたいかがわかっています．

JC As we watch this interview, what should we look at? What should we look for?

DVDを見る時には，どのようなことに注目すべきですか？

JB There're several things. One is to see the structure of the interview because this is a very typical interview. We're checking the mood, setting an agenda, discussing an important problem, teaching the patient some skills, giving a homework assignment, summarizing and getting feedback. So that's one part. I think the second part to look at is affective shifts in the patient. You can see as she's feeling very depressed and overwhelmed and then suddenly she looks brighter. And then try to figure out when she's looking brighter, what has been the cognitive change. And I think underlying most of the shifts is a feeling of being less helpless, less inadequate. I'm always looking for opportunities through the tape to undermine these beliefs that I hypothesize her there about inadequacy and helplessness.

いくつかあります．これは非常に典型的な面接ですので，まず構造を見てください．気分をチェックし，アジェンダを決め，重要な問題を話し合い，患者さんにいくつかのスキルを教え，宿題を出し，まとめとフィードバックをしてもらっています．次に，患者さんの感情の起伏を見てください．非常に落ちこんでいる患者さんが，突然明るくなります．どんな認知の変化があったのか考えてください．どうしようもなく能力不足だという度合いが軽くなっています．私は常に，そういう信念を弱めるチャンスを探しています．

②セッションの構造化
⑦セッション中のホットな認知を見逃さないこと

JC I think it also would be important that we always watch how you do that, how carefully you challenge some of these dependent personality issues she has through empowering her and really get into her to see her strength she has within herself. You did that frequently throughout the interview.

あなたはそういう依存パーソナリティの問題に対して，患者さんを力づけ，彼女自身の中にある強さに気づかせるよう注意深く働きかけていらっしゃいますね．それにも注目すべきですね．

JB	You know, the one difficulty I had with her was that she was agreeing with me too quickly.	この患者さんとのセッションでの難しさは，彼女があまりにも素早く私に同意するということでした．
DK	Yes, yes.	そうですね．
JB	And I had the sense that I had started to make a little movement with her, but that was unrealistic to expect that she'd really change to thinking that much in any given segment. So that's why I think you'll oftentimes see me going deeper and really trying to assess to what degree she really believed in her gut what I was saying and how much she was trying to please me.	私は少しばかりの治療を進められたとはいえ，短時間に彼女が変わるというのは現実的ではありません．だから私はより奥深く，彼女が心の底でどう考えているか，どの程度私を喜ばせようとしているのかを探っています．
JC	I think we're all excited about this interview. Let's let the viewers watch.	では DVD を拝見することにしましょう．
JB	OK.	

23分

セッション開始．まずセッションの導入部．

JB	Thank you for coming in tonight. If this were our regular session in regular therapy, what I'd do is to have you come in for an evaluation first where I'd ask you a lot of questions to find out what exactly your diagnosis was and how the problems developed and what your symptoms were. But we do that tonight we won't have any chance to do therapy, so I'm just going to jump right in.	今日はよくお越しくださいました．普段のセッションではまずあなたにたくさん質問して，あなたの正確な診断や，問題がどのように生じてきたのか，どんな症状があるのかなどを確かめていくのですが，今夜はそういう時間はないのでさっそくセッションに取り掛かりたいと思います．
C	OK.	

§1 ここから

JB	It's really helpful that you filled in this depression inventory and you have the score of 41, which usually indicate that the depression is in the severe range. How long have you been feeling like this?	あなたのベック抑うつ質問票のスコアは 41 です．これはあなたが重度のうつ状態にあることを示しています．いつからこのように感じていますか？	②セッションの構造化：症状チェック
C	Since the summer of 1996.	1996 年の夏からです．	
JB	What was going on then?	何があったのですか？	
C	I lost my brother and I was starting to do a lot of erratic things.	弟が亡くなって，私はいろいろよくないことに手を出しました．	④ソクラテス的問答

Judith Beck『うつ病』

JB	Such as?	たとえば？	
C	I was arrested and convicted and....	逮捕されて有罪になって…．	
JB	For what?	何の罪で？	
C	Delivery of controlled substance. And it just changed my life a whole lot.	薬物の運び屋をやって．それで私の人生はすっかり変わりました．	
JB	So you got depressed then?	それで落ちこんだわけですね？	
C	Yeah	はい．	
JB	And you've been depressed ever since?	それ以来ずっと落ちこんでいる？	
C	I think so.	そうだと思います．	

§1 ここまで

§2 ここから

JB	Now what I'd like to do at the beginning of the sessions is to set an agenda. So that's what I want to do with you tonight.	まず，セッションの初めに，今夜話し合うアジェンダをあなたと一緒に決めたいと思います．	②治療の構造化：アジェンダの設定 ④協力的実証主義
C	OK.		
JB	And that's to review what problems you're having and to pick one or maybe two of them to go over.	あなたがどんな問題を抱えているのかを見て，1つか2つ，話し合うことを決めましょう．	①問題解決モード ⑤心理教育：認知行動療法の教育
C	OK.		
JB	So can you tell me a little what's going on in your life now? What are some problems you might want to work on tonight?	ではあなたのことを少し話してください．今夜話し合いたいことをいくつか．	③認知行動モデルにより，患者の問題の全体像を把握しようとする
C	Right now, I think the biggest problem I'm having is... okay I work part-time even though I have two, three children I've got to see and I was finally felt like I was really ready to get out on my own, raise them in my own household and it has just been a struggle trying to find out an affordable house for myself. And I think just coping every day with... live with my mother. My father's been gone for a year now over a year now and just a grief... the ongoing grief is just comes and goes it's like you never know and...	今一番の問題は…私はパートで働いています．面倒見なくちゃならない子どもが3人います．やっと自立する気持ちになって，今の家を出て自分の家で子どもたちを自分で育てようと思って…．でも手ごろな家を探すのも大変で，毎日を…母と暮らす毎日をやっとの思いで過ごしています．父がいなくなって1年以上ですが，この悲しさ…ずっと続いている悲しさがあって…．	

JB	Your mom's grief or your grief?	あなたのお母さんの悲しさですか，あなたの悲しさですか？
C	Both of ours.	両方です．
JB	And grief over...	何についての悲しさですか？
C	Over my father and brother's death.	父と弟が亡くなったことです．
JB	OK. And you said coping with your mother?	わかりました．それと，お母さんに対処することも？

§2 ここまで

C	Yes.	はい．
JB	Tell me more about that.	そのことをもう少し話してください． ④ソクラテス的問答
C	She's helping a lot and she's done so much for me. But I feel sometimes like she just could be having a bad day over it and I could be in a better mood than I was before and I see her in that grieving or unsure it makes me scared and kind of unsure. So I have to deal with that day to day. I don't know what each day is going to be like. I know they're all different but it's like... I don' know.	これまでも今も母は私にいろいろしてくれます．でも時々調子の悪い日があって…私は前より気分よく過ごせることだってあるのに，そうやって悲しんでいる母を見ると怖くなるし心細くなります．そういう毎日を過ごしていかなくちゃならないんです．その日1日がどんな日になるのか私にはわかりません．毎日が違うってわかってるんですけど…わからなくなります．
JB	So you feel scared and unsure when you see your mom's grief.	お母さんが悲しんでいるのを見ると，あなたは怖くなり，心細くなるのですね．
C	Yeah.	ええ．
JB	And then another piece seems to be what will today bring?	そしてもう1つは，今日はどんな1日になるだろうということですか？
C	Yes.	はい．
JB	And when you're feeling really depressed, what do you think today is going to bring?	すごく落ちこんでいる時，今日はどんな日になると思いますか？ ④ソクラテス的問答
C	I don't know.	わかりません．
JB	Any problems as opposed to happy moments?	楽しい時と違って何か問題が？ ④ソクラテス的問答

§3 ここから

C	Sometimes it's like... I'm just wishing that it's better, hoping it gets better at some point.	時々…ただ，あれさえもっとよければいいのに，いつかもっとよくなるように，と．
JB	When you say wishing it'd get better, what's the "it"?	あれさえもっとよくなるように，というあれとは，何のことですか？ ④ソクラテス的問答：患者固有の言い回しを明確化する

Judith Beck『うつ病』

C	Just... feeling so burdened, so many things.	ただ…いろいろなことがすごく重荷に感じること．
JB	What kind of things?	どんなことが？
C	Being a parent, being a mom.	親，母親であること．
JB	Uh, that's true.	それはそうですね．
C	So I feel so burdened and in the end I feel I do have obligation to my mother. She's moving in with us in a year, U.S. citizens a year and I come from a large family and I just feel kind of burnt to meet expectations what they are expected me of and sometimes it's not easy.	すごく重荷に感じて，結局のところ私は母に対して責任があると感じます．母はアメリカの市民権を得て私たちと同居して1年です．私は大家族で育って，みんなの期待に応えることに燃え尽きたような感じがします．期待に応えるのは簡単じゃないから．
JB	And these expectations are what kind of things?	期待とはどういったことですか？ ④ソクラテス的問答　§3 ここまで
C	Finishing college. I think my mother was a great mother to her. She had eleven children and I can just see there's difference between us. I always waste the times. I'd like to be more like her in a sense of being a mother to my kids, you know, being there. She was there all the time. She was a homemaker. So I think it's a big difference. It makes a big difference.	大学を卒業すること．母は11人の子どもを育てたすごい人です．私とは違うことがわかっています．私はいつも時間を無駄遣いします．自分の子どもたちにとって，母のような親になりたいです．いつもそこにいてやれるような．母は専業主婦でしたから，私とは違うけれど．大きな違いです．
JB	Sure. So you work part-time at a dresser as a cashier?	あなたはパートで美容院のレジ係をしているのですね？
C	Yes, I work part-time and I'm a full-time student.	はい．パートで働いて，フルタイムの学生もしています．
JB	And a full-time student.	フルタイムの学生ですか．
C	Yes.	
JB	It's understandable that you feel burdened. Maybe there's something we can do to that, trying to lift the burden a little bit. Any other problems you haven't mentioned already? Any problems with work or other relationships?	あなたが重荷に感じているのはわかります．その重荷を少し軽くするような何かがここでできるかもしれませんね．そのほかには何か問題がありますか？　仕事やそのほかの人間関係では？ ①問題解決モード ③認知行動モデルにしたがって，まず広く問題候補をとらえよう
C	No. I would like a better job, but I guess I just have to better my skills. But while working there now I like it because I feel I'm in a nice environment of people, coworkers. But I really wish I could do better.	いいえ．もっといい仕事があればとは思うけど，それには技能を上げないと．今の仕事は気に入ってます．いい人たちに囲まれてると思うし．もっと仕事がうまくなりたいです．

JB	Yeah. And how about other relationships? Any problems with friends, family members?	人間関係はどうですか？　友達や家族との間に問題はありますか？
C	Well, friends, I don't really feel like I have friends right now, not many, one or two. And one friend's been friends with me for a while. She's been a great friend.	友達ですか．今はあまり友達がいるとは思いません．大勢はいません．1人か2人．1人，いい友達がいます．
JB	And you wish you had more friends? Or are you okay with what you have?	もっとたくさん友達がほしいですか？　それとも今のままでいいですか？
C	I think I'm okay with that.	今のままでいいと思います．

§4 ここから

JB	OK. Well, let me go through the problems you've mentioned and then maybe we can pick one to start working on.	では，あなたが話してくれた問題を見て，どれについて話し合うか決めましょう．	①問題解決モード ②セッションの構造化：アジェンダの設定
C	OK.		
JB	So the first thing is the housing problem. I'm not sure if I have much to offer right now, but maybe more of a practical thing.	まず最初に，家のことがありますね．でもこれについては，今ここで私にできることはあまりありません．	
C	Right.		
JB	The second thing is coping better with your mother. Especially when you get into a spiral where your mother is feeling a lot of grief and you start to feel unsure and scared. So that's one thing we can talk about. Then another thing we can talk about is feeling burdened about your role as a parent.	2つ目は，お母さんともっとうまくやっていくこと，とくに，お母さんが悲しんでてあなたも心細くて怖くなるという悪循環に入りこむということについて．これについては話し合うことができます．それからあなたが親としての役目を重荷に感じていることについて．	
C	OK.		
JB	And the third thing we can talk about is feeling obligated to your mom.	3つ目は，お母さんに対してあなたが感じている義務感です．	
C	OK.		
JB	And I guess there's a forth thing is meeting family's expectations for finishing college and so forth. And this sounds as if you're comparing yourself to some of your other brothers and sisters.	4つ目は，大学を卒業するという家族からの期待に応えることについて．これは，あなたが兄弟姉妹と自分とを比べているように聞こえますが？	
C	Well, I do because you hear it a lot, at home. I get the comparisons a lot.	比べています．家でもよく比べられますから．	

Judith Beck『うつ病』

JB	All right. So which one of those would you like to talk about tonight?	わかりました．では，今夜はどのことについて話し合いたいですか？	①問題解決モード ②セッションの構造化：アジェンダの設定 ④協力的実証主義
C	I think dealing with the grief, with my mom in it.	母の悲しみにどうつきあうかについて．	

30分

§4 ここまで

以上でアジェンダを設定した．ここまで7分．ここからアジェンダに入る．

JB	OK. Now did this kind of situation come up during this very week, where as your mom was having a lot of grief and then you started to feel scared and unsure?	この問題はこの1週間に起こりましたか？ お母さんが悲しんでいてあなたが怯えて心細く思うことが？	① 問題解決モード：大きな問題は解決できない，具体的な問題から
C	Yes.	はい．	
JB	Do you remember when that was?	それはいつでしたか？	
C	It was Tuesday morning, I believe.	火曜日の朝だったと思います．	
JB	OK. So, tell me a little bit about what was happening.	どんなことがあったのか話してください．	④ソクラテス的問答
C	Er... I was... I was feeling... I was feeling okay... and er... I was... preparing myself to leave for school. And er... my mom... er... she just... she just.... She's a real nice, sweet person but when she's been having a bad day, it's... automatic. You know as soon as you see her. And er... it's like... I don't know, I think I let a paper towel or something out. And she just... it was like... I don't know... I'm tired of picking it up.... It was just... I don't know where it came from. Sort of just... but it just came out and...	私は普通の気分で，大学へ行く支度をしていました．母は…母はとてもやさしくていい人ですが，調子の悪い日というのはひと目見たらわかります．その時私はペーパータオルか何かを出しっ放しにしていたのだと思います．それで母は…私はもうそういう母の様子に気づくのもいやなのですが…とにかくただそれが始まって…．	
JB	She started yelling at you or criticizing you, or...?	お母さんはあなたに向かってどなり始めたのですか？ 非難し始めたのですか？	
C	Criticizing a lot.	非難です．すごく．	

JB	Yeah. And you ended up feeling emotionally sad? Or scared, or unsure? What was the issue?	そしてあなたは悲しくなった？ 怖くなった？ 心細くなった？ 問題はどれでしたか？	③認知行動モデルのうちまず感情に注目
C	All of those.	全部です．	
JB	All of those. Now, what was... what went through your mind when she said... or she's started criticizing you for leaving the paper towels out?	全部．お母さんが，あなたがペーパータオルをそのままにしたことを非難し始めた時，あなたは頭の中で何を思いましたか？	⑧-a 自動思考の同定
C	That if I had my own place I wouldn't have to listen to her criticizing me about the paper towel.	自分の家があれば，お母さんの言葉を聞かなくてもすむのに．ペーパータオルのことを言われなくてもすむのに．	
JB	Right. So if I were in my own place I wouldn't have to listen to this.	別のところで自分で暮らしていれば聞かなくてもすむのに，と．	
C	Right. You know, how it can end dealing with it. How she's doing it end, go home.	はい．自分の家に帰ってしまえば，それにつきあわなくてもいいのに．終わりにできるのに．	
JB	That's right. And did you have... particularly any thoughts that were particularly sad?	そうですね．とくに悲しいという思いはありましたか？	⑧-a 感情ごとに自動思考を同定 ④ソクラテス的問答
C	Er... I just thought about... I... how much she missed my father. I'm not... I really... I felt sad about just... it really didn't done on me, I don't think... all this year how much she could really be missing him and how lonely she could actually be feeling	ただ…父が亡くなったことを母がどれほど悲しんでいるか，と思いました．この1年，母がどれほど父に会いたがっているか，寂しがっているか…．	
JB	I see. So you had thoughts like she must really miss my father. She must be lonely.	お母さんはお父さんがいなくなって悲しい，寂しいのだろうと思ったのですね．	
C	Yeah.		
JB	And those thoughts were connected with the sadness?	そういう考えは，悲しさとつながっていますか？	
C	Yes.	はい．	
§5 ここから			
JB	What thoughts do you think were connected with feeling of being scared or unsure?	怖いとか心細いという気持ちとつながっているのは，どのような考えですか？	⑧-a 感情ごとに自動思考を同定

Judith Beck『うつ病』

C	I thought that... just seeing her... just seeing... she's so different now. She just.... She seems real, real short-patient now. And what made me scared is just a thought of losing her and just a thought of... if I was wondering... okay, my... when my dad... when my dad died I lost... I feel like I lost a lot of things, I don't know, seem like things just started to go away, I don't know. And what I'd have felt... I was just... scared... I know I'm just... I just feel scared. I feel like... that I might lose her. And it scares me a lot.	今の母は，昔とぜんぜん違って見えます．今の母はすごく短気に思えます．私が怖いと感じるのは，母を失うかもしれないと思う時…父が亡くなった時，私はものすごくたくさんのものを失った気がしました．何もかもがなくなってしまうような…母をも失うような…よくわからないけど，とにかくただ怖いです．	
JB	Yeah. And what's your thought, if I lose her then what? What are you afraid would happen?	もしお母さんを失ったら？　あなたが思うのはどんなことですか？　どうなることが怖いのですか？	⑧-a 感情ごとに自動思考を同定 ④ソクラテス的問答：下向き矢印法
C	If I lose her... I won't have anybody like, on my side.	私の味方をしてくれる人は誰もいなくなります．	
JB	If I lose her I won't have anybody on my side, and then, what are you afraid would happen then?	お母さんがいなくなったら，誰も味方をしてくれる人がいなくなって，そしてどうなるのですか？	⑧-a 感情ごとに自動思考を同定 ④ソクラテス的問答：下向き矢印法
C	I'm afraid that, I don't know, what I might do. That's what I'm afraid most. I don't know. I'll... what'd happen to me if I... if I make it. That's what...	私はどうしたらいいのかわからないということが怖いです．どうなるかわかりません．私はやっていけないかもしれない．それが怖いです．	
JB	So you have the thought that I might not make it.	あなたはやっていけないかもしれないということが怖いのですね．	
C	Yeah.	はい．	
JB	Yeah. And do you have an image or a picture in your head of not making it?	やっていけないというイメージや様子が頭の中に思い浮かびますか？	③認知行動モデルのうちイメージに注目 §5 ここまで
C	Er....	さあ…．	
JB	Can you kind of see yourself in the future, not making it in some way?	うまくやっていけない自分の未来の様子を思い浮かべますか？	
C	Er....	さあ…．	

JB	When you think of the future, and you are scared she might not be in your future, where do you see yourself? Do you see yourself in the same place as you're living now?	自分の未来を思い浮かべた時，そこにお母さんがいないことが怖いのですね．あなたはどこに住んでいますか？ 今と同じところに暮らしている自分を思い浮かべますか？
C	No.	いいえ．
JB	Where do you see yourself?	あなたはどこにいますか？
C	Er... I don't know. I don't... I don't really see myself like... anywhere that would... that makes me feel good. I don't know.	わかりません．私には自分がどこか幸せなところで暮らしているのは見えません．わかりません．
JB	Do you see yourself out on the street? Or being alone in some place?	自分が路上で暮らしているのを思い浮かべますか？ あるいはどこかでひとりぼっちですか？
C	Er... it's not... I don't think I'm out on the street. I don't see myself on the street. I see myself like... just... how I'm doing as well...	路上ではないです．路上生活をしている自分は見ません．よくわかりません．
JB	And feeling unhappy?	不幸せな気分で？
C	Yes.	はい．
JB	Or finding it harder to cope?	うまくやっていくのがもっと難しいと感じて？
C	Yes.	はい．
JB	But you don't see yourself in a specific physical place?	でもあなたは，自分がどこか特定の具体的な場所にいるとは思わないのですね？
C	Er... physically... er.... No, I see myself in Chicago. That's it. But... and I always said I don't wanna move back there, but I always see myself back in Chicago.	具体的…シカゴにいる自分を思い浮かべます．それだけです．私はいつもシカゴに戻りたくないと言っていました．シカゴにいる自分です．
JB	I see. Where in Chicago is that?	シカゴのどこですか？
C	West where we grew up, where I grew up.	西部です．育ったところです．
JB	So when you have this thought I might not make it you see yourself back in a place where you grew up?	あなたはうまくやっていけないかもしれないと思う時，自分が育ったシカゴにいることを思うのですね？
C	Yes.	はい．
JB	Being unhappy, not coping very well? Feeling really, continued to feel burdened, not very effective.	そこにいるあなたは不幸せな気分で，うまくやっていけなくて？ 重荷を背負っていると感じ続けていて，何もできないと思っている？
C	Yes.	はい．

Judith Beck『うつ病』

JB	Well, it's understandable then why you feel so scared if you have that kind of image. Now, when your mom was criticizing you for the paper towel, did you... do you think you had the picture in your mind? Did it kind of flash though your mind? Of you being back in Chicago? Or is that just something you thought of now?	もしあなたがそういうイメージを持っているのなら，怖いと感じるのももっともですね．お母さんがペーパータオルのことであなたを非難している時，そのイメージが頭に浮かびましたか？ シカゴに戻っている自分の姿が頭の中を横切りましたか？ それともこれは今思っただけのことですか？
C	Er... well, no, I kind of... I think I have thought about that... that... when I think back of the times, I thought, well, if I lose her what's gonna happen to me? Always, like I said, I see myself back in Chicago, but... er... the day when she was criticizing me about the paper towel... I don't know, I was so confused I don't... I don't really remember... That's another thing I'm having trouble with a lot of times just remembering simple things like that. I don't really remember... er... exactly, you know, what... how I...	いえ…ただ，母を失ったらと思う時に自分がシカゴに戻っていることを思い浮かべたことはあります．でもペーパータオルのことで母に非難されていた日は，わかりません．私はとても混乱していてよく覚えていません．私はそういう簡単なことを覚えていられないことがよくあって，それにも困っています．あの時の私の正確な考えが何だったのか…．
JB	Well, that's fine. But this is a typical kind of image that you have, you're back in Chicago where you grew up and not doing as well.	それは構いませんよ．でも，育ったシカゴに戻っているけれどうまくいっていないというイメージは典型的なものなのですね？
C 37分	Uh, right.	はい．

以上で，アジェンダの1について具体的な状況に即して自動思考とイメージを聴取した．ここから認知再構成に行こうとするが，先だって疾病と認知行動療法の技法についての心理教育をする

JB	Now, just as an aside, do you know why you're having more problems with your memory now?	今話していることとは少し違いますが，あなたはなぜ最近記憶力が悪いのか，わかりますか？ ④ソクラテス的問答
C	Er... I think it's just I don't get enough sleep.	さあ…睡眠不足だからかな．

JB	That's probably part of it. And probably also what's part of it is that you're depressed. Now, when you... this is a depression test, and all of these symptoms you saw here are symptoms of depression. So you're more pessimistic, you're more sad, you feel like a failure, you don't enjoy things as much. You feel guilty, you have trouble making decisions, you feel more confused and so forth. Those are all symptoms of the depression. And once we see the depression lifting, we should see all of these symptoms getting somewhat better too.	それもありますね．でもおそらくは，あなたが落ちこんでいるからということもあります．これはうつ病の検査ですが，ここにある症状はすべてうつ病のものです．あなたは以前よりも悲観的，悲しい，敗北者だと思っている，楽しくない，罪悪感がある，ものごとを決められない，混乱している，など，すべてうつ病の症状です．うつ病が治ればこれらの症状も軽くなります．	⑤心理教育：疾患
C	Oh, okay.		
JB	So, it's just important for you to know that it's... that you have a real illness called depression. And no wonder you're having symptoms like this.	ですから，あなたはうつ病という病気にかかっていて，そのためこのような症状があるのだということを知っておくことは大切です．	
C	OK.		

Judith Beck『うつ病』

JB	Let's get back to the situation where your mom was criticizing for the paper towel. Now, do you see that the reason you're feeling sad and scared was because of what was going through in your mind at the time? Now, if you'd had a different kind of thought, you might have felt a different kind of emotion. So if you had a thought such as "How dare mom talk to me like that," then you might have thought angry. Or if you had a thought like "Oh, that's just like mom blowing out steam, and I don't have to pay too much attention to her," then you might have ended up feeling, you know, okay. Right?	では，お母さんがペーパータオルのことであなたを非難していた時の話に戻りましょう．あなたが悲しくて怖いと感じていたのは，その時頭の中で考えていたことのためだということはわかりますか？　もしその時に違うことを考えていたら，違う気持ちを感じていたでしょう．たとえば，「お母さん，よくもそんなことを言うものだわ」と思っていたら，あなたは怒りを感じたかもしれません．あるいは，「またお母さんが八つ当たりしている，そんなことに耳を貸す必要はないわ」と思っていたら，平気だったかもしれません．そうですね？	⑤心理教育：認知行動モデル
C	Right.		
JB	So, is it clear to you how what you think in the situation affects then how you feel?	つまり，その状況であなたの考えていることがあなたの気持ちに影響しているということがわかりますか？	
C	Yes.	はい．	
JB	OK. Now, then, I think you need to know about depression is that everybody who's depressed has thoughts like this. They have depressing kinds of thoughts. Frequently they have scared kinds of thoughts, too. And that oftentimes these thoughts are not true. Or they are not completely true.	もう1つ，うつ病についてあなたに知っておいてもらいたいのは，うつ病の人はみんなこういう気持ちを感じているということです．落ちこんだ考えがあり，怖いという考えもありますが，そういう考えは，事実ではない，あるいはすべてが事実ではないということです．	
C	OK.	はい．	
JB	But at the moment, you have the thoughts. Usually you really think that they probably are completely true. You don't even think to say to yourself, "Wait a minute. Maybe this is just a depressed thought. Maybe this isn't true."	でも今のところ，あなたはそう考えています．絶対に事実だと思っていて，そうじゃないかもしれない，うつ病だから考えるだけのことかもしれない，とは考えません．	
C	Right. OK.	そうですね．	

JB	So, one of the things I'd like to do now is to teach you how you can figure out what your thoughts are, and how you can find out to what degree they're true. If it turns out your thoughts are true, then you need to solve the problem. It's calling there to be solved. If the thoughts turn out to be not true, then you change your thinking around. And I'll teach you how to do that. And then when people change their thinking around, usually then they start to feel better.	そこで今からやりたいのは，あなたが自分の考えを知り，その考えがどの程度事実なのかを自分で見つける方法です．もしもあなたの考えが事実であることがわかったら，あなたは問題解決に取り組まなければなりません．もしも考えが事実ではないことがわかったら，あなたは自分の考えを変えなければなりません．今からあなたにそのやり方をお教えします．自分の考えを変える方法を学んだ人は，たいてい気持ちが楽になっていきます．	①問題解決モード
C	OK.	はい．	

39 分

概要の心理教育に続いて認知再構成に行くが，ここで，Judith Beck は患者にとってなるべく中心的な自動思考を取り上げようとしていることに注意．それは「お母さんがいなくなったら，私はやっていけない」である．まず「お母さんがいなくなったら」を取り扱う．

JB	So... seems to me one of the key thoughts is... what... oh, I might not make it. If I lose mom, I might not make it. So I guess there's two things that we can do. The first question is "What's the likelihood that you will lose your mom?"	中心となる考えの1つに，「もしもお母さんを失ったら私はやっていけないかもしれない」というのがあります．ここではできることが2つあります．では最初の質問です．お母さんを失うというのは，どの程度現実にありそうですか？	③最初から認知行動モデルを作り，中核信念についての仮説から自動思考を選んだ ⑧-b ソクラテス的問答による認知再構成：可能性を聞く
C	Well... I think that is... she seems healthy at this point, at this... at this stage of her life, but which is that... if things go like they usually is, parents usually die first. And I know that... it's inevitable, but... I don't know.	母は今のところ年齢から考えれば健康だと思います．でも普通，親が先に死ぬわけだから避けようがありません．よくわかりません．	

Judith Beck『うつ病』

JB	When you have the thought she's criticizing you about the paper towels and you think, "Oh, no, what if I lose her," are you thinking what if I lose her 20 years from now or 30 years from now? Or are you thinking what if I lose her very soon?	お母さんがペーパータオルのことであなたを非難していて、あなたは、もしお母さんがいなくなったらどうしようと思った時、あなたは、20年、30年先にお母さんがいなくなったらどうしようと考えていたのですか？ それとも近いうちに、ですか？	
C	It was more about losing her very soon.	すぐに、という気持ちでした．	
JB	Yeah. Now do you have any evidence that you are gonna lose her very soon?	そうですか．すぐにお母さんが亡くなりそうだという根拠があるのですか？	⑧-b ソクラテス的問答による認知再構成：根拠を聞く
C	No.	いいえ．	
JB	Do you have any evidence on the other side that you probably won't lose her very soon?	その逆，お母さんがすぐに亡くなったりはしないだろうという根拠はありますか？	
C	I don't know what very soon is. I mean... it's like... like saying the years to come I hope and pray every day that it's... that I die before her or something.	すぐに、がどれくらいかはわかりません．この先の年月を考える時、私は自分のほうが母より先に死にますように、と祈ります．	
JB	Well, another symptom of being very depressed. Thinking a lot about death.	それもうつ病の症状ですね．死のことをしばしば考えるというものです．	
C	Yeah.		
JB	What's the likelihood that she will die, say, in the next five years?	この先5年間のうちにお母さんが亡くなる可能性は、どれくらいありますか？	④質問による発見
C	Er... probably small. Probably... not very likely.	たぶん，低いです．あまりありそうもないです．	
JB	And at the moment when she was yelling at you about the paper towels and you thought "What if I lose her?" were you thinking "Oh, no, there's very small of that would happen"?	お母さんがペーパータオルのことであなたにどなっていて、もしお母さんを失ったらどうしようと考えていた時、あなたは、それはあまりありそうもないことだ、と考えましたか？	
C	I did. I did... toward the end at she blew me out. 'Cause... she seem a lot strong.	はい，母が怒り続けている最後の頃には、母はずいぶん強いから…．	
JB	Oh, I see. She seems pretty strong when she was criticizing you.	なるほど．あなたを非難している時のお母さんは強そうなのですね．	
C	Yeah.		
JB	That's good that you were able then to let in the evidence of what was going on in front of your eyes.	それはいいですね．あなたは目の前のできごとから根拠を取り入れたわけです．	
C	Yeah.		

JB	And when you thought she seems pretty strong, then how did you feel emotionally? A little bit better?	それで，お母さんは強そうだと考えた時，あなたの気持ちはどうでしたか？ 少しは軽くなりましたか？	⑦ホットな認知（感情と認知の関係）についてソクラテス的問答
C	Somewhat. It was like it took a while, I was so... for me to come to that... for me to... to... get the concept of that...	少しは…そう考えるようになるまでに少し時間がかかりました．	
JB	Well, that's wonderful. Do you see what you did? You did exactly what I'm trying to teach you to do, which is you have the thought, "Oh, no, what if I lose her," and in fact kind of the meaning to you was I may lose her pretty soon. And then you went away from the situation and you thought about it. And you realized that she was actually being very strong. And that was evidence against the fact that you're gonna lose her.	すばらしいですね．あなたはその時に自分のしたことがわかりますか？あなたはまさに私が教えてあげようとしていることをやったのです．つまり，あなたは，「もしお母さんを失ったらどうしよう」と考えました．それはつまり，すぐにお母さんが死んでしまうかもしれないということです．次にその状況の外へ出た時にもう一度考えると，実はお母さんはとても強い，そしてそれは，お母さんがすぐに死んでしまうということに反する根拠です．	⑧-b 認知再構成
C	Oh, okay, yeah.	ああ，そうですね．	
JB	And then you felt a little bit better when you did that.	そしてあなたは少し気持ちが軽くなった．	
C	Yeah.	はい．	
JB	So, this is exactly what I'm talking about. Taking the thoughts that go through your head when you're feeling upset, and looking at them more objectively.	これがまさに私が言おうとしていることです．自分が動揺している時に頭の中にある考えを取り上げ，その考えをもっと客観的に見るということです．	⑧-b 認知再構成 ⑤心理教育
C	OK.		

Judith Beck『うつ病』

JB	Now, I think another.... Sometimes the thoughts are in a word form like "What if I lose my mother?" and sometimes they may be images or pictures, like pictures of yourself back in Chicago.	考えというのは，言葉になっていることもあります．「もしお母さんがいなくなったらどうしよう」というように．また，イメージや絵のこともあります．シカゴに戻っている自分の姿を思い浮かべたように．
C	Right.	
JB	Then maybe we should talk about the Chicago picture for a minute. So, you see yourself in Chicago at the particular house you grew up?	シカゴのイメージを話した時のことを思い出してください．あなたが育った家のことを思っていましたか？ ⑧-c イメージ 書き換え
C	Yes, in that area. Yes, in that particular building.	はい，その地域です．ええ，その家のことも．
JB	In a particular room in that house?	その家であなたは，特定の部屋の中にいたのですか？
C	Yeah, the room I grew up in.	はい．私の部屋です．
JB	OK. What are you doing? Did you see yourself in that room?	あなたはそこで何をしていますか？　その部屋の中にいる自分が見えますか？
C	It's just... I wonder... I used to look out. I can see downtown Chicago. And I'm just looking out from the window. I spent so much time looking out that window... thinking about what I was gonna do when I grew up and all that stuff.	窓からシカゴの街が見えます．昔よく見ました．私は窓から外を見ています．窓の外を見ながら，大きくなったら何をしたいかというようなことを考えていました．
JB	And here you see yourself back in that same room, still looking out the window.	今あなたは，またその部屋で窓の外を見ている自分を思い浮かべていますね？
C	Yeah.	
JB	And what does that mean to you that you're back in the room looking out the window again?	その部屋にまた戻っている，また窓の外を見ているということは，あなたにとってどんな意味がありますか？
C	When I used to look out the window, I used to think about all the places that I wanted to see downtown, and all the things that I really wanted to do, what I wanted to be. It was just... When I think about it now talking about it, it was... kind of comforting.	昔その窓から外を見ていた頃は，ダウンタウンにある，行ってみたいいろいろな場所のことを考えていました．自分がやってみたいことやなりたいもののことなどです．今こうしてまた考えてその話をすると，ほっとするような気がします．
JB	So without the mystic when you were younger.	まだ何も起こっていない子どもの頃ですね．
C	Yeah.	

JB	Now when you have the image of being back in that same room, and you have the thought "I might not make it," then are you having the same kind of perspective, when you look out the window?	今こうしてその部屋に戻り，うまくやっていけないかもしれないと考えている自分をイメージして，窓の外を見ながら，今も同じことを考えていますか？
C	It's like... er... When I'm looking out the window, it's like... I don't know, the room is empty. That's all I know. The room is completely empty. The house is completely empty. And it's like... the only thing that... even bring life to that room is just the view out the window. And so... I don't...	窓の外を見ていると…部屋の中は空っぽです，それだけはわかります，家も空っぽです．窓からのあかりがあるだけです．だから…わかりません．
JB	Do I get the sense that it says if the room is empty and then your life is empty?	部屋の中が空っぽということは，あなたの人生が空っぽだという感じがしますが？
C	Something... I may feel like that, I think.	そうかもしれません．
JB	I might be putting the words in your mouth?	私が勝手に言葉にしてしまいましたか？
C	No.	いえ，そんなことはありません．
JB	Do you think that's right?	あなたはそう感じますか？
C	Yeah, I think that er... that's one thing I was fixed... that the house is just empty. It's empty.	はい．家はとにかく空っぽです．
JB	And do you feel as if it's a step back if you went back to that room?	その部屋に戻るということは，逆戻りをすることのように感じますか？
C	Yes.	はい．
JB	Why would that be a step back?	なぜ逆戻りだと思うのですか？
C	Because... where I grew up wasn't the greatest place. I think that... I don't know, just the view just gave me comfort, but I don't wanna physically be there. I don't wanna ever physically be there.	私が育ったところはいいところではなかったから．その景色にはほっとしますが，実際にそこにはいたくないです．もう二度と行きたくありません．
JB	All right. So, when you have these kinds of thoughts that are in word form, then oftentimes it's very helpful to respond to them in word form as you did with the thought "What if I lose my mother?" You thought more about it in words and you said yourself well look how strong she is, she's just been criticizing me. I'm not gonna lose her soon.	わかりました．こういう考えを言葉として思う時は，言葉で答えると役に立ちます．あなたは「もしお母さんを失ったら」と言葉で考え，それからまた言葉で「お母さんはとても強い，すぐに死んでしまう可能性は低い」と考えました．
C	Right.	

Judith Beck『うつ病』

§6 ここから

JB	If you're having the kind of thought in a picture form, sometimes it's more helpful to try to change the picture, try to change the picture itself instead of only trying to change the words. Now, let's take the same picture where you're back in that room and looking out the view. Is there someway that you could figure out to change that picture in your mind so that actually you're feeling stronger and feeling as if you're moving ahead in your life?	もしそれを絵として思い浮かべた時には，その絵を変えてみます．言葉を変える代わりに，絵そのものを変えてみます．部屋に戻って窓の外を見ている絵を思い浮かべてください．その絵を変える方法はありますかね？あなたがもっと強い気持ちになれるような絵に？人生の先に進んでいくような気持ちになれるような絵に？	⑧-e 行動実験
C	Put some furniture?	家具を置いてみる？	
JB	Put some furniture in there. Okay, that's one thing.	家具．それも1つですね．	
C	Yeah, I think I could change the picture.	絵を変えることはできると思います．	
JB	What kind of furniture would you put in that room?	どんな家具を置きますか？	
C	Well.... We had a great apartment. I liked it. Er... a nice couch in the bedroom. I mean, a nice couch will fit. Er... a bed, pictures... family pictures.	そうですね…あれはいいアパートでした．ベッドルームにはちょっといいソファとか．家族の写真を飾ったり．	
JB	Would you like to imagine your kids are jumping on the bed or something?	あなたの子どもたちはベッドの上で飛び跳ねていますか？	
C	OK. yeah.	はい．	
JB	Having fun in the room?	部屋の中で楽しそうにしている？	
C	Yeah.	はい．	
JB	What do you see them doing? You know them. I don't know them. So what are they doing?	子どもたちは何をしていますか？	
C	Jumping in the bed. That's what they're probably doing. Jumping on the bed.	ベッドに飛び乗って，飛び跳ねています．あの子たちはそうするでしょうね．	
JB	OK. So now when you have this picture in your head and the room is furnished, it's got pictures on the wall, there's a couch and a bed and you see you've got three kids, they're jumping on the bed, how does that make you feel emotionally?	そのような絵を思い浮かべた時，部屋の中にはソファやベッドがあり，壁には写真が飾ってあり，あなたの3人の子どもたちはベッドで飛び跳ねている様子を思い浮かべた時，どんな気持ちになりますか？	⑦ホットな認知：感情の重視

C	Better.	これまでよりいい気持ちです．
JB	Does it?	
C	Yeah.	
JB	Now the fact of the matter is that we don't know whether or not you'll ever end up in that room again. My guess is somebody else probably lives there now.	実際には，あなたがまたその部屋に戻ることになるのかどうか，あなたにも私にもわかりません．たぶん現在は，ほかの人がその部屋に住んでいるのでしょうね．
C	Yeah.	
JB	Is that right? So it's unlikely that you're gonna end up in the room. So it's just something that you had a fantasy about.	つまり，あなたがまたその部屋に戻るというのはありそうもないことです．
C	Right.	
JB	So what I'm suggesting is that you take, since it's just a fantasy, it's not true anyway, take that fantasy and improve it in a way that makes you feel better.	単なる空想であって事実ではないのですから，あなたにやってもらいたいのは，自分の気持ちが軽くなるようにその空想をいい方向に変えてみることです．
C	OK.	はい．

§6 ここまで

JB	What do you think, having pictures on the wall, nice furniture, kids on the bed, why does that make you feel better? What does it make you realize?	壁には写真が飾ってあり，ソファやベッドがあり，子どもたちがベッドの上に乗っている．それを思い浮かべるとなぜ，それまでよりいい気持ちになるのですか？ どんなことに気づきますか？	④ソクラテス的問答：まとめをする
C	It just makes me realize that the house is full. I mean, I grew up... what a full house, you know, family and everybody was always there, and I think that just being in the room by myself, growing up, without brothers and sisters, is... is just scary.	家の中がいっぱいだということに気がつきます．私は大家族で育ちました．いつも誰かがそこにいました．兄も姉もいない部屋の中に自分1人でいるのは怖いです．	
JB	No wonder you feel scared when you see that kind of image. So now every time when you have that kind of image, see if you can say to yourself, "Now wait a minute. I'm gonna improve on that." And then add things to them.	そういうイメージを持つと怖くなるのは当然ですね．これからは，そういうイメージが浮かんだら，「ちょっと待って，私はこの絵をもっといい絵にする」と考えてください．そしていろんなものをそのイメージに付け加えてください．	
C	OK.		

48分

自動思考の前段「お母さんがいなくなったら」について思考の修正とイメージの修正を行い、次に自動思考の後段「私はやっていけない」を取り上げようとするが、

§7 ここから

JB	Maybe we ought to talk now about the thought that you have in words, which is "I might not make it." Especially, "If mom's not around, I might not make it."	今度は、言葉になったあなたの考えを見てみましょう。「私はやっていけないかもしれない」という考えです。とくに、「もしお母さんがいなくなったら私はやっていけないかもしれない」という考えです。	⑧-b 認知再構成
C	OK.	はい。	
JB	Now there's no doubt about it, say, if your mother died at some point in the next few years, you would probably feel really at a loss. You've been very grief stricken at first. You've had several losses already. So this would be another one on top of that. She sounds very important to you. But I wonder if you could see that... although you would be extraordinary pained at first that you'd be able to continue on with your life. And that grief might get a little bit less as time went on. Do you think that's possible?	万一、この2、3年のうちにお母さんが亡くなったら、あなたは大きな喪失感を味わうのは間違いないでしょう。これまでに家族を亡くしていますから、それに加えて大きな悲しみでしょう。あなたにとってお母さんはとても大切な人のようですから、でも、最初の大きな悲しみの後、前に進む自分を考えられますか？時間が経ったらその悲しみが少し軽くなるということを考えられますか？そんなことが可能だと思いますか？	④質問による発見
C	Yeah.	ええ。	
JB	Is there something that makes you think you might go downhill and stay downhill?	自分がそのまま坂を転げ落ちていってそのままどん底にいるだろうと思うようなことがありますか？	
C	I don't know.	わかりません。	
JB	Feel like you need your mom in order to make good decisions?	正しい決断をするためにはお母さんが必要だと思いますか？	

C	I feel like… I need to gain independence from her beforehand in order to, you know, … I wanna be independent. Before anything happens I don't wanna to force me to… I don't wanna anything happen to her to force me having to be responsible and having to be, you know, I don't wanna… I just don't wanna that to happen.	何かする前に母から自立することが必要な気がします．母に何かあって，私が自分で責任を持たなければならないような場面に置かれたくありません．とにかくそういう目に遭いたくないのです．	
JB	I think it's a good plan. Do you know what to do first in order to get more independent? Or are there things you've already done, trying to get more independent?	それはいいことですね．もっと自立するためにはまずどうすればいいかわかりますか？ これまでにどんなことをしてきましたか？	④ソクラテス的問答
C	I'm… I'm trying to get more independent, but it's like… The hard part for me is having everybody telling me, "You should do this first," "You should do this first." And that is to me is another burden in part. Everybody telling me, "You should do this and do this," "You should do this in this way." It's like trying to figure out on my own. I don't have a clue now because it's like I have so much input from everybody else, maybe by the end… I get the way I should go is like everybody saying take this road and ten people are telling me to take ten different roads…	私はもっと自立しようとは思っているのです．でも難しいのは，みんなが私に，「まずこうしなさい，まずああしなさい」と言うことです．私にとってはそれも重荷です．こうすべきだ，ああすべきだ，と．まるで今の私には何もわかっていないみたいに．10人が10通りのことを言うので．	
JB	Yeah. Maybe there's something I can teach you tonight that might be helpful to you.	あなたの役に立つことを今夜教えてあげられるかもしれません．	⑧-f メリット・デメリット分析
C	OK.		
JB	Can you tell me what a couple of those different roads might be?	10人が言う10通りのことのうちのいくつかを話してもらえますか？	
C	OK. It's like… my one sister used to call me, she called me to say, "You have to get a car first." Then my other sisters said, "No, you have to get your place first." And my other sister said, "If I was you I'd move out of mom's house 'cause then you're gonna never have anyone for anything." That's not what I wanna do. Then my other sister, she says like, "Well, I think you should move out of the state so you can really know what independence is."	1人の姉は，「まず車を買いなさい」別の姉は，「まず家だ」と言います．「私だったらまずお母さんの家を出る，そこにいたら自分のことは何もできない」と言います．わかるけどそうしたくないし，もう1人の姉は，「州の外へ出なさい，そうすれば自立がどういうことかわかるから」と言います．	

Judith Beck『うつ病』

JB	Right. And at this point you're feeling pretty confused?	そして今のあなたはどうしていいか混乱している？
C	Yeah.	はい．
JB	Is there any one of these things you think you can knock off? Say, "No, I don't think that's right for me right now"?	これらのうち，無視できるものはありますか？「それは私が今やりたいことじゃない」と？
C	Er... moving out of the state.	州外へ引っ越すこと．
JB	OK. So you can cross out one off right away. See, now you're only down to three.	1つ消えましたね．あと3つだけです．
C	OK.	はい．
JB	OK. Now, a car first or a place first. A car first or a place first is really.... Isn't that really a decision?	では車か家か，というのは？ まず車か，まず家か，これは本当に決断が必要ですね？
C	Right.	はい．
JB	Because "don't move" goes along with "a car first." Is that right?	というのは，「引越しをしない」というのは，「まず車」ということになりますね？
C	Yeah, I guess it does.	ええ，たぶん．
JB	Or maybe I'm missing something?	何か私がわかっていないことがありそうかな？ ⑦セッション中のホットな認知を見逃さないこと（患者の口調の変化に注意）
C	Er... No, I think, what I think I should do is to move first.	私が自分でまずすべきだと思うのは，引越しです．
JB	Move first.	まず引越しですか．
C	Yeah.	
		§7 ここまで
JB	OK. And you feel confident in that decision? Or not completely?	あなたはその決断について，自信がありますか？それとも絶対の自信ではないですか？ ④質問による発見 ⑧-n 相対化（数量化）
C	I feel confident in the decision. It's what I share with everybody else.	私は決断に自信がありますけど，みんながそうではないから．
JB	I'm sorry. Can you say that again?	もう一度言ってもらえますか？
C	I feel confident in the decision of me wanting to move first. I share with everybody else, with my mother and my sisters, everybody. And then it's like that's what all the pain is coming.	引越しをしたいという自分の決断には自信があります．でも母や姉たちがみんなそう思っているわけではないので苦痛です．

JB	I see. Right. Some people agree with you and some people don't agree with you.	なるほど．あなたに同意する人もいれば，そうでない人もいるのですね．	
C	Right. They agree that I should move. They agree to think I should get a car first. Then I don't think that it's that important. Even though they do, they think I need to have a way to get around. But I think that I wouldn't need that. Somewhere to live, to be.	そうです．みんなは私の引越しには賛成で，だからまず車を買えと言います．車があれば出かけるにも便利だから．でも私はそうは思いません．それは重要なことだとは思いません．私は引っ越すためにはまず住むところだと思います．	
JB	To be, yeah. Well, it certainly sounds sensible to me. Sometimes when you have to make a decision, it's helpful to look at what are the advantages of, say, moving first, and what would be the disadvantages of moving first.	確かにそれがよさそうですね．決断を下す時には，その決断のメリット，デメリットを考えることも役に立ちます．まず引越しをする，ということのメリットとデメリットです．	⑧-f メリット・デメリット分析
C	OK.		
JB	And then you can also look at what are the advantages of getting a car first and disadvantages of getting a car first. And I think if you do that, you're probably right about moving first since you seem to feel it pretty strongly in your gut.	それから，まず車を買うということのメリットとデメリット．もしあなたがそういうことを考えてみるなら，私はあなたの，まず引越し，という考えは正しいと思います．というのは，あなたは心の底で強くそう思っているようにみえるからです．	
C	OK.		
JB	But I think if you put it down on paper, it may then help you answer your family members who are saying, no, you should do something different.	紙に書いてみると，意見が違う家族と話すのに役立つかもしれません．	
C	OK. OK.	はい．	
JB	Does that sound sensible to you?	納得できますか？	④ソクラテス的問答：うなずきが弱くなった患者の感情の動きを見逃さない
C	Yes.		
JB	What would be some of the advantages of moving first?	まず引越しをすることのメリットには，どんなことがありますか？	
C	I'll have more time to study.	勉強する時間が増えます．	

Judith Beck『うつ病』

JB	Yeah. You know what? Why don't we have you write some of these down? So you can remember them. So, you just put a line down in the middle of the page and put advantages on one side and disadvantages on another side. We'll just start this a little bit so I can do some of other things with you. And maybe you can finish this either on your own or with one of your sisters or with your mom. So this is advantages and disadvantages of moving first. And you said one advantage would be to have more time to study.	そうですね．紙に書いてみましょうよ．覚えておけるように．紙の中央に線を引いて，片方にメリット，もう片方にデメリットを書きましょう．ここでは少しだけやってみましょう．そうすればあなたはお母さんといる時，お姉さんたちといる時に，また自分でできるでしょう．これは，まず引越しをすることのメリットとデメリットです．メリットの1つは，勉強する時間が増えるということでしたね． ⑧-o 書き留める
C	Uh, hum. I'll have a lot more time to study.	はい．
JB	Yeah. And how about another advantage?	ほかにはどんなメリットがありますか？
C	Er... I'll be the only person, I will be the only adult that has the first and formal say for my children.	私が唯一の大人だから，子どもたちに対して発言力があります．
JB	Absolutely. So I think you'd better write that down.	確かにそうですね．それも書いてください．
C	OK.	はい．
JB	You know, my sense is that you're doing this so well that you can probably continue to do this without me.	とてもうまくできますね．私がいなくても自分でできますね．
C	OK.	はい．
JB	You think so? Or would you rather continue to do with me?	そう思いますか？ それ ④協力的実証主義 とも一緒に続けますか？
C	Yeah, I... I think that... just talking about it is getting me to thinking.	こうして話していると，考えることができます．
JB	That's good. I'm really impressed, I have to tell you. By the fact that your depression score is 41, you seem to be very clear thinking about this. So, somehow, you're able to overcome the depression to do this.	それはいいことです．あなたのうつ病のスコアは41ですが，それにしてはあなたははっきりとものごとを考えることができています．うつ病を克服してこれができているようですね．
C	Yeah, I think that's what I really wanna do.	私はそうしたいのだと思います．
JB	That's the way it sounds to me, too.	私にもそう思えますよ．

C	I think it's like I'm just... to a point where I feel like I have to.	絶対にそうしなくちゃとすら思います．
JB	Yeah. OK. That sounds very sensible to me. OK. So one of the things I'll have you do for homework, you didn't know you're gonna get homework tonight, is you're gonna continue this list about advantages and disadvantages of moving. And then if you'd like, you can also do advantages and disadvantages of getting a car first.	そうですね．では宿題です．今夜宿題があるなんて思っていましたか？宿題は，まず引越しをすることのメリットとデメリットを考えることです．できるならば，まず車を買うことのメリットとデメリットも考えてみてください． ⑥宿題の設定
C	OK.	
JB	And then I think you'll feel stronger in being able to talk back to your sister. Your sisters who are saying, no, you have to get a car first. Don't move, save up your money, stay with mom longer.	そうすれば，もっと強い気持ちでお姉さんに反論できると思いますよ．引越しは後にしてお金を貯めてまず車を買うべきだ，もうしばらくお母さんと一緒に暮らすべきだと言っているお姉さんに．
C	Yes.	はい．
JB	Now, will you have trouble standing up for yourself?	自分の意見を言うことは難しいですか？ ⑧-ⅰ アサーション訓練
C	Er... only to the extent that I feel as though I have been the one that has... like my father would think... I put in a lot of time with my parents because er... I know that they're getting older, they would get older that my mom... I have always the one that if they need to get an appointment as in everything, I felt, I made sure that they did that, and whatever that they needed if I can do it then I've tried to do it. So, I didn't have a problem putting them first, but now I think that they see, they know that if I move, I'm not gonna be there like I used to be. And so...	父が病気だった時も，私が両親とはたくさんの時間を過ごしてきました．両親は年をとってきてますから．病院の予約などがあれば，ちゃんと病院に行くようにさせてきたのは私です．両親が何か必要な時には，私にできることであれば私はやってきました．だから意見を言うことはできました．でも今は，もし私が引っ越せば私はこれまでのようにはいなくなるわけですから…．
JB	So maybe they have an interest in... they didn't stay there.	つまり，あとどれだけあなたがそこにいるかは，お姉さんたちにも関心のあることなのですね．
C	Exactly.	

Judith Beck 『うつ病』

JB	So another advantage to moving sooner is that you'll be able to put more energy toward you and your kids instead of toward your mom. Either your mom would take up your slack or some of your brothers or sisters will take up the slack.	そうすると，引っ越すことのもう1つのメリットは，お母さんにではなく，あなた自身と子どもたちにもっとエネルギーを使えることですね．そしてお母さんはあなたが抜けた穴を自分で埋めるか，あなたの兄弟姉妹が埋めるかですね．	
C	Exactly. That's true.	その通りです．	
JB	Now, will you have trouble, you think, telling your sister who wants you to stay with your mom that you've made a decision and that you're gonna move out? Is she hard to talk to?	あなたにそのままお母さんのところにいてほしいと思っているお姉さんに対して，引っ越す決断をしたと言うことは難しいですか？　このお姉さんに話すのは難しいですか？	④質問による発見 ①問題解決モード
C	Er... No, she's not hard to talk to. She is the oldest of us, all of the eleven, and I think that she's had a lot of responsibility put on her, and she's taking it very well. I think that she understands that advantage of moving. I think that she really does. You see, my mother doesn't drive. And so I think that plays a big part in it, too. Er... but I don't think I'll have a problem talking to her.	いえ，話しやすい姉です．11人のうちの一番上の姉です．彼女は大きな責任を負ってきたし，それをこなしてきたと思います．彼女は，私が引っ越すことのメリットをわかってはいると思います．でも母は運転しないので，それも大きいと思います．でも，彼女と話すのは難しいことではありません．	
JB	OK. That's great. So, then another homework assignment is to talk to your sisters who think that you shouldn't move, and just tell them in a nice but firm way that now this is the decision that you've made. That you've really looked at all the advantages and disadvantages.	そうですか．ではもう1つの宿題は，あなたが引っ越すべきではないと考えているお姉さんたちと話すことです．感じよく，でもはっきりと，そう決めたのだと話すことです．メリットとデメリットをよく見てくださいね．	⑧-iアサーション訓練
C	OK.	はい．	

58分

自動思考の後段を取り上げようとしたら，患者が，姉たちがばらばらのアドバイスをするので決められないという問題を持ちだしてきたので，メリット・デメリット分析と，それを利用したアサーションをカバーした．いよいよ，もう一度後段の自動思考「私はやっていけない」の認知再構成に入る．

§8 ここから

JB	OK. But let's get back to a related topic. Er... it sounds as if you have a kind of thought that goes like this; if I lose mom before I become independent, then I might not make it.	では関連することに話を戻しましょう．あなたはこういうふうに考えているように思えるのですが．「もしもわたしが自立する前にお母さんを失ったら，やっていけないかもしれない」	③認知行動モデル
C	I feel like that.	はい，そう感じます．	
JB	Yeah. Now, what is... whether a kind of another looking at it might be... "If I become independent first, it would be easier on me if I lose mom. If I'm not independent first, it's going to be harder, but perhaps not necessarily impossible"	別の見方をしてみましょう．「もし私が先に自立したら，万一お母さんを失っても，そうじゃない時と比べたら楽だろう．もし私が先に自立していなければ，もっと大変だろう．ただし不可能とは限らない」	⑧-b 認知再構成：別の見方
C	That's true.	そうですね．	
JB	You agree with that?	同意できますか？	
C	Yes.		
JB	Is that something you think that would be helpful to remember?	覚えておくといいと思いますか？	④質問による発見
C	Yes.	はい．	
JB	Why don't I have you write down something about that?	それも書き留めてください．	⑧-o 書き留める
C	OK. So... if I become independent first...	もし私が先に自立したら…	
JB	Yeah. ... it'll be easier.	…少し楽だろう．	
C	OK. It'll be easier.	少し楽だろう．	
JB	If I lose mom.	万一お母さんを失っても．	
	But if I'm not independent first...	でも，私が先に自立しなければ…	
C	OK.	はい．	
JB	... it would be harder, but not impossible.	大変だろう．でも不可能ではない．	
C	OK. ...but not impossible.	…でも不可能ではない．	
JB	Now, how much do you believe that last statement you just wrote down that it would be harder but not impossible?	最後の部分，大変だろうけど不可能ではない，をあなたはどのくらい信じますか？	④ソクラテス的問答 ⑧-n 相対化（数量化）

Judith Beck『うつ病』

C	Um... I believe... I believe it... If I become independent first, it'll be easier, but if I'm not, it'll be harder but not impossible. I believe it a lot.	信じます．もし私が先に自立しなければ大変だろう，でも不可能ではない…とても信じます．	
JB	Is there any part of you that doesn't believe it?	心のどこかで信じていないところはありますか？	⑧-n 相対化（数量化）：患者がたとえば80％と答えたなら，残りの20％には何がありますかと聞くことができる
C	Er... I don't know. I believe... I want to believe it. I really want to believe this. So, I believe it, I do believe it... that I... I don't know although sometimes...	わかりません．信じたいです．本当に信じたいです．だから…信じます．よくわかりません．	
JB	You know, everybody needs help from time to time, especially in a period when you're gonna be grieving. I assume your sisters will be grieving as well. Do you think you'll have your sisters for support?	誰でも助けが必要な時はあります．とくに悲嘆にくれている時は．あなたのお姉さんたちだって悲しむでしょう．あなたはお姉さんたちからのサポートがちゃんと得られると思いますか？	
C	Yes.	はい．	
JB	And is there anyone among your sisters who might be able to help you in a way that your mom helps you now?	お姉さんたちの中で，今お母さんがあなたを助けてくれているようにあなたを助けてくれる人はいると思いますか？	④質問による発見
C	No.	いいえ．	
JB	What kinds of things does your mom do for you now?	今あなたのお母さんは，あなたにどんなことをしてくれていますか？	④質問による発見
C	Er... baby-sit. Er... support... support... I guess the financial advantage is greater.	子どもたちの子守りです．支えてくれること…経済的援助のほうが大きいと思います．	
JB	No question about that. Anything else?	当然ですね．ほかに何か？	
C	Er... no, that's really it.	それだけです．	
JB	Well, why don't we take just a minute to take a look at these three things and see whether it'll be impossible to get these three things from other people, or whether just be harder?	ではこれら3つのことをほかの人から得ることはできないかどうか，見てみましょう．	⑧-b 認知再構成 §8 ここまで
C	OK.		

JB	Baby-sitting. What will you do about baby-sitting if you lose your mom?	子どもたちの子守り．もしお母さんがいなくなったら，子守りはどうしますか？
C	I don't know. I would have to... I would have to find someone to baby-sit. I would have to...	わかりません．ベビーシッターを探さなくちゃならないと思います．誰か見つけないと．
JB	Right. You would have to find somebody. And you think that would be hard but not impossible?	それは難しいけど不可能ではない，と思いますか？
C	If... it would be hard, but not impossible.	大変だけど，不可能ではないです．
JB	OK. Well, who knows, you might even trade off some baby-sitting with your sisters. You know, I'll watch your kids for a few hours and you watch mine.	お姉さんたちとお互いに子どもを，みあえるかもしれませんね．自分の子をみてもらったり，お姉さんの子をみてあげたり．
C	Yeah.	
JB	OK. Now how about emotional support? If your mom's not there to give it to you, is it possible that you can give it to yourself?	気持ちの上でのサポートはどうですか？お母さんからサポートを得られないとしたら，自分で自分をサポートすることは可能ですか？
C	Well, coming from myself... er... I don't know. I used to feel confident that I could... er... I guess I could.	私自身の中から…わかりません．以前は自分でできるという自信がありましたが…たぶんできるでしょう．
JB	It might be something that you need to learn how do again. If you're once more confident in yourself, then you can get there again. No one with the depression score that I know of 41 feels very confident. But maybe once you're over the depression you'll find your confident come back and then you're really able to support yourself emotionally better.	もう一度，どうやってそれをするのか学ぶ必要があるかもしれませんね．もう一度自信をもってできるように．うつ病のスコアが41で自信がある人はいません．でもうつ病がよくなれば，自信が戻ってきて，自分で自分の気持ちをもっとサポートすることができるかもしれません．
C	OK.	
JB	How about the possibility of emotional support from any of your sisters?	お姉さんたちからのサポートはどうですか？
C	They'll be there for me.	みんな支えになってくれると思います．
JB	They'll be there for you? OK. So, it's not quite as easy as getting emotional support from your mom, but there's always you and there's always your sisters.	そうですか．お母さんからほど簡単ではないけれど，いつでも自分がいるし，お姉さんたちがいますね．
C	Right.	
JB	And possibly your kids.	子どもたちも支えてくれるかもしれませんね．
C	Yes.	はい．

Judith Beck『うつ病』

JB	Financial support. Now you're getting help from your mom and you're living in her place and stuff. So, finance is gonna be a problem if she's gone. Is that right?	経済的援助．今はお母さんに援助してもらっているし，お母さんといっしょに暮らしています．お母さんがいなくなったらお金は問題ですね？
C	Yeah.	はい．
JB	Now, does that mean that it's impossible to get your financial resources together or just more difficult?	それは経済的にはまったく不可能ということですか？　それとも今より大変になるということですか？　⑧-b 認知再構成
C	It'll be more difficult, and I think what I worry about is... my kids. Like now, we're out looking for a place and they compare everything with their grandma's house. It's not like her house. It was just lodges...	今より大変です．私が心配なのは子どもたちです．今，家を探していますが，母と住んでいる家とは違います．今の家は大きいですから．
JB	That must have been hard.	それは大変ですね．
C	Yeah, it was hard...	
JB	All right, here's thinking for you. You go out and look at some place new and you say to your kids, "We're gonna do a little game. Let's see who can find the most good things about the next place we're gonna look at. Right? Let's see who can say the fewest things about comparing it to grandma's place." Do you think they would like that? Could they do that? How old are they again?	ではヒントをさしあげましょう．新しい家を見にいく時，子どもたちにこう言います．「ゲームをしよう．次に見に行く家について，誰が一番いいことを見つけられるだろう？　おばあちゃんの家と比べる回数が一番少ないのは誰だろう？」子どもたちはそういうゲームが気に入ると思いますか？　何歳でしたっけ？　④質問による発見
C	They're... my oldest will be nine. They're nine, seven and three.	9歳，7歳，3歳です．
JB	Well, the three-year-old can't do it, but the other two, I bet, could do it.	3歳の子には無理ですけど，あとの2人はできますね．
C	Yeah, they could.	はい．
JB	See, kind of making it to a little game for them?	そんなふうにちょっとゲームをしてみてはどうでしょう．
C	OK.	
JB	Wanna write that down too?	それも書いておきましょう．　⑧-o 書き留める
C	Sure.	はい．

JB	OK. Let's get back to this thought. "If I don't have my independence first before I lose mom, I might not make it." What's another way of looking at that now?	ではもう一度，「もしお母さんを失う前に自立しなかったらやっていけないだろう」という考えに戻りましょう．違う見方をするとどうなりますか？	⑧-b 認知再構成：別の見方 ④ソクラテス的問答でセッションの途中でまとめを入れる
C	Uh... quiz... Another way of looking at it? I guess if I have my independence now, I would feel a lot more secure.	テストですね．別の見方…もし今自立していれば，もっとずっと安心できるでしょう．	
JB	That's right. But not having your independence now, does that necessarily mean that you won't be able to make it?	そうです．でももし今自立していなかったら，それは，やっていけない，ということですか？	④ソクラテス的問答
C	It seems like that's... I'm.... It seems that way because... just because how things are now... it really does seem that way. It almost seems like that if I don't make it out of here now while... So it's like... I wanna prove to her that I can make it.	そういうふうに思えます．だって今の状態を考えればそうですから．そう思えます．もしここから出ていけなかったら…私は母に対して，私にだってできるということを証明してみせたい，という感じがします．	
JB	Well, I think it's a good idea to do that. The only thing I'm trying to do is to try to have you not be quite so anxious about it. And have you see that even if the worst happened and you were to lose her soon, that it would be hard, but that you would eventually make it.	そうしてみるのはいいことですね．私がやろうとしているのは，あなたがそんなにも心配しないようにすることです．そして，もし仮にすぐにお母さんが亡くなってしまうような最悪の事態になったとしても，大変でしょうけれど，最終的にはあなたはちゃんとやっていけるとわかってもらうことです．	
C	OK.	はい．	
JB	You seem less sure than you did a few minutes ago.	さきほどよりも確信がないようですね？	⑦セッション中のホットな認知を見逃さない ④質問による発見

§9 ここから

C	Yeah... I want that though. I really do.	ええ，そう思いたいのですが．
JB	Well, maybe another important thing to remember is I want independence so badly that I'm making the steps toward it. You're certainly going out looking for apartments. That's very good.	もう1つ大切なことは，私は本当に自立したい，だからそれに向けて一歩踏み出す，と覚えておくことかもしれませんね．アパートを探しにいくのはいいことです．
C	OK.	

Judith Beck『うつ病』

JB	When we talked about, at first you said you're confused about what to do next. And we talked about it for another minute and you were very clear about what to do next. So my sense is that you really are going in the right direction. You have a good head on your shoulders and you know what to do. The depression is probably holding you back a little bit. And your fears may be holding you back a little bit too. But what I see is that you're plowing ahead. You're looking at your apartments. You're doing things to try to make your life better. What do you think that says about you as a person?	最初あなたは，次に何をしたらいいのか混乱していると言いました．でもあなたは，次に何をしたいかとてもはっきりしていました．だから私は，あなたは正しい方向に向かっていると思いますよ．しっかり考えていて何をすべきかわかっています．うつ病がじゃまをしているのでしょう．あなたの怯えもね．でも私には，あなたは前に進んでいるように見えます．あなたはアパートを探していて，人生をよくすることを考えています．あなたという人について，それはどういうことを意味していると思いますか？	④認知行動モデルによる理解 ⑤それによる心理教育 ④ソクラテス的問答
C	That I'm trying...	頑張っている？	
JB	I wonder if you're stronger than you think you are.	あなたは自分で思っているより強いのではないですか？	④質問による発見：認知行動モデルから，肯定的なデータを強調しないと患者は学習しないと考えて，肯定的なデータを強調している
C	I don't know. I wonder. I want to be stronger. I want to be stronger and independent, and not feel so sad and burdened, but... I really do.	わかりません．もっと強くなりたいです．もっと強く，自立して，そんなに悲しまないように．本当にそう思います．	
JB	I think you're making some good steps toward it.	あなたはそれに向かっていい一歩を踏み出していると思いますよ．	
C	OK.		

JB	The other thing I was trying to get across tonight is that the reason you feel so sad and anxious sometimes are because of thoughts that you have.	今夜あなたにわかってもらいたかったことは，あなたがそんなにも悲しくて不安に感じることがあるのは，あなたの考えが原因だということです．	⑤心理教育：認知行動モデル
C	OK.		
JB	You have thoughts like... if I lose mom before I get my independence, I won't make it. This kind of thoughts are gonna undermine you, make you feel really anxious or sad. You can't necessarily stop the thoughts from coming into your head. But once they come into your head, you can say yourself, "Now wait a minute, how do I know that's true?"	私が自立する前にお母さんを失ったらやっていけない．そういう考えがあなたを崩れさせています．あなたを悲しませ，不安にさせています．そういう考えが頭に浮かぶことを止めることはできないかもしれませんが，そういうことを考えた時，自分で自分に向かって，「ちょっと待って，どうしてそれが事実だとわかるの？」と聞いてみましょう．	⑧-b認知再構成
C	OK.		
JB	Maybe it's not really true.	そうではないかもしれません．	

§9 ここまで

C	OK.	
JB	Maybe it's not as true as it feels right now. And as you gave me an example before about mom, oh, even the thought I might lose mom even then you thought that over later and you said to yourself, now wait a minute, here she was criticizing me, she's actually very strong. So that's the kind of thing that I'm talking about.	今あなたが感じているほどそうではないかもしれません．先ほどお母さんの話で，そういう考えが浮かんだけれど，お母さんに非難されている時に，ちょっと待って，お母さんは強い人だ，と思いましたね．そういうことなのです．
C	OK.	はい．
JB	When you are feeling really anxious or depressed, just look for thoughts or pictures that are going through your head. And then kind of evaluate them critically. Think to yourself how true they are.	すごく不安な時，落ちこんでいる時，頭の中の考えや絵を探してみてください．そしてそれを批判的に評価してみてください．どれくらい本当だろうか，と．

Judith Beck『うつ病』

C	OK. OK. How true are the thoughts...	はい．その考えはどれくらい本当だろうか，と．	⑧-o 書き留める(ここで患者がすでに自分で進んで書き留めるようになっていることに注意！)
JB	If it's a picture going though your mind, then you can try to change the picture in the way that we did before.	それが絵だったら，絵を変えてみましょう．さっきやったみたいに．	
C	OK. Change the picture...	はい．絵を変える．	

69分

以下，セッションのまとめに入る

JB	So, if you could summarize a little bit about what we talked about tonight. What do you think was important?	では今夜話したことをまとめてみてください．どんなことが重要だと思いますか？	②セッションの構造化：セッションのまとめ
C	Um... standing firm with the decision that I need to move.	引っ越すことをはっきりと話す．	
JB	Good.	いいですね．	
C	Er... what else...	ほかには…	
JB	You can look at your page.	書いたことを見てもいいですよ．	
C	Er... about... just advantages also of moving. The thing to about becoming independent first even be...	引っ越しのメリット．まず自立すること．	
JB	And what a good idea that is, but not to scare yourself so much if it doesn't happen.	いいことですね．でももしそうできなくても怖がらなくていいですよ．	
C	Yeah. OK.	はい．	
JB	And let's see, anything else we talked about tonight? Oh, and then when you do find that you're having some scary thoughts or depressing kind of thoughts, just to say to yourself how do I know that this is true?	ほかには？　そうそう，落ちこむような考えが浮かんだら，どうして本当にそうなるとわかる？　と自分に尋ねてみること．	
C	Right. "How true are the thoughts?" OK. And try to change the picture.	はい．「どれくらい本当だろうか」それから絵を変えること．	

§10 ここから

JB	Yeah. Now, was there anything that I said tonight that you thought I'm misunderstood? Or anything that bothered you?	今夜の話の中で，私が誤解しているようなことはありますか？ あるいはお気に障ったことは？	②セッションの構造化:フィードバックを求める
C	No, no.	いいえ．	
JB	OK. Anything you particularly liked about at all in what we talked about?	話の中であなたがいいなと思ったことは？	
C	Yes, about writing down the advantages and disadvantages of making a decision.	決める時にメリットとデメリットを書きだすことです．	
JB	OK. That'll help you with other decisions as well.	ほかのことを決める時にも役立ちますね．	
C	Yeah... It makes a lot of sense.	はい．そう思いました．理解できます．	
JB	Yeah. Most of the time people just have these advantages and disadvantages swimming in their heads. But it's much easier if you put them down on paper and you can really get a better idea.	メリットやデメリットを私たちは普通考えますが，書き留めるとわかりやすいですね．	
C	Right.	はい．	
JB	Good. Well, thanks for coming in tonight. It was pleasure talking to you.	今夜はお話できてよかったです．	
C	Thank you.	ありがとうございました．	

71分

§10 ここまで

以上でセッションは終わり．カウンターは71分．以下，セッションの要所要所をプレイバックしながら，解説が入る．

JC	Judith, is this a good example of cognitive therapy?	これは認知療法の典型的な例ですか？	
JB	Well, I think in general it is. I think it shows the structure of the therapy session from doing a mood check and setting agenda, specifying a problem to work on, teaching the patient tools to summarize and feedback. So I think in that was it is. And I think in meeting the goals of a therapy session it is as well. It is taking a problem and starting to do some problem solving toward it.	一般的にそうだと思います．気分のチェック，アジェンダを決める，取り組む問題を特定する，患者さんに方法を教えることから，まとめをしてフィードバックまでの構造を見せていると思います．これが認知療法で，セッションの目標にも合っていると思います．目標とは，問題について話し，それに向かって問題解決をすることです．	②セッションの構造化 ①問題解決モード

Judith Beck『うつ病』

JC	If you had the opportunity to do this interview again, would you do anything differently?	このセッションを再び行う機会があったら，違うやり方をするというところがありますか？	
JB	Well, one thing I'm curious about is whether she has a substance abuse problem or did in the past, and how that might relate to the depression and to her ongoing problems. To be honest with you, because it was a cognitive therapy of depression tape, I shied away from even asking about it.	そうですね，1つ私が興味を持っているのは，彼女が薬物乱用者，あるいは過去にそうであったかどうか，そしてそれが現在の彼女のうつ病にどのように関わっているかということです．正直なところ，これはうつ病の認知療法の録画なので，私はそれについて尋ねることをしませんでした．	
JC	OK. What would you do next with her if you would meet with her in a week or two?	なるほど．1週間か2週間先にまた彼女と話すとしたら，どうなさいますか？	
JB	Well, the first thing I would do is to find out what problems she wants to work on next week, and I'll also do some follow-up from this session and see whether she got the homework done or where she is toward solving a problem of becoming more independent.	まずはその時に彼女がどの問題に取り組みたいかを知ることです．それから，このセッション後のフォローアップをして，彼女が宿題をやったかどうか，自立するための問題解決に向けてどのくらい進んだかを見ます．	①問題解決モード ②セッションの構造化
JC	And would that be the eventual goal, to have her become more independent, or would it be to resolve the depression, or just where are you headed?	もっと自立するというのは最終的な目標ですか？ それともうつ病を治すことですか？ あなたはどこへ向かっているのでしょう？	
JB	Well, there really are several goals. One goal, the most obvious goal is to get the depression into remission. Also hope to teach her things during the course of therapy that actually she'll use not only in the coming weeks but five years from now or ten years from now. So relapse prevention is the second very important goal.	いくつかの目標があります．もっとも明白な目標は，うつ病を寛解に持ちこむことです．同時に，セッションを続ける中で彼女に教えたことを，その次の週だけでなく5年後あるいは今後の人生で実際に使ってもらうことを願っています．つまり，再発防止は2番目に重要な目標です．	
JC	In this first clip we're gonna watch, you did a mood check with her. And you also used the Beck Depression Indicator and came up with a score of 41. Can you talk about that?	これから観る最初の部分では，あなたは彼女の気分チェックをなさいました．ベック抑うつ質問票も使って41という結果が出ました．これについてお話しいただけますか？	②セッションの構造化：症状チェック

JB	Well, that score is in the severe range. And it's very helpful for me to know that her score is 41 and not 27 or something like that.	それは重度の範囲にあるスコアです．彼女のスコアが，たとえば27などではなく41である，と知ることは非常に役に立ちます．
JC	And the cutoff of that is... is that 29 or 30?	境界線は29か30ですか？
JB	Approximately in that range in order to meet the criteria for depression. So she really is quite depressed. I can't really get that information without her filling out the scale unless I asked her a great number of questions. So the depression inventory allows me very quickly to see what are her depressive symptoms, that allows me from week to week because I would give it to her every week to check whether some symptoms are getting better or worse. And for both of us to see whether the total score is coming down over time so we have an objective check in addition to her subjective account of how she's feeling week to week.	うつ病の診断基準を満たすためには，それがおおよそその範囲です．つまり彼女のうつ病はかなり重症だということです． この尺度に記入してもらわないと，非常にたくさんの質問をしない限り，そういう情報を得ることはできません．抑うつ質問票により，彼女のうつ病の症状を素早く知ることができます．毎週これをやってもらいますので，良くなったり悪くなったりしている症状があるかどうか，毎週知ることができます．合計スコアが時間の経過とともに下がっているのかどうか，彼女も私も知ることができ，彼女が毎週どう感じているかという主観的な話に加えて，客観的なチェックができます．
JC	Well, let's watch the mood check right now.	ではその気分チェックを観てみましょう．

—§ 1—

JC	As we looked at that example, was it hard for you not to query more about how she lost her brother, and she was convicted, maybe has a substance abuse problem?	弟がなぜ亡くなったのか，その後どういう経過で有罪になったのか，あるいは薬物乱用の問題があるかどうかについての質問をしないでおくのは難しかったですか？

Judith Beck『うつ病』

JB Well, what I really wanted to do was to go beyond that point and find out the whole scope of her problems and then give her the choice of where we wanted to start. My sense was that she looked a little embarrassed when she was talking about the drug problem and I sensed in order to really build a relationship it was probably better not to go into it in depth at that point. In any case my goal in the first part of the session is to hear the range of problems that the patient has, particularly in the first session and then help her choose which one to work on.

私が目指していたのは，そのこと以上に，彼女の問題全体を知り，どこから始めるかを彼女に決めてもらうことでした．薬物のことを話している時の彼女は少し恥ずかしがっているようでしたから，彼女との関係を築くためにはあの時点ではそれを追求しないほうがいいだろうと感じました．いずれにしても，セッションの最初，とくに初めてのセッションでは，患者さんが抱える問題全体を聞き，患者さんがその中から取り組みたい問題を1つ選ぶ手助けをすることが私の目標です．

④協力的実証主義
④の前の，すべての精神療法の基本としてのラポールの形成
③認知行動モデルをベースに，
①患者が抱える問題リストをとらえる

JC And that's what you do in the next segment. It sounds like we're just gonna continue on and what you do here is to set an agenda. Let's watch that.

次に観るのがその部分です．あなたはアジェンダを設定しています．観てみましょう．

—§ 2—

JC It seems like you're working here identifying a variety of different concerns she has. Are you usually so collaborative like that?

ここではあなたは，彼女が抱えるさまざまな心配事を特定しようとしていますね．通常もこんなに協力的なのですか？

JB	Always. That's really the hallmark of cognitive therapy, used to be collaborative with the patient, and one way of being collaborative is to make sure that when they start talking at the beginning of a session you don't just have the patient continue to talk about whatever he/she wants to talk about, but the therapist structures it so that the patient sees clearly what are the choices in talking about various problems and doesn't just talk about the first thing out of her mouth.	いつもです．それがまさしく認知療法の特徴です．患者さんと協力的であることです．協力しながらやっていく1つの方法は，セッションの最初に患者さんが話し始めた時，好きなことをどれだけでも話してもらうのではなく，治療者が構造化するということです．そうすれば，患者さんはさまざまな問題について話をしながらも選択肢がわかり，最初に口をついて出たことを話すだけではなくなります．	④協力的実証主義 ②治療の構造化
DK	And you really say this is what we're gonna do now and this is what we're gonna do now, so that she feels a sense of direction or security then with you.	彼女が方向性を感じ，あなたと話すことに安心感を持つように，あなたは，今からこれをしましょう，これからこれをしましょう，と言っていますね．	
JB	And what I try to say too is, is that okay, this is what I'd like to talk about next, how does that sound.	はい，そしてまた，それでいいですか，私は次にこれについて話したいと思いますがどうですか，とも言うようにしています．	④協力的実証主義
DK	Yeah. And I noticed you taking notes.	そうですね．それから，メモをとっていらっしゃいましたが．	
JB	Right. I think it's very important. What I'm trying to do is to take notes in a way that I can remember the most important things to go over with her without interfering with our relationship, or the rapport we have. So I try to kind of sneakily take notes then maintain eye-contact.	はい．非常に重要だと思います．私がやろうとしているのは，彼女との関係，ラポールを妨げないようにしつつも彼女にとってもっとも重要なことを覚えておけるような形でメモをとることです．ですからなるべく目立たないようにメモをとり，アイコンタクトを維持することを心がけています．	④の前の，すべての精神療法の基本としてのラポールの形成

Judith Beck『うつ病』

JC	In the next clip we're gonna watch you take this list and getting more and more specific. Is that the protocol?	次に観る部分では,あなたはリストを取り上げてどんどん具体的な話をしていきますね.これは通常のやり方ですか?	
JB	Right. Patients usually come in with big problems like my life is a mess or I'm very unhappy, or I don't know what to do. We try to take these big problems and specify them because those are too big to work on. We try to narrow them down so that it's something that we can really talk about and start to solve in that session.	そうです.普通,患者さんは,私の人生はめちゃくちゃだ,とても不幸だ,どうすればいいのかわからない,といった大きな問題を抱えてやってきます.でもそれは取り組むには大きすぎるので,我々はそういう大きな問題を具体的なものにしていきます.話ができるように問題を絞っていき,そのセッションで問題解決に取り組みます.	①問題解決モード ⑧-j 問題解決技法
JC	Let's watch you specify the problem.	ではあなたが問題を特定する様子を観ましょう.	

—§3—

JC	You've already zeroed in on her problem here. I like the way you clarify the "it" for her and it seems like that's really meaningful.	あなたはここですでに焦点を絞っていますね.私は,あなたが彼女のために「あれ」を明確にしてあげている様子がとてもいいと思います.意味があることのようですね.	④ソクラテス的問答:患者固有の言い回しを明確化する

JB	Right. I think when patients first come to therapy they don't necessarily have the skill of being able to specify their problems. They just feel really overwhelmed frequently by their emotions. As you said before, both the structure and narrowing down of the problems I think gives them some sense of control, gee maybe there's something I can do about these problems.	そうです．患者さんは初めて治療に来る時には問題を特定するだけのスキルを必ずしも持ち合わせていません．自分の感情に圧倒されていることが多いのです．先におっしゃったように，構造と問題の焦点を絞ることの両方が，患者さんに，コントロールできるという気持ちを持たせます．これらの問題について何かできるかもしれない，という気持ちです．	①問題解決モード
DK	Yeah, picking them apart.	はい，たくさんの問題を細かくしていくのですね．	
JC	And the word choice was really important that you got her to focus "it" now became a whole sentence and exactly what it was.	そしてあなたの言葉の選び方が非常に重要だと思います．あなたは彼女に焦点を絞らせ，「あれ」が完全な文になり，何のことなのか正確にわかりました．	
JB	That's right.		
JC	In the next piece, we're gonna have you look at some of her problem list and have her look specifically and go over the problem list and to choose what she wants to work on, follow that collaborative theme. And that's what you're attempting to do for sure?	次の部分では，あなたは彼女に問題のリストを見てどれに取り組みたいか選んでもらっています．協力的であるというテーマに確かに従っているわけですね？	④協力的実証主義
JB	That's right.		
JC	Let's watch it.	では観てみましょう．	

—§4—

JC	There's no doubt who the therapist is. You really take a very active role.	誰が治療者なのか間違いようがないですね．あなたは実に積極的な役割を担っています．

Judith Beck『うつ病』

JB	Right. She's a very depressed patient and she doesn't know how she's going to get better. By listening to her problems and conceptualizing what's going on I have a sense of what direction we need to go. I never know in advance whether or not any particular intervention is going to work or not, but at least I have a game plan in my mind.	はい．彼女は重度のうつ病患者であり，どうやって病気を治していけばいのかわかっていません．彼女の問題に耳を傾けそこで起こっていることを概念化することにより，私にはどの方向に進めていくべきかがわかってきます．どの介入方法が成功するかなどということは前もってわかりません．しかし少なくとも私は，心の中に進め方の計画を用意します．	③認知行動モデルによる概念化
DK	I almost as I was watching it this time I had a feeling that she's feeling that these were piling on her shoulders and then when you asked her to pick one, huh, there's a bit of a sigh, she said oh you know.	この部分を見ていて私は，問題が両肩に積み上がっていると感じていたところへ，あなたが，1つ選んでくださいと言ったことで，彼女はほっとして息を吐いたように見えました．	
JB	So just listing the problems itself did seem to make her feel somewhat overwhelmed, but then horning in and working on a specific one made her a little bit more hopeful.	たくさんある問題をリストにしていくと彼女は参ってしまったようでしたが，1つに焦点を絞り，その特定の問題に取り組むことで少し希望を持てるようになりました．	
DK	That was my sense.	私もそう感じました．	
JC	In the next piece we're gonna watch, you're gonna focus on the loss of her mom or this loss theme in her life, which might actually be core beliefs...	次に観る部分では，あなたは母親を失うこと，彼女の人生におけるこの喪失というテーマに焦点を当てています．これは中核信念かもしれませんね．	
JB	I think it's tied to her core belief.	私は中核信念に関係あると思います．	
JC	What would you think the core belief might be for her?	彼女の中核信念は何だと思いますか？	

JB	It's interesting. To her losing her mom means losing her sense of support, financial support, emotional support or help with making decisions and so forth. And it seems to me that underneath of it all she really believes she's at least to some degree helpless and inadequate and she really needs her mom to make it, maybe even to survive.	彼女にとって母親を失うことは，経済的なサポート，感情面のサポート，あるいはものごとを決める時の助けを失うことを意味しているというのは興味深いことです．私には，それらすべてのことの根底で，彼女は自分が，少なくともある程度，どうしようもなく能力不足であり，うまくやっていくために，もしかしたら生きていくために，母親が必要だと信じているように思えます．	③認知行動モデル
JC	And you're gonna follow this up segment by trying to get some of the automatic thoughts that come up. Can you let our viewers know just what to look for here specifically that you're gonna be doing?	そしてあなたは，これから観る部分では，自動思考を引き出そうとしていますね．これを観ている皆さんに，あなたがとくに何をしようとしているのかご説明いただけますか？	
JB	What I'm trying to find out from her is in a specific situation that came up this week what were the thoughts that went through her mind right at the time. And these are thoughts that are directly connected with her discomfort feelings. She has two sets of thoughts, one are kind of sad thoughts and the other ones are anxious thoughts. So I'm gonna try to elicit both kinds and then make a decision about which thoughts seems to me the most important on to go after.	私が見い出そうとしているのは，今週起こった特定の状況の中で，そのことが起こっている最中に彼女の心の中にどんな考えがあったかということです．それは彼女の持っている，自分はだめだという気持ちと直接結びついています．彼女は2種類の考えを持っています．1つは悲しいという思い，もう1つは不安な思いです．そこで私はその両方を引き出し，どちらが取り組むべき，より重要なものであるかを決めようとしています．	⑧-a 自動思考の同定 ⑦ホットな認知：感情の重視，感情から自動思考へ
JC	Let's watch.	では観てみましょう．	

Judith Beck『うつ病』

JC She seems to be very comfortable with your questions. She didn't seem to have any trouble coming up with the thoughts once you asked the right questions. Is this typical?

彼女はあなたの質問にまったく無理をしていませんね.あなたが的確な質問をすると,自分の考えを口にすることにはまったく問題がないようでした.これは普通のことですか?

JB Well, there's really a range we find in a therapy. Some patients like this where all you have to do is to ask for the thoughts or ask questions about what's going through your mind and they usually are able to come up with their automatic thoughts. Other patients, or the other extreme are much more difficult. These are patients who say I don't know or who keep in tone with their emotion and have more difficulty initially eliciting their thoughts.

治療においてはほんとうにいろいろな場合があります.この場合のように,何を考えていましたか,あなたの心の中にはどんな考えがありましたかと尋ねるだけで,自分の自動思考を答える患者さんもいます.それとは極端に異なる場合,もっと難しい患者さんもいます.そういう患者さんは,わかりませんと言ったり,自分の感情にのまれていたりしますので,最初は考えを引き出すことがもっと困難です.

⑧-a 自動思考の同定

DK Her thoughts though as she talked about them, there was a great deal of emotional undertone there you see. One part I thought she was just at the edge of tears.

彼女の場合は,考えを話している時にその根底に大きな感情がありましたね.泣きだしそうに見えた時もありましたが.

JB	I think so too. So what that shows me is that that's probably a very important thought to go after in therapy. Now she may have had thousands of thoughts during the week, thousands of negative dysfunctional thoughts, but there's only time to go into one or two or maybe three in a therapy session. So I'm looking for thoughts that produce a lot of emotion, a lot of negative emotion that are clearly distorted in some way that seemed very typical to come up often in the past and may come up often in the future.	私もそう思います．それはつまり，おそらく治療で取り組むべき非常に重要な考えであろうということを示していると思います． 彼女はこの1週間，さまざまな考え，否定的でうまく機能しない考えを持ったでしょうが，セッションでは1つか2つ，あるいは3つくらいしか取り組む時間がありません．ですから私は，何らかの意味で明らかに歪んでいて，過去にしばしば出てきたし，今後も出てくるであろう，たくさんの否定的な感情を生みだす考えを探しています．	⑦セッション中のホットな認知を見逃さないこと ③認知行動モデルに則って治療を進める
DK	So that emotional tone gives you a hint of where you wanna go.	つまり，彼女のあの感情的な雰囲気が，どこを探せばいいのかというヒントになるわけですね．	
JB	Exactly.		
DK	Actually more than a hint	実際にヒント以上ですね．	
JB	Right.		
JC	You finished a segment by talking about an image and we're gonna jump ahead to where you actually get her to change an image. Is doing this kind of work with imaging an important part of cognitive therapy?	あなたはこの部分をイメージの話で締めくくりましたね．ここで少し先に飛んで，あなたが実際に彼女にイメージを変えさせているところに行きましょう．このようにイメージに取り組むというのは認知療法の重要な要素ですか？	

Judith Beck『うつ病』

JB	I think it should be an important part of cognitive therapy. I think even a lot of cognitive therapists neglect this one area though. They just assume that patients' thoughts are always in verbal form and they don't even know to look for thoughts are in the form of images. But the images can be quite powerful and really lead to a lot of negative emotion. So it's important to help patients uncover them indeed they are there.	そうあるべきだと思います．認知療法の治療者にはこのことを軽視する人が大勢いますが，そういう人たちは，患者さんの認知はいつも言語化されていると決めてかかり，イメージという形の認知をみようともしません．しかしイメージは非常に強いことも多く，実際たくさんの否定的感情に繋がります．ですから，そういうイメージが実際にそこにあるということを患者さんに気づかせてあげることは重要です．	⑧-c イメージ 書き換え
JC	Do you ever go further with this and get somebody to really relax, deeply, maybe even use some hypnosis techniques and help them lessen these?	あなたはこれをもっと追求して，患者さんを本当に深くリラックスさせたり，催眠法などを用いて，軽減に取り組むことはありますか？	
JB	There're some therapists who do use hypnotic techniques. I think it's probably better not to do that unless you absolutely have to because if you're using hypnosis it's putting more of the control in the therapist seat instead of the patient seat. We found that really patients are pretty much able to recall important memories and thoughts without the use of hypnosis. We do use imagery experiential kinds of techniques particularly with personality disorder patients when we're looking at how some of their beliefs originated in childhood trauma and get patients to re-experience that trauma and then try to restructure the meaning of some of these experiences though guided imagery.	催眠法を用いる治療者も確かにいます．私は，どうしてもそうする必要がある時以外は催眠法を用いないほうがいいだろうと思っています．催眠法を用いると，患者さんではなく治療者側がより大きなコントロールを握ることになるからです．実際のところ我々は，催眠法を用いなくても患者さんは重要な記憶や考えをかなり思いだすことができるとわかっています．我々も，イメージで経験する技法(imagery experiential techniques)を用いることはあります．それはパーソナリティ障害の患者さんで，その人の信念がどのようにして子ども時代のトラウマに端を発しているかを探求している時です．患者さんにそのトラウマを再体験してもらい，イメージに働きかけることによってその経験の意味を再構築してもらいます．	
JC	In this clip you're actually gonna change an image. Can you help our viewers know just what to look for?	この部分ではあなたは実際にイメージを変えていますね．観ている皆さんが注目すべきことを説明していただけますか？	

JB	The part right before here as I elicited an image that seems to occur to her over and over again and this is where she's alone in the room where she grew up and the room was completely empty. This spontaneous image comes to mind quite a lot to her and causes her quite a lot of distress. Now it's not anything that ever has happened to her in the last few years or likely to happen, but when the image occurs to her it still makes her very upset. So just teaching her one technique of kind of taking control of that image and changing it so that she doesn't feel so upset.	この直前の部分で私は，患者さんが何度も何度も思うイメージを引きだしました．彼女が育った部屋に1人でいるというものです．部屋は空っぽです．これは彼女がしばしば思う自然発生的なイメージで，大きなストレスを与えています． 過去数年の間に実際に生じたことでもなければ，これから起こりそうなことでもありません．でもこのイメージが浮かぶと彼女は非常に動揺します．そこで，そのイメージをコントロールして変える方法を1つ教えてあげて，彼女がそんなに動揺しないようにします．
JC	Taking a useless image and making it into a more useful one, at least a neutral one.	むだなイメージを取り上げ，もっと意味のあるもの，少なくとも中立的なものに変えるわけですね．
JB	Right, exactly, kind of undercutting the impact.	そうです．影響力を弱めます．
JC	Let's watch it.	では観てみましょう．

—§6—

JC	Not only did you seem to change the image for her but she seems to enjoy the work.	あなたがイメージを変えるというだけでなく，彼女はその作業を楽しんでいるように見えますね．
JB	She did. Really could see the change in her affect where she went from a lonely room to what would probably be a more realistic picture anyway, whatever apartment she eventually moves to, she will have furniture, she will have kids jumping around, will not be empty.	彼女は楽しんでいましたね．彼女の表情の変化に見て取ることができました．ひとりぼっちの部屋から，より現実的な絵に変わりました．結局のところどんなアパートに引っ越すにしても，家具があるでしょうし，子どもたちは飛び跳ねているでしょう．空っぽではありません．
JC	And she seemed at least more alive, less depressed, more empowered	少なくとも彼女は，落ちこみが軽くなり，もう少し生き生きとして力を得たように見えました．
JB	That's right.	そうです．
DK	This is interesting because the first part of the image was a really abandoned person in this empty place and all of a sudden now she's got this fun kind of piece to it.	興味深いですね．最初のイメージは，空っぽの部屋にいる見捨てられた人でした．それが突然，楽しそうな様子が加わりました．

JB	That's right and in fact what we did was to really change it to a more realistic image. She probably will not be alone in the room as long as she has three kids.	そうです．事実，私たちがやったのは，最初のイメージをもっと現実的なイメージに変えるということです．3人も子どもがいるのですから，部屋でひとりぼっちということはないでしょう．
DK	That's true.	そうですね．
JC	In the next piece you begin, at least prior to beginning, she's talking about wanting to be independent and then she's soliciting advice from all of her sisters about how to be independent, so she does things in this very dependent way.	この次の部分では，彼女はもっと自立したいと話していますが，同時にお姉さんたちからはどうやって自立すべきかというアドバイスを引き出しています．つまり彼女はこのように非常に依存したやり方でものごとをするのですね．
JB	She does. What I'm trying to do is first of all to find out from her what particularly is the decision that she has to make, what kinds of advice has she gotten and actually to my surprise it turns out she's already made the decision. And what I tried to do is just support that since it seemed to be a reasonable choice. And to reinforce in her the idea that she's made this decision already and then we look at advantages and disadvantages of the decision itself so that she can learn a technique to use in the future when she needs to make decisions but also so that she can learn to stand up for herself with her very well-meaning, well-intentioned sisters who are kind of undermining the sense of independence.	はい．私がやろうとしているのは，まず第1に，彼女がとくにどのような決断をしなくてはならないか，どのような助言をこれまでに得ているのか，ということを知ることです．驚いたことに，彼女はすでに決断をしていました．それは正当な決断であると思われたので，私はそれをサポートし，彼女の中にある，自分はもう決めたのだという考えを強化しようとしました．そして一緒にその決断のメリットとデメリットを考えました．そうすることにより彼女は，将来決断をする必要が生じた時に使えるテクニックを学ぶことができるだけでなく，善意からではあるのですが彼女の自立心を損なっているお姉さんたちに立ち向かうことができるようになります．
JC	I think that's important for our viewers to look at, because rather than fitting in with her sisters also offering advice for her, you brought it out from her to let her know that she can make her own decisions that she did that this solution was already within her.	それは，ご覧になっている皆さんが注目すべき重要な点だと思います．助言してくれるお姉さんたちに合わせるわけではないですからね．あなたは彼女に対して，すでに自分で決断していて問題解決を手にしていると気づかせましたね．	④**協力的実証主義：運転席に座っているのは患者だ**
JB	Yes.	はい．
JC	Let's watch how you did that.	どんなふうにやっていらっしゃるのか観てみましょう．

JC	With the dependent clients or someone with these dependent traits like she has how do you keep from providing what she wants, telling her what to do?	彼女のように依存性の高い患者さんや、そういう性格特性を持った患者さんに対し、あなたはどのようにして、その人が求めている、どうすべきか、という指示を与えないようにしているのですか？	
JB	I think in some cases it is important to give her some advice and to make suggestions for her but as much as possible if she has the skills to do it herself and I have some data to think she's gonna be successful in that then I always try that first because again my conceptualization is that underneath she feels very helpless and inadequate and I'm very conscious during the session of providing as many opportunities as possible to undercut that belief.	場合によってはいくらかの助言を与えたり提案をすることは重要だと思います．しかし患者さんが自分でできるスキルを持っている場合，手元のデータからうまくできると思われる場合はいつも，最初は指示を与えないようにします．なぜならば，彼女は根底で非常にどうしようもなく能力不足だと感じているというのが私の概念化ですから，私はセッションの間，彼女がその信念を弱める機会を提供することを非常に意識しています．	③認知行動モデルによる理解（概念化）が常にベースにあることを説明
JC	What about you have a powerful therapist and she is an oppressed client, how do you stop her from giving you superficial kinds of feedback agreement, just saying what you want to hear?	強力な治療者とうつの患者さんの場合，患者さんが表面的に同意して，治療者が求めるようなフィードバックをすることをどうやって止めますか？	

Judith Beck『うつ病』

JB	Well, I think you've put your finger on something very important and I think she is an overly compliant patient. We often see that in dependent kind of patients. There were several times during the session when I did feel as if she was superficially agreeing. So then I would ask questions such as is there part of you that doesn't believe that, or what would it mean not to make it.	それは非常に重要なご指摘です．この患者さんは非常に迎合的だと思います．依存するタイプの患者さんにはよくあることです．セッション中も何度か，彼女が表面的に同意していると私は感じました．そこで私は，あなたはどこかでそのことを信じていないということはありませんか，それができないということはあなたにとってどんな意味がありますか，というような質問をします．	⑦ホットな認知：感情の重視
JC	Well, in this next clip I thought that was what's going on and you picked up on it and you had her to do some writing. Is that an important part of cognitive therapy to get people to write?	次に観る部分では，それが起こっていますね．あなたはそれを察知して，彼女に書かせています．患者さんに書かせるというのは認知行動療法の重要な要素ですか？	⑧-o 書き留めさせる
JB	We do try to get patients to write. If they can't write, we write for them or we might have them put an audio tape in for the last couple of minutes of the session to summarize the most important points. Research have shown that patients forget almost everything that happens in the doctor's office. So a good rule of thumb is anything you want the patients to remember really needs to be recorded in some way. Sometimes we have patients just write down something toward the end of the session not necessarily throughout the session although there are other times especially with the very dependent patient where it is very useful to have them write throughout the session as you have concluded talking about something important because then it gives them the opportunity to kind of take control and to write down something for themselves, so it's giving them an important message.	我々は患者さんに書いてもらうようにしています．患者さんが書けない場合は，我々が代わりに書いたり，セッションの最後の数分間を録音して，もっとも重要なことをまとめてもらいます．患者さんは診察室の中でのことをほとんど全部忘れてしまうということが研究からわかっています．ですから経験則に従い，患者さんに覚えておいてもらいたいことは何らかの形で記録する必要があるのです． セッションのすべてではなく最後のほうで書いてもらうことがありますが，非常に依存性の高い患者さんの場合は，セッションの最初から最後まで，重要なことは書きとめてもらうと役に立ちます．自分で書くことで彼らはコントロールする機会を得ることになるので，重要なことを伝えることにもなります．	

DK	It seems to me in her case it also gives her a weapon in a sense or some armor to use with those sisters.	彼女の場合は，お姉さんたちに対する武器，手段にもなるように思えますが．	
JB	Exactly.		
DK	You know, I went to this therapist and she told me, or this is what I came up with.	私は治療を受けにいってこんなことを言われたのよ，あるいは，私はこんなふうに考えたんだけど，というような．	
JB	That's right. My sense was that she has ten people telling her what to do. So what was going through my mind is how can I make a difference for her outside of the session.	私には，彼女にはどうすべきか指図する人が10人もいるように感じられました．ですから私は心の中で，どうすればセッションの外で彼女にとって役に立つことができるだろうか，と考えていました．	
DK	Well, at one point we don't know we show it during this part, but she actually says she has ten different opinions and you can count.	次の部分に含まれるかどうかわかりませんが，彼女は実際に，10人が違う意見を言うと述べていますね．	
JB	That's right and my sense was that if I didn't have her write something down that she would quickly swamped in the moment she left the session.	そうです．私は，彼女が書きとめておかないと，セッションが終わった瞬間にそういう人たちの意見に飲みこまれてしまうだろうと感じました．	⑧-o 書き留める
JC	And she would forget about it. So maybe that's why we're administering to take notes because she's really serious now wants to remember things. Let's watch how you do this with the client.	そして忘れてしまうでしょうね．だから書いておいてもらうわけですね．彼女は真剣に覚えておきたい様子でしたから．では，あなたがこれをなさる様子を観ましょう．	

—§8—

JC	I really appreciated your continued solicitation and the use of not just verbal but nonverbal cues and the way that you were able to keep probing whether or not this was a yes ma'am response, something more deeply felt.	あなたが言葉だけでなく非言語的ヒントも駆使して，それが何でも同意することによる返事なのか，もっと深いところで彼女が感じていることなのか，彼女から引きだそうと粘るのがとてもいいと思いました．	⑦ホットな認知：感情の重視

Judith Beck『うつ病』

JB	Yes, there were two things. One is I watch for her face whether that was changing her body posture and so forth and I was also thinking to myself if I had had a very strong belief in the way she does would I change my beliefs so quickly and the answer was no. So that was another cue to me to probe more deeply and make sure that she really understood what we were talking about.	はい，2つのことがありました．まず私は彼女の表情の変化や身体の姿勢などを見ています．同時に私は，もし私が彼女のような強い信念を持っていたらそんなに簡単に信念を変えるだろうかと自分自身に問いかけました．答えはノーです．それもヒントとなって，私はより深く探り続け，話し合っていることを彼女が本当に理解していることを確かめようとしました．	
JC	I continue to be impressed with the way you solicit and you use verbal as well as the nonverbal feedback that you're getting from her. Is that a hallmark of cognitive therapist to really interpret this nonverbal behavior?	あなたが彼女に対し，言語的，非言語的フィードバックの両方を使っている様子に感銘を受けました．非言語的行動を解釈するというのは，認知療法家の特徴ですか？	⑦ホットな認知：感情の重視
JB	Oh yes, it's very important. With this particular patient I have the sense from her nonverbal cues that she's really agreeing with me superficially but that it really hasn't made any cognitive shift kind of her gut. And I keep on thinking to myself if I had thoughts as she did would I be able to change my mind so quickly and when my answer was no, then I used that plus her nonverbal cues as a cue to myself to go deeper.	もちろんです．それは非常に重要です．この患者さんの場合は，私は非言語的ヒントから，彼女は表面的に私に同意しているだけであって，心の底では認知の転換は生じてはいないと感じていました．ですから私は心の中で，彼女のような考えを持っていたら私はそんなに簡単に気持ちが変わるかと問い続け，私の答えはノーでした．そこで私は，そのことと，さらに彼女の非言語的ヒントを用いて，さらに深く進みました．	
JC	And when you did with her you actually had her think about what she said and she took her time, paused and thought about it. She actually did agree with it but I think that really was the first time she thought about it.	あなたは彼女に自分の言ったことを考えさせ，彼女は時間をかけて考えていました．彼女は実際に同意しましたが，私はその時が彼女が初めて本当にそのことを考えた時だったと思います．	④ソクラテス的問答の様子を，第三者から見るとこういうふうに見えるのでしょう
JB	Yes, she really had to let it sink down more in order to think more deeply about it and make this cognitive shift.	はい．もっと深く考え，この認知転換をするためには，彼女はそのことを本当に心の底にしみこませなくてはなりませんでした．	
DK	It's helpful that she has such wonderful expressions that you can pick up a great deal from watching her face.	彼女が表情が豊かで，顔を見ているだけでそれがわかるというのは助かりますね．	

JB	She does and she's an easier client in that way. The more difficult ones are the ones who have more of a mask and who don't really let you know how they're feeling right at the moment. It's very important to be able to figure out whether the patient is having interfering automatic thoughts during the therapy session itself.	そうです．そういう意味では彼女はやりやすい患者さんです．もっとも難しいのは，仮面をつけ，自分の感じていることをその場で表面に出さない患者さんです．セッション中には，その患者さんが，妨げとなる自動思考を持っているのかどうか見極めることができるというのは，非常に重要です．	⑦セッション中のホットな認知を見逃さないことが非常に重要
JC	In this next segment you're moving towards a closing piece. And as you do that you have positive confrontation, not negative confrontation but positive confrontation and encouragement was there. Can you talk about how you use that?	次にお見せする部分では，あなたは締めくくりに向かっています．それをする時に，あなたは否定的ではなく肯定的に彼女に直面していますね．そこには励ましがあります．どのようにそれを用いるのか，お話しいただけますか？	
JB	I think it's particularly important with depressed patients because they only see the negative. They screen out because of depression. They're not really letting in the positive data. So I try to point out to depressed patients the positive things that I do see going on, so I'm really giving honest encouragement, positive encouragement in order to help her see that some of her thoughts are inaccurate and especially her view of herself is not completely accurate.	それはうつ病の患者さんの場合はとくに重要だと思います．彼らは否定的なことしか見ないからです．うつ病のために，それ以外のことを排除してしまい，肯定的な情報を取りこもうとしません．ですから私は，うつ病の患者さんには，そこで起こっている肯定的なできごとを指摘するようにしています．患者さんの考えには正確でないものがあること，とくに自分自身をどう思うかということについては正確ではないということが患者さんにわかるように手助けをするために，率直な励まし，肯定的な励ましを与えます．	②セッションの構造化：まとめを入れる ③認知行動モデルに則って介入する

Judith Beck『うつ病』

JC	Let's watch how you create a perceptual alternative for her.	それではどのようにして彼女のために別の見方を提供してあげたのかを見てましょう	⑧-b 認知再構成
JB	Yeah.	はい．	

—§ 9—

JC	In that segment I saw you kind of switch from beginning as a cheerleader and then moving on to becoming a teacher.	この部分では，チアリーダーとしてセッションを始めたあなたが，先生になっているのがわかります．
JB	Right. That's right	そうです．
JC	And it sounds like that's the kind of thing you wanna do at the end is to leave somebody with some hope still in them and then very specific suggestions for what it is they're gonna do?	あなたがセッションの最後になさりたいのは，患者さんがセッションを終えて帰る時に希望を感じるようにさせること，自分がこれから何をしようとしているのかという非常に具体的な提案をすることのようですね．
JB	Yes, we tell patients when they first come to therapy that it's not enough just to come for 45 or 50 minutes a week, that they need to learn certain things in therapy that they're going to use for the rest of the week and hopefully for the rest of their lives.	はい，我々は患者さんが最初に治療に来た時に，週1回の45分か50分のセッションに来るだけでは十分ではないこと，そして治療で学んだことをその後の1週間，できればその後の人生でずっと活用する必要があるということを伝えます．
DK	She kept saying OK, OK, and I know I was thinking, as I was watching, she had that pen in her hand, I was wondering why you didn't suggest to write down one of those statements or one of those points	彼女がオーケー，オーケーと繰り返し，しかも手にペンを持っているのを見ていて，私は，なぜあなたが彼女にいくつかのポイントを書き留めるように言わないのだろうと考えていました．
JB	Which point?	どのポイントですか？
DK	You were talking about I've already made a decision, or I'm already moving on, and I wondered if it would be helpful for her to remember those.	もう決めた，すでに動きだしている，などです．それらを覚えておくことは彼女にとって助けになるのでは？
JB	It probably would have been helpful, and to be honest I don't remember at that time why I didn't have her write down. My sense is that I thought I had given her enough to write down. Giving her more at this point might be confusing to her or overwhelming to her. I think that's what's going through my mind at the time.	そうだろうと思います．正直なところ，私はその時なぜ彼女に書いてもらわなかったのか覚えていません．私は，彼女にもう十分書いてもらっていて，その時点でさらに書くように言うことは，彼女を混乱させたり多すぎるかもしれないと感じました．たぶんその時，私はそう考えていたのだと思います．

JC	In this final segment we're gonna look at the closing piece. And in this, you continue to solicit feedback from her. Is that how you close an interview?	さて次は最後の部分を見ます．ここではあなたはまだ彼女からフィードバックを引き出そうとしています．あなたはこういうふうにセッションを終えるのですか？	②セッションの構造化：まとめ
JB	Yes, getting feedback from clients is very important. As I was saying earlier, if we see that patients are having an emotional shift right in the session, suddenly looking unhappy or scared or hopeless or irritated, right at the moment we ask for feedback, what's going on in your mind right at this minute, right now. If we don't see those kinds of shifts then by the end of the interview we wanna ask what did you think about the interview, anything you thought I got wrong, or anything bothered you. Because we really wanna tailor the therapy for the patient. If the patient is having automatic thoughts, negative thoughts about herself, or about the therapist or the therapy, it will interfere with what we are trying to do with her.	はい．患者さんからフィードバックを得ることは非常に重要です．すでにお話ししたように，もしも患者さんがセッションの中で感情の変化を生じたとわかったら，突然悲しそうに見えたり，怖がっていたり，もうだめだと思っていたり，あるいはイライラしているなどに見えたら，我々はその場でフィードバックを求めます．今この瞬間，あなたは心の中で何を思っているのですか，と．そういった変化がなければ，セッションの終わりまでには，セッションをどう思いましたか，私が何か誤解していると思いましたか，何か嫌だったことがありますか，と聞きます．我々はその治療を本当にその患者さんに合わせたいですから．もし患者さんが自動思考，自分について，あるいは治療者や治療対して否定的な思考を持っていたら，それは我々がその患者さんと一緒に行おうとしていることを妨害することになるでしょう．	⑦セッション中のホットな認知を見逃さないこと ②セッションの構造化 ④協力的実証主義

Judith Beck『うつ病』

JC	It seems to me too that tailoring is really important to make sure that your treatment sticks. I know that the hallmark of your approach is to focus on relapse and the prevention of relapse. So that someone leaves they don't feel good or they don't feel good in a couple of hours they're back to where they were before. How do you do that with relapse?	治療がきちんと続くために，私も患者さんに合わせるということはとても重要だと思います．あなたのアプローチの特徴は，再燃と再燃の防止に焦点を当てることだと思います．患者さんがセッションを終えた時にいい気分でなかったら，あるいは1, 2時間のうちにいい気分にならなかったら，彼らは元に戻ってしまいます．あなたは再燃についてはどのようになさるのですか？
JB	Well, one part is through teaching them specific skills during the course of therapy itself. Then what we try to do is to space out sessions towards the end of the therapy so if they are coming once a week we try to get them once every two weeks and then we move to three or four weeks. And in between, have them practice the skills they have learned during therapy itself.	1つには，治療そのものの期間中に，特定のスキルを教えます．それから，我々は治療期間の終了に向かってセッションの間隔をあけるようにします．毎週来ていたのなら，2週間に一度にして，それから3週間とか4週間にします．そしてその間に，患者さんには治療で学んだスキルを練習してもらいます． ②治療全体の構造化
JC	And then tailoring the piece to make sure that it's the right solution for her problem?	そしてそれをその患者さんに合わせ，その人の問題の正しい解決であることを確認するのですね？
JB	Exactly.	その通りです．
JC	Let's watch how you conclude the interview.	あなたがセッションを締めくくる様子を観ましょう．

— § 10 —

JC	Visibly we see a change with her. She doesn't look like a 41 on the Beck Depression Scale	彼女は目に見えて変化しています．ベック抑うつ質問票で41点の人には見えません．

JB	That's right. I think what has happened is that we've been able to undermine her belief that she's helpless and inadequate. In particularly what she liked was the advantage/disadvantage analysis I taught her. I think she saw that by doing this kind of technique she could make decisions better and probably she could stand up to her family better.	そうですね.自分がどうしようもなく能力不足だという彼女の信念を弱体化させることができたのだと思います.とくに彼女が気に入ったのは,私が教えてあげたメリットとデメリットの分析です.彼女は,こういうことをすることにより,自分がよりうまく決断ができ,おそらくは家族に対してもうまく対峙することができるということがわかったのだと思います.	
DK	Right. She has something concrete. I've thought this through. The other thing I thought interesting was when you asked her for some negative feedback. It was like you're kidding look on her face.	そうですね.彼女は具体的な何かを手にしました.私はずっとそう考えていました.もう1つ,私が興味深いと思ったのは,あなたが否定的なフィードバックを求めた時です.彼女の顔には,冗談でしょ,という表情が浮かびましたね.	②セッションの構造化 ④協力的実証主義
JB	Yeah. Patients often have that reaction at first and in a real therapy session I might have gone into more of a rational as to why I'm asking these questions	はい.患者さんは最初はそういう反応をすることがよくあります.本当のセッションだったら,私は,なぜそういう質問をするのかという説明をしていたかもしれません.	⑤心理教育
DK	That certainly showed great respect for her	それは彼女に対して敬意を示すことになりますね.	
JB	Right. Part of that is the collaborative nature. Together, we have to figure out what's going to help you.	そうです.それも協力的であるということです.あなたの助けになることを一緒に考えていかなくてはならない,ということです.	
JC	Thank you for collaborating with us and letting us see some inside into your work.	私たちと協力して,あなたのお仕事の内側をお見せいただき,ありがとうございました.	
JB	My pleasure.	こちらこそ.	

Judith Beck『うつ病』

Aaron T. Beck 1『絶望感―初回面接』（Disc 2）

登場人物　**Aaron T. Beck**（以下 **AB**）
　　　　　患者　　　（以下 **C**）

AB	I understand that you came here because you're feeling depressed?	あなたは落ちこんでいるのでここにいらっしゃったのですね．
C	Yeah.... I've seen a television show. That's why I came.	ええ…テレビで見て，それで来ました．
AB	Uh.	
C	Well, I didn't come because of the television show, but that's how I got here...and I just felt that I needed somebody, something to help me, so... so many states I go through...	いえ，テレビ番組を見たから来たわけじゃありませんが，でもそうやって来たので…．ただ，誰か，何か助けが必要だと感じたので．いろいろなことがあって…．
AB	Can you tell me a little bit about these states?	そういった状態について少し話していただけますか？ ④**質問による発見**
C	Well, then... er... sad, tiring... I don't usually have any energy to do anything.. umm... usually wanna do anything...I'm always like in a confused state. I don't know which way to turn... anything...er... like I just don't know... I feel like I don't know too much about what to do..	ええ…あの…悲しくて，疲れていて…．普段，何をする気力もありません，何も…．いつも混乱状態にあるみたいで．どちらに向かえばいいのかわからないし…何もわからないのです．何をしたらいいのか，よくわからない気がします．
AB	Uh.	はい．
C	I found that when I decided to come here, the thing that made me decide was my husband losing his job and he... how he reacted to it, like it was the end of the world..	ここに来ようと決めた時，そう決めたのは，夫が失業したからでした．その時の彼の反応です…まるで世界が終わったみたいな態度だったので．
AB	Uh.	
C	I've finally seen what I was doing... making it worse than it really is.	私はやっと自分のしていることがわかりました．ものごとを実際よりさらに悪くしていました．
AB	Uh... Can you tell me a little bit more about how you discovered that you were making it worse than it really was?	ものごとを実際より悪くしていたことが，どのようにしてわかったのですか？ ④**質問による発見** もう少し話してもらえますか？

C	Well...er.... I don't know about any other time, but I know that that one time... I went...oh, let's see... he lost his job and I ... I got ... well.... I was like a mad person so it's like, I couldn't sit still, I couldn't think straight, I could... hmm... everything was wrong, as though everything was just wrong... and now... I didn't... I couldn't figure out how we were gonna get back to ... normal.	えーと…ほかの時のことはわかりませんが，あの時だけは私は…あの…夫が失業して，私は…あの…私は気が狂ったみたいでした．じっと座っていられなかったし，ちゃんと考えることもできなかった．すべてがだめでした．まるで何もかもが間違っているみたいに．そして…私たちがどうやって元に戻ればいいのか，私にはわかりませんでした．
AB	Uh.	
C	And I would sit and think about it for hours and hours and hours, and my mind would just go round in circles... And then I ... I ... er ... after like three or four days of doing that, I went out... And I went over to my mother's and my mother was having like the same sort of problems...with money... And... t'was ... before I got there though that I thought ... I don't know how I thought it.... it just... must've hit me... that thing ... the thing ...er.... Oh, I know what it is. He got ...er... compensation, unemployment?	何時間も何時間も座ったまま考えて，私の考えはぐるぐる回って…．それから私は…3，4日間そんなことばかりした後，出かけました．母のところへ行きましたが，母自身も似たような問題を抱えていて…お金のことでした．母のところへ行く前に私が考えたのは…どうしてそう考えたのかわかりませんが，思いついたのです．あれを…夫はあの…そう，補償を，失業の補償金をもらいました．
AB	Uh.	
C	And I thought well now that's not the end of the world 'cause now we have some money coming in somewhere.	それで私は，この世の終わりではないと思いました．入ってくるお金が少しあるから．
AB	I see.	なるほど．
C	And before that, I wouldn't think ... that there was any hope at all.	それまでは，まったく希望もないと思っていました．
AB	Is that the way you feel right now?	あなたは今もそのように感 ⑦ホットな認知 じていますか？
C	Umm.... about my future? Yeah...	将来についてですか？
AB	You said no emotion?	それとも何も感じていない？
C	About... I feel like that about my future. Yeah, we're... and what's gonna come, that way.	将来について，そう感じます．これからどうなるのだろうかと，そんなふうに．
AB	So you're feeling more or less ... kind of lack of feeling? Or you feel sad?	つまりあなたは，どちらかというと何も感じないような状態ですか？　それとも悲しいですか？
C	Right. I feel sad at... er.... I feel sad about it. I don't wanna... look that way sometimes, but I ... I feel that, I mean.... I've been thinking that.	悲しいです．そのことについては悲しいと感じます．そんなふうにものごとを見たくないと思う時もありますけど，私は…ずっと考えています．

C	Like... today on my way here I was thinking about.... most of my best friends have died... that that's sad thoughts... you know... like... you know?	今日もここへ来る途中に考えていました．親しかった友達はほとんど亡くなったし…そういう悲しい考えです．
AB	Uh.	
C	Yeah... er... depressed.	ええ…落ちこみます．
AB	You say, mostly you sad most of your best friends have died.	親しい友達のほとんどは亡くなって，主に悲しいのですね．
C	Well, I don't know, I...	
AB	... Such a young person...	その若さで…．
C	I don't know, I don't know. Well, there was...	
AB	How old are you? 24 or..?	おいくつですか？ 24歳くらい？
C	Uh. The friends that I loved the most.. yeah, they... dead...	ええ…．私が一番好きだった友人たちが亡くなりました．
AB	Were they old people?	それは年配の友人たちでしたか？
C	No, they're around my age... or a little older.... One girlfriend got this really strange disease, I don't know what it was. It was bad....	いいえ，私くらいの年齢か，少し上でした．女友達の1人は，よくわからないけど，とても珍しい病気になりました．何の病気か知りません．ひどかった…．
AB	Uh.	
C	And it showed... it wasn't a disease that she didn't show. Like cancer, you can't say it, you know, it's just there, and it might hurt and all. But this disease, she got it you could see it all over her, like she just ... it was bad... Then another friend got in a car accident and then he died... so like, ... er...	見てわかりました．彼女の病気は見えない病気ではありませんでした．がんだったら，わからないけど病気はそこにあって痛みもあるでしょ．でも彼女の病気は身体中にあるのが見えて，ひどかった…．それから別の友達は交通事故で…彼も亡くなりました．だから…．
AB	It's like what?	だから？
C	I don't know... it's just like, like.... Thank God, none of my family died 'cause I think that would be really bad.	わかりません．ただ…ありがたいことに，私の家族に亡くなった者はいません．もし家族が亡くなったら本当に大変だろうと思います．
AB	Now were you about to say it's as though fate has something...?	あなたは今，運命のようだと言おうとしましたか？
C	...Fate? Well, no.	運命？ いいえ．
AB	You didn't mean it that way?	そういう意味ではない？
C	No. 'Cause it's happened to other.... If it was happening now, I would say, yeah, fate did it, you know?	いいえ．だって，ほかの人に起こったことだから．もし今起きていることなら，ええ，運命のせいだと言うかもしれません．
AB	Uh.	

Aaron T. Beck 1『絶望感―初回面接』

C	But since it was just friends....	でも友達だけだったから….
AB	Now, when you come in here, you said these thoughts went through your mind. How does that connect up with your husband's problem?	さて，あなたはここへ来る途中，そういった考えが頭に浮かんだとおっしゃいました．そういう考えは，あなたのご主人の問題とどうつながるのですか？ ④質問による発見
C	...They're all bad things.	…全部，悪いことです．
AB	So you're having thoughts right now about bad things happening to you.	つまりあなたは，あなたに起こっている悪いことについて今，考えている．
C	...Well...	…ええ…．
AB	Or...	それとも…．
C	Yeah...	
AB	Well, happening in a sense that you've lost as far as the impact on you of... you lost good friends.	あなたにとっての衝撃という意味では，親しい友人を亡くしたというできごとですね．
C	...Right...	…そうです．
AB	As far as the event with your husband, you lost your husband in a sense as far as...	ご主人についてのできごとは，ある意味で，ご主人を失ったようなことですか． ④質問による発見
C	Yeah, I...don't know if I ever had one or not.	ええ，私には何が起こったのか…．
AB	You mean...	つまり…．
C	Because he's like... it's... he's there... but he's not... he's not anybody I could talk to, or... be open with... I tried talk and tell him, he's not... he's not... he doesn't wanna talk.	だって夫は…彼はそこにいますけど，でも話のできる相手じゃないし，気持ちを打ち明けることのできる相手でもない．私は話をしようとしましたが，夫は…話したがらないのです．
AB	Uh.	
C	Like I'll ask... may.... Like the other night, I said to him... well... "You don't wanna work do you?" And he says, "Yeah, I wanna work." But I know like he's not telling the truth, you know, it's like... and I just think it's hopeless, like he's gonna continue on... doing things he shouldn't... and now... continuing on, worrying about the whole...	このあいだの夜も，私は夫に話そうとして…言ったのです．「あなたは働きたくないのでしょう」と．彼は「働きたい」と言いますが，私にはわかっています．彼は本当のことを言っていません．それで…私は絶望的だと思うだけです．彼はやるべきじゃないことをやり続けるつもりなのです．今もずっと心配で…．
AB	Uh, now you say that you can't talk to him. You can't share your own feelings with him?	あなたはご主人に話ができない，自分の気持ちをご主人に打ち明けられないのですね？
C	...I don't think he's interested in anything I know, a bit, well...	夫は，私の知っていることに関心があるとは思えません．

AB	Do you ever try to talk to him about how you felt?	自分がどう感じているかを話そうとしたことはありますか？ ⑧-iアサーション訓練
C	Uh, huh. Yeah... I've tried... I think a lot ... but I don't think he's interested.	ええ…話そうとしました．いろいろなことを考えて….でも彼が関心を持っているとは思いません．
AB	What happens when you talk to him?	あなたがご主人に話をすると，どうなりますか？ ④質問による発見
C	He shuts up. And he doesn't... he doesn't wanna really know what I have to say.	夫は黙りこみます．彼は私が言いたいことなど本当は知りたくないのです．
AB	So he just doesn't respond?	つまりご主人は返事をしない？
C	... Right.... And if he does, he usually whisper... respond, he usually responds by starting an argument... may, er.... It's not that he doesn't feel that I'm trying to talk to him. He feels I'm trying to tight with him.	…そうです．返事をしてもほそほそ言うだけです．返事をする時は，夫は言い争いを始めるのです．彼は私が話しかけようとしていることを感じていないわけではないのですが，私が厳しいことを言うと思っているのです．
AB	So, even if you're talking about yourself, he still takes it as it...	つまり，あなたが自分の話をしていても，ご主人はあなたが彼のことを…．
C	Yeah that he's...	
AB	That he's let you down in some way?	ご主人はあなたを落ちこませることがありますか？
C	Yeah.	はい．
AB	Do you feel that he's let you down?	あなたは，ご主人があなたを落ちこませたと感じますか？
C	... Yeah	…はい．
AB	Why is... do you feel he's let you down?	なぜご主人はあなたを落ちこませたのですか？
C	... In some way... some ways he's not... he's not ... because I... he's let me down and er... staying out of trouble... and he let me down because he's... he doesn't really wanna work... even though he's laid off right now, he now, he doesn't wanna work anyway.... he just... you know...	ある意味で夫は…彼は私を落ちこませて…自分が問題に関わらないようにしています．彼が私を落ちこませるのは…彼が本当は働きたくないからです．今は失業中ですが，どっちみち彼は仕事をしたくないのです．
AB	So you said earlier that you feel sad, like retiring... You don't have any energy to do anything.	先ほどあなたは，悲しくて引きこもった感じで，何もする気力がないと言いましたね．
C	Uh.	ええ．
AB	Can you tell me more about that?	それについてもっと話してもらえますか？ ④質問による発見
C	Well... it's... er. the last... Let's see... last night, I'm like... I'm all nervous I can't stop fidgeting, you know.	ええ…あの…そうですね…夕べ私は…とても神経質になって落ち着きませんでした．

Aaron T. Beck 1『絶望感―初回面接』

C	Usually it's not like that, though usually I don't wanna get out of bed. I wanna stay there, I wanna just keep the covers up to my head, just stay there, you know. Er... I don't wanna do anything, I just wanna be left alone, and just keep everything out, keep everything away from me.	普段はベッドから出たくないのです．布団を頭までかぶって，ただそこにいたいのです．私は何もしたくなくて，1人にしておいてほしくて，何もかも私に関わりのないようにしておいてほしいのです．
AB	You feel better when you get under the covers and shut everything out?	布団をかぶって何もかも遮っているほうが気分がいいのですね？
C	Yeah.	はい．
AB	You do feel better.	そのほうがいい気分なのですね． ⑦ホットな認知：感情の重視
C	Uh. Yeah, I feel…. I feel better in that way.	はい，そうしているほうがいいです．
AB	So how much time do you spend doing that?	どのくらいの間，そうしていますか？
C	Now? Lately?	今ですか？ 最近？
AB	Yeah.	はい．
C	Er... I don't get to do it too much… because I have two kids… I don't really get to do it all that much. I'd love to do it more but… I mean I feel… I feel… safe, sort of secure. Like things that are staying … like the… on the other side of the wall near me.	あまりそうしていられません．子どもが2人いるので…そんなに長い時間はできません．もっとそうしていたいけど…だって私は…私が感じるのは…安心，じっとしていると安心していられる感じです．ものごとは壁の向こうにあるみたいな感じ．
AB	Uh. Now after you spend some time in the covers how do you feel about yourself?	ええ．では，布団の中にしばらくいたあと，自分についてどう感じますか？ ⑦ホットな認知：感情の重視
C	…From laying there? I don't know.	…布団の中で横になっていたあとに？ わかりません．
AB	Let's say...	ではたとえば…．
C	…I don't usually have any bad feelings about…. Oh, yeah, I do… I feel I shouldn't be laying down, doing nothing. You should've been doing this, should've been doing that… should've got up and done something whatever that's supposed to do… And even though I'm laying, I'm thinking that I'm not making any solutions to any problems. I'm just there...	たいていは，悪い気持ちはないです．ああ，あります，何もしないで横になっているべきではないと感じます．これをするべきだ，あれをするべきだ，起きてやらなくちゃならないことをするべきだ，と．横になっていても何の問題も解決できていないと考えています．ただそこにいるだけ…．
AB	So on the one hand you seem to enjoy, but on the other, you...	つまり，その状態を楽しむ一方，もう一方では…． ④ソクラテス的問答
C	Well, I... I... it's not that I do it... so I feel safe.	私は…何かするということではありませんが，安心だと感じます．

AB	Uh.	ええ．
C	I feel like I don't have like... as long as I stay there they'll like... nothing's gonna happen... not that nothing's gonna happen to me, I mean like somebody could come in and do anything, you know, but... I don't know, it just feels like.. I can just... if I can just lay there, just not think about nothing.	そこにいる限り，何も起こらないと…感じます．私に何も起こらないということではなくて…だって誰かがやってきて何かするかもしれないから…．でも…わかりません．そこで横になっていれば，何も考えなくていい…．
AB	When you do get out of bed, if you say you start dealing with the children how do you feel about yourself?	ベッドから起き出した時，④**質問による発見** 子どもたちの相手をし始めた時，自分のことをどう感じますか？
C	About the children?	子どもについてですか？
AB	Uh.	ええ．
C	I usually feel bad about the kids because I don't... I should be taking them out to play... I should be playing with them myself... and I feel mad at them because I can't do what I wanna do... like I'd just, I would rather lay down and I can't do it so I'm sort of a little mad at them... mad at myself for being mad at them because it's not their fault, you know, it's like in a circle... it's er....	子どもたちに対しては，たいてい私は申し訳なく感じます．外に遊びに連れだしてやるべきだし，いっしょに遊んでやるべきです．それから子どもたちに対して腹が立ちます．だってやってやりたいことができないから…．私はただそこで横になっているだけで何もできないから，だから少し腹が立ちます．子どもたちに対して怒っている自分に腹が立ちます．だって子どもたちが悪いわけじゃないし…．堂々巡りみたいな感じです．
AB	You say you feel you should take them out and do other things with them. Do you believe you're not doing as much as you should do with the kids?	あなたは子どもたちを外に連れていったり，いろいろなことをいっしょにすべきだと言うのですね．子どもたちにしてやるべきことを自分がしていないと思いますか？
C	Yeah, if I had... it's not that... I feel when I'm there... I feel like I can't do it, I can't get up, I can't.. I just can't do it. Umm, I... it's physical tired it's more emotional tired I think tired worrying, tired... my brain is just not functioning.	ええ，ベッドの中にいる時は，私はできない，起きられない，とにかくできないと感じます．私は身体が疲れているというより，気持ちが疲れています．心配することに疲れます．私の脳みそはとにかく働いていません．
AB	So you're saying when you're laying in bed you feel you cannot do some of these active things.	つまりあなたは，ベッドで横になっている時には，そのような活動的なことができないと感じるというのですね？
C	Right.	
AB	And er...	そして…
C	I can't... I might want to, I still... even if I want to, sometimes I can't.	私は…やりたいのかもしれないけれど，それでも私は…できません．
AB	As long as you're laying in bed.	ベッドで横になっている限りは．

Aaron T. Beck 1『絶望感―初回面接』

C	...Yeah.	…はい．
AB	Now what happens when you get out of bed? You find you can do certain things that you've been thinking?	では，ベッドから出たらどうなりますか？ 考えていたことが何かできますか？
C	Yeah, sometimes I can't... No, 'cause it... I just wanna sit and play with my kids, sometimes I can't... I don't have the... er.... whatever it takes to do it.	ええ，時々は…．でもできません．私はただ座って子どもたちと遊びたいと思いますが，できない時もあって…．そうするだけの気力がないというか…．
AB	Uh.	ええ．
C	The patience, or... It's not patience, it's... I just don't have the strength to play with them.	忍耐力というか…忍耐力ではないですね．私には子どもたちと遊ぶだけの体力がありません．
AB	What happens when you're playing with them?	子どもたちと遊んでいるとどうなりますか？ ④質問による発見
C	...Nothing terrible happens. It's just that I don't have the... I don't know... just... my mind won't center on just that... like it's... like I said, always in the back of my mind is... what's gonna happen, what am I gonna do... look I can't take... er... the time for them because all these other problems I'm thinking about....	何も大変なことにはなりません．私には…わかりません．私の心は集中できなくて…．さっき言ったみたいに，心の奥にあるのは…どうなるのだろう，どうしよう…ということです．いろいろな問題のことを考えているので，子どもたちのために時間をとることができなくて…．
AB	Uh. Do you think we might be able to help you?	ええ．あなたは，私たちがあなたの助けになりそうだと思いますか？
C	I hope so. I mean this is my last hope...	そうだといいと思います．だってこれは私の最後の望みで…．
AB	Now, you had your intake interview previously with Julie, right?	あなたは担当者と初診面接をしましたね？
C	Yeah.	はい．
B	Right now you look pretty sad when you said "This is my last hope".	今しがた，あなたは「これは私の最後の望み」とおっしゃった時，ずいぶん悲しそうでした． ⑦ホットな認知
C	(crying) ... I think I'm all right....	私は大丈夫だと思います…．
AB	You all right? What was going through your mind when you said "This is my last hope"? Did you have some kind of a picture in your mind?	大丈夫ですか？「これは最後の望みだ」と言った時，あなたの頭の中にはどんなことが浮かんでいましたか？ 心の中に何か絵が浮かびましたか？ ⑦ホットな認知を見逃さず，⑧-a 自動思考を同定
C	...Er... yeah... If it doesn't work out... that I don't think I could take living with this the rest of my life.	もしうまくいかなかったら…私はこの先の人生をやっていけません．

AB	Uh. It doesn't work out, then what?	うまくいかなかったら，何なのですか？ ④質問による発見
C	...Then I wouldn't really care what'll happen to me.	…そしたらどうなったって構わない．
AB	You have something more concrete in mind?	もっと具体的なことを考えていますか？ ④質問による発見
C	...All right, this minute I'll think I would commit suicide, maybe if afterwards I thought that there's nothing left I hope... I don't know though... 'cause I've thought about suicide before... I've never been able to bring myself to do it... come close... never been able to succeed...	…そうです，この瞬間，私は自殺することを考えています．何も希望は残っていないし…．私はこれまでにも自殺を考えたことがあります…．できなかったけど…しそうになったことはあって…でもうまくできたことはなかった…．
AB	Uh.	ええ．
C	I know... I know little certain things start me like, er... my kids, I don't think... even though I think I'm sometimes not as good a mother as I could be, I think they'd be a lot worse off with my husband.	ささいなことがきっかけになるとわかっています．子どもたち…私はいい母親ではないけれど，それでも子どもたちにとっては父親といるよりはまだましだと思います．
AB	Uh.	
C	Er... I think it would destroy some other people like my mother if I did something like that, you know, and er... that's what I think mainly stops me, my children and my mother, just that, you know, they would... I guess... I'm afraid if I did something my mother would think that she failed somewhere which is not true, I don't think... and... it's just, well, my kids, I couldn't trust my husband with my kids, like... even though I'm messed up I think that he would mess them up more.	もし私がそんなことをすれば，ほかの人を，母を，打ちのめすだろうと思います．それが私を思いとどまらせているのだと思います．子どもたちと母です…．私がそんなことをすれば，母は自分がダメな母親だったからだと思うだろうし，それは違うのですけどね．それに…子どもたちも…夫は信頼できません．私もひどいけど，彼は子どもたちをもっとだめにしてしまうと思います．
AB	Are these some of the reasons for not committing suicide?	自殺をしないのはそういうことが理由ですか？
C	Uh.	
AB	What are some of the reasons why you wanted to do, you think?	自殺したいと思った理由は何ですか？ ④質問による発見
C	'Cause it's sometimes it's just hopeless... there's no solutions, there's no... it just continues... constantly the same way, all the time	だってとにかくもう絶望的な時があって…．解決策はないし…この状態が続いて…いつもいつも同じです．
AB	It's hopeless, there's no solutions and continues constantly.	絶望的で解決策がない，常にそういう状態が続いている．
C	Uh, it doesn't let up... sometimes it's better for a little while and then, bam! They come down harder... you know...	ええ，よくなりません…．少しいい時があってもほんのちょっとの間で…またダメになります．もっとひどくなります．

Aaron T. Beck 1『絶望感—初回面接』

AB	When you say it doesn't let up, you mean the hopelessness?	よくならない，というのは，絶望が，という意味ですか？	
C	...Right...	…そうです．	
AB	So you have this sense of hopelessness, a sense of hopelessness and leads you to wanna commit suicide. When you think of the children and your mother and then you think I'll try to put it off.	つまりあなたにはこの絶望感があり，それがあなたを自殺したい気持ちにさせている．子どもたちとお母さんのことを思うと，思いとどまろうとする．	②セッションの構造化：セッションの途中でも要所要所でまとめ
C	Well, I... there was one time that... when I was really, really, really dead set on doing it, like I care at all, I mean I would just do I had, I had two kids... I think it was right after I came home with my second, I... I don't know somehow I felt my mother and my father and my whole family had abandoned me... like they left me. I don't know why I felt it, I just felt that way.	一度…私は本当に，本当に，本当に実行するつもりでした．もうどうでもよくなって．2人目を産んで家に戻ってきたすぐ後だったと思います．私は…どういうわけか，母からも父からも家族みんなから見捨てられたと感じました．みんなが私から離れていったみたいに．なぜか分からないけど，そう感じたのです．	
AB	Uh.		
C	And that's when I was really dead set on doing it 'cause then that was like... okay, I didn't have a husband, I didn't have my family, you know, like they don't give two shits. I don't need that, you know... that was one time when... if I could've... I went around to see somebody to get some pills, they didn't have as many as I needed to do it... I did take some...	その時私は，本当に自殺するつもりでした．夫もいない，家族もいない，何もない．それが私が…もし自殺できたとしたらその時でした．誰か薬をくれる人がいないかと探しました．でも必要な数は手に入らなかった…．	
AB	Uh.		
C	But just put me to sleep though.	ただ眠っただけでした．	
AB	How many pills did you take?	薬を何錠飲みましたか？	
C	Er... I think three or four.	3錠か4錠だったと思います．	
AB	Uh.	はい．	
C	Well, but I know they put me to sleep and calmed me down...	でもそれで眠ってしまって，私は落ち着きました．	
AB	Can you remember what you took?	何を飲んだか覚えていますか？	
C	Can I remember what I took?	何を飲んだか覚えている？	
AB	Yeah, what kind of pills?	はい，どの薬を？	
C	I don't know what kind they were. I just took them... He said, I said, give me something, I don't care what it is, you know. He didn't know what I was doing.	何だったかわかりません，ただ飲んだだけで…．私は，何でもいいから何かちょうだいと言いました．夫は私が何をしているのか知りませんでした．	
AB	Uh.		

C	...You know, I said to him can you get me some more, you know... I just acted like I was... I just wanted to do drugs, you know, I didn't act like I wanted to... kill myself... do is... well, I don't know.... If I would've got more, I would have done that time though.	私は夫に，もっとあるかと聞いて，ただ薬を飲みたいというふうに装いました．自殺したい様子は見せませんでした．もっと薬があったら，あの時に自殺していたかもしれません．
AB	You say you think you would have.	自殺していた，と思うのですね．
C	Oh, yeah, I think so.	ええ，そうです．そう思います．
AB	... One of the factors then was that you felt abandoned.	原因の1つは，見捨てられたと感じたことですか．
C	I thought... well... abandoned... I didn't have any... anybody at that point, that's how I felt... I just had... me... Me wasn't good enough.	私は…見捨てられて…その時は誰もいないと感じました．自分だけ…自分だけでは十分じゃなかった．	②セッションの構造化：セッションの途中でも要所要所でまとめ
AB	And er... Let alone, abandoned, just you, who's not good enough, that's all you had...	見捨てられただけではなく，自分しかいなかった，不十分な自分だけ．
C	At that point... yeah.	その時は…そうです．
AB	Remember you started just a few minutes ago you started to feel sad. I presume when we talked about you coming here. How this was the last resort. Is that correct?	数分前，あなたは悲しいと感じ始めていました．このセッションが最後の頼みの綱だ，と．そうですか？	⑦ホットな認知
C	Well, I can't depend on anybody, any... well, I'm sort of dependent on it, this, you know, but...I can't depend on my family or my mother, I told you about my mother, er...	私は誰も頼る人がいません．このセッションを頼りにしているのです．家族にも夫にも頼れないし，母のこともお話しましたよね…．
AB	Yeah.	ええ．
C	...My sisters and brothers... and they can't help me I realize that now. They can't... there's nothing they can do...	姉や兄も…私の助けにはならないことがわかりました．みんなにしてもらえることは何もありません．
AB	Uh.	ええ．
C	There's nothing my husband can do... well, he could... he make like a little easier, but... he does nothing about, he can do... really about how I think...	夫にできることも何もありません．彼は…少しは楽にしてくれるかもしれないけど，でも彼にはできません．私がどういうふうに考えるか，は…．
AB	So what you seem to be saying is that the problem that nobody can seem to help you with is how you think.	つまり，誰にも何もできない問題というのは，あなたの考え方を手助けするということですか？

Aaron T. Beck 1『絶望感―初回面接』

C	...Right... Yeah...	…ええ.
AB	And what made you think that and believe that we might be able to help you with... the way you think.	あなたがどうしてそう考えるようになったのでしょう？ 私たちにはあなたの考え方を手助けすることができるかもしれない，と？
C	...You're telling me you're not gonna be able to help me?	私を助けることはできない，ということですか？
AB	That was the thought. That's an interesting thought you just had. I was telling you that we would be able to help you.	それは興味深い考えですね．私は，私たちはあなたを助けることはできるだろうと言ったのです． ⑦ホットな認知
C	Yeah, that's a negative thought, huh?	どうも否定的な考えでしたね．
AB	That's right. That's very important, a good discovery. If you get any more negative thoughts like that, will you tell me?	そうです．重要なこと，大切な発見です．もしこの先も否定的な考えが浮かんだら，私に話してくれますか？ ③心理教育：認知行動モデル ④協力的実証主義
C	Okay... er... I forgot the last now.	いいですよ….何の話でしたっけ？
AB	The question was, when you decided to come to the clinic, how did you have a sense that you needed someone to help you, how to think and I just was wondering the way you thought how we might be able to help you. What do you think?	問題は，あなたがこのクリニックに来る決心をした時，あなたの考え方を助けてくれる人が誰か必要だ，とどうして思ったのかということです．そして私たちがここでどのような助けになるとあなたが考えたのか，知りたいと思います．どうですか？
C	I don't know.	わかりません．
AB	Now you have the sense that if we could help you to work these things out inside your own head, that the things would be better for you and your life in general.	あなたは今，もし私たちがここであなたの頭の中のことを解決する助けになれば，ものごとはよくなるだろうし，あなたの人生全般がよくなるだろうと感じていますね． ②セッションの構造化：要所要所でまとめ
C	Yeah.	はい．
AB	Seemed to me that that's what you're saying before, about somebody helping you how to think, your husband couldn't help you how to think better, your family couldn't help you in that way.	先ほどあなたがおっしゃっているのはそういうことのように聞こえました．誰かが自分の考え方を手助けしてくれますように．ご主人にはできないし，家族にもできないし．
C	Right, er... If some.... Yeah, I feel if someone can help me how to make decisions, like... instead of just going around in a circle all the time...	そうです．もし…ええ，もし私が何かを決める時に，堂々巡りをするだけではなくて誰かが助けてくれたら…

C	if I can make myself, or force myself to... make a decision and then stick to it, and not let anybody change it or...	もし自分で決めることが，自分に決めさせることができて，それを実行することができたら，他の人に変えられてしまうのではなくて…．	
AB	So you feel if you can make a decision you'd feel better about yourself?	つまり，自分で決めることができれば，あなたは自分のことをもっとよく思うことができる？	④質問による発見
C	...Yeah.... That will be a first step I think.... 'Cause I don't think I've made any in a long time.	ええ．それが第一歩だと思います．もう長い間，自分で何かを決めたことがないから．	
AB	Uh, well, why don't we see, maybe we can get started on something and see where it goes. Is there any kind of decision you'd like to think about or talk about right now?	ええ，では，ここでやってみましょう．今あなたが話したいこと，決めたいことはありますか？	⑧-e 行動実験 ②セッションの構造化：アジェンダの設定
C	... Well... er... there... there's.... The main decision I think is scary to me, it's like... I don't know if I wanna face it.	えーと…大きな決心は怖いです．それは…そういうことには向き合いたくないかもしれません．	
AB	Uh.	ええ．	
C	And that's... if my husband and I could work things out or if it's just a waste of time, you know, and I can't make a decision on that.	それは…夫と協力して解決することができるのかどうか，それとも時間の無駄なのか，私には決めることができません．	
AB	And the decision is whether to split.	その場合の決めることとは，別れるかどうかということですね．	
C	Right.	そうです．	
AB	That's kind of a big one. That would take a lot of time. So it's important to talk to him, talk about him. Talk to Julie about it, too. Now, are there any other smaller decisions that you could make that would affect your life right away?	それは大きな問題です．時間がかかるでしょう．ご主人に話すこと，ご主人について話をすることは重要です．担当者にもその話をしてください．ほかに，すぐにあなたの人生を左右しそうな，もっと小さい決め事はありますか？	①問題解決モード

23 分

以上で導入部を終え，アジェンダを設定したことになる．ここまで 23 分かかっているが，初回セッションなので仕方がない．

C	...Well, I don't know... I guess... er... just trying to. I don't know... for a long time I've been wanting to go out and do other things like, I don't know, join something, feel like I'm a part of something, you know. And I haven't been able to do it. I don't know if it's financial, why I haven't been able to do it, I mean that's excuse that I come up with.	さあ…えーと…．ずっと長い間，私は外に出かけて他のことをしたいと思っていました．何かに参加するとか，仲間であるという感じです．でもずっとできませんでした．できなかったのはお金の問題なのかどうか…それはたぶん私が思いついた言いわけですね．
AB	Uh.	
C	But... I think sometimes that it's not financial. Sometimes I just don't get up and do it.	でも…それはお金の問題ではないと思うこともあります．ただ起きだしてそれをする，ということを私はしないから．
AB	Uh. Was there some specific group that you have in mind?	あなたが考えている，具体的な仲間がいますか？
C	Well.... I don't know... I guess that's another decision... I can't make... I think, I'm... like everything interests me enough to interest me.	よくわかりませんけど…それも決めることですね．私には決められなくて…私が興味を持てるほどのことがあれば…．
AB	Why don't we make a list and see what happens. The list, you know, what are some of the things you'll be interested in doing?	リストアップしてどうなるか，見てみましょうか．興味があってやってみたいと思っていることには，何がありますか？ ⑧-e 行動実験 ⑧-h 行動活性化
C	Bowling.	ボーリング．
AB	Uh.	はい．
C	I haven't done that for a long time.	もう長い間やっていません．
AB	Now, does this involve joining a bowling group or team?	これは，ボーリングのグループやチームに参加するということですか？
C	Uh, yeah. Well, that's... what I wanna do.	ええ…．それは…やりたいです．
AB	You know people who belong to...?	誰がメンバーか，知っていますか？
C	No.	いいえ．
AB	Uh.	なるほど．
C	I know other people, but they don't belong to... in Philadelphia.	知っている人もいますけど，その人たちはフィラデルフィアのグループじゃないから．
AB	Uh.	ええ．
C	Well, they do, but I guess it's...	メンバーだけど，でも…．
AB	How would you go about finding out about a bowling team?	ボーリングのチームを，どのように探すのですか？ ④質問による発見 ⑧-m 行動用語で記述
C	You only have to go down to the nearest bar in L.A. and it's there.	ロサンゼルスでは近くのバーに行けばそこでわかります．

AB	What would happen when you went down there?	そこに行くとどうなりますか?
C	I don't know, I mean, I don't know the procedure, I don't know. I've never been to one.	さあ…どういう手続きなのか,私は知りません.私は行ったことがないから.
AB	What do you think you could do when you got there?	そこに行ったら,あなたに は何ができると思いますか? ④質問による発見 ⑧-m 行動用語で記述
C	Obviously, I'd just... I don't see... I've never... I don't know how many people are in one group, I don't know if the whole group go down with you and say, okay..., we wanna be a team... But I guess there's, you know, some people, be sure to form a group and you can get on that team, you know.	それは…私は行ったことがないし…グループに何人いるのかも知りません.グループ全員で行くのかどうかも…たとえば,そこにいる人たちでグループを作るのか….でもまあ,誰かはいるだろうし,きっとグループを作るだろうし,そうすればチームに参加できるでしょうね.
AB	Uh.	
C	I guess... I'm not sure.	
AB	So how could you get that information about when...	では,そういう情報をどのようにして得ますか? ④質問による発見 ⑧-m 行動用語で記述
C	I guess it I went down there.	そこへ行ってみるのでしょうね.
AB	Uh, you think that you can get the information if you went down there?	そこへ行ってみれば情報が得られると思うのですね?
C	Yeah, yeah.	ええ,はい.
AB	Uh. You find out whether you join as individuals or as a group, or how many, need somebody to fill in?	個人で参加するのか,グループとして参加するのか,何人いるのか,人数が足りないのかどうか.
C	Right, uh.	そうです.
AB	How do you feel about doing that?	それをやってみるというのは,どうですか?
	Kinda stupid (laugh).	ちょっとバカみたい(笑う).
AB	'Cause it seems so trivial?	あまりにも些細なことだからですか?
C	Yeah, ...Like, well, why didn't I do it before?	ええ….だって…そんなこと,どうして私はこれまでにしなかったのか….
AB	There are good reasons why you didn't do it before. That was because you were so caught up in hopelessness.	これまでにしなかったのは,理由があるからです.あなたは絶望感にとらわれすぎていたからです.
C	Right... right.	そうですね,ええ.
AB	When you're hopeless you tend to deny as it were cut off parts of both solutions...	絶望的になっていると,どの解決法もダメだというように否定する傾向があります. ⑤心理教育:疾患

Aaron T. Beck 1『絶望感—初回面接』

AB	Remember when your husband lost his job and you said you refused to accept the fact that he get compensation. So when you gets caught up in hopelessness, this is what happens, such a thing.	ご主人が失業した時，あなたは補償金という事実を認めようとしなかったと自分で言っていたのを覚えていますか．絶望感にとらわれると，そういうことが起こるのです．	⑤心理教育：疾患
C	Yeah.	はい．	
AB	So rather than be down on yourself 'cause you hadn't thought of it before, why don't we carry you right through? So go to the bowling alley, and you get information, and then what would you do?	では，これまで考えつかなくて落ちこんでいたという状態からあなたを連れだしましょうか．ボーリング場に行って，情報を得て，それからどうしますか？	⑧- h 行動活性化 ⑧- m 行動用語で記述
C	Find out... OK, find out what you have to do get on the team, and then you just go.	チームに入るために何が必要かを聞いて，そして参加する．	
AB	And how do you get on the team? Say, once you get the information.	情報を得た後，どうやってチームに参加しますか？	
C	I don't know. I don't.... It depends upon...	さあ，わかりません…．	
AB	So, how do you feel about between now and Wednesday, do you think you might have the motivation to go to the bowling alley and at least get that information?	では，今から水曜日までの間に，あなたはボーリング場まで行って，少なくとも情報を得るだけの気持ちがあると思いますか？	
C	Yeah.	はい．	
AB	That's all you need to do, get the information.	情報を得る，することはそれだけです．	⑧- k 段階的課題設定
C	Yeah. Yeah, I think I'll go. Somebody's told me to do it, too.	はい，ええ，行けると思います．行きなさいと言ってくれた人がいるから．	
AB	I didn't tell you to do it. I just asked if you were willing to.	私はあなたに行きなさいと言いませんでしたよ．行きたいと思いますかと聞いただけです．	
C	No, well, I know. Yes. I feel like I'm motivated.	わかっています．はい，行きたい気持ちがあります．	
AB	You feel motivated to do it now?	今あなたは，行きたい気持ちがあるのですね？	
C	Yeah. Yeah. Before, I didn't have any reason for doing it. Oh, I did, but I guess I didn't feel like I did. I felt... like... just because I wanted to do it maybe it isn't... worthwhile?	はい．さっきまでは，私にはそうする理由がありませんでした．いえ，理由はあったけど，そういう気持ちがしなかったのです．私は…自分がそうしたいと思うだけではたぶんする価値がないと思っていました．	

28分

行動活性化が一通りすんだので，認知再構成を進めようとするが，

AB	You do seem to be a little down on yourself. Is that correct?	あなたは自分のことを低く評価していますね．どうですか？	④質問による発見
C	Yeah.	はい．	
AB	'Cause you just said "Because I wanted to do it, it can't be very worthwhile". You have a sense that you're not a very worthwhile person.	あなたは「今，自分がそうしたいと思うだけではする価値がない」と言いました．あなたは自分のことをあまり価値のない人間だと思っていますね．	
C	Yeah, a lot of times. I mean I know other people who blame everybody else for their problems. It's always somebody else did it to them. I don't feel that way. I feel it's... I did it to myself.	ええ，よくそう思います．自分に起こった問題を他人のせいにする人たちがいますよね．いつだって他人のせいでそうなった，と．私はそうは思いません．私は…自分でやったと思います．	
AB	So you blame yourself and you consider yourself not worthwhile?	つまりあなたは自分を責め，自分は価値がないと思うのですね．	
C	Sometimes.	時々ね．	
AB	How about right now?	今はどうですか？	⑦ホットな認知
C	Right now? Yeah, sometimes... half and half I guess.	今ですか？ ええ，時々…半々でしょうか．	
AB	Do you think that part of you at least feels worthwhile enough to go on and make a real life for yourself, a better life?	あなたの中には少なくとも続けていくだけの価値があり，自分の人生をより良くしていくだけの価値があると考える部分もありますか？	⑧-b 自動思考への反論
C	...I don't know. I don't know.	…さあ．わかりません．	
AB	The hopelessness, the thought that you have right now might suggest you might be able to make a better life yourself?	その絶望感，今のあなたの考えは，もっといい人生にすることができるという可能性を感じさせますか？	
C	That would be very hard. It would take a lot of strength.	難しいですね．強くないと．	
AB	Well, if you cut it up into little pieces, do you think maybe it would take as much strength?	問題を小さく砕いたら，それほど強くなくてもいいかもしれないと思いますか？	⑧-j 問題解決技法 ④ソクラテス的問答
C	I don't know. It sort of really single but how?	わかりません．1つのことを取り上げたら…．	
AB	Yeah, but as you say, your mind has a way of greatly magnifying things, just as when your husband lost his job.	ええ，しかしあなたもおっしゃったように，あなたは心の中でものごとを巨大化しています．ご主人が失業した時のように．	

Aaron T. Beck 1『絶望感―初回面接』

AB	You thought that you were destined and it turned out, what's turned out since then? Just standard of living going down?	その時あなたは，もう終わりだと思ったけれど，その後どうなりましたか？　生活水準が下がりましたか？	④質問による発見
C	Well, it's a little lower but...	ええ，ちょっとだけ…．	
AB	But things did work out.	でも何とかなった．	
	Yeah.	はい．	
AB	So, it sounds from what you say your mind has a way of making things very bad.	つまり，あなたの言葉からは，あなたは心の中でものごとを非常に悪くしてしまうことがわかります．	
C	Uh.	ええ．	
AB	And perhaps one of the approaches is to take things just one step at a time, like going to the bowling alley may seem silly to you in a way, but it's the first step.	アプローチ法の1つは，1度に1つだけ取り上げることです．ボーリング場に行くというのはばかげたことのようですが，第一歩であるということのように．	⑧ - k 段階的課題設定
C	Right. First steps are really hard for me.	そうですね．第一歩が私には本当に大変です．	
AB	But here first steps are hard for everybody, but that's why there's an old expression that you only have a thousand miles starts with a first step.	第一歩は誰にとっても大変ですよ．しかしだからこそ，千里の道も一歩から，という言い回しがあるのですよ．	
C	Very good.	上手ですね．	
AB	So that first step, it's very important to take the first step.	ですから，一歩目，第一歩がとても重要です．	
C	Uh.	ええ．	
AB	If you've taken the first step, and the second step, the third step and so on, all you have to do is take on steps. You don't have to take on giant steps.	第一歩を踏みだせば，二歩目，三歩目と続きます．歩き続けるだけです．大きな一歩ではなくて構わないのです．	⑧ - h 行動活性化
C	Yeah, I can see that now. I don't think I've seen it before. I think before, I was thinking every step would be just as hard as the first step.	はい，前はわからなかったけど，今はわかります．以前は，どの一歩も，一歩目と同じように大変だと思っていました．	
AB	Uh.	ええ．	
C	Maybe it's not that way.	そうじゃないのかもしれません．	
AB	That would be interesting to see, wouldn't it? I said that would be interesting to find out.	やってみるといいですね？本当はどうかを発見できるとよいですね．	

AB	So if you take the first step between now and Wednesday, then we can talk after that about the second step, then see if it does get easier.	今日から水曜までの間に第一歩を踏み出したら，二歩目について話し合いましょう．そして最初よりも簡単になるかどうかみてみましょう．	⑧-e 行動実験
C	Right. Well, the first step is probably the hardest, and then the second step will still probably be hard because that would probably involve meeting the people on the team.	そうですね．一歩目がたぶん一番難しいですが，二歩目も難しいでしょう．チームの人たちと知り合いになるということが必要ですから．	
AB	Uh.	ええ．	
C	You know, like...	それは…．	
AB	And then step number two would be meeting them.	二歩目は知り合いになること．	
C	Right.	はい．	
AB	And then step number three would be what?	では三歩目は何ですか？	④質問による発見 ⑧-k 段階的課題設定
C	How well could you bowl?	ボーリングがどのくらい上手か？	
AB	That's the pay off.	それは努力の成果ですね．	
	Well, what people think of you is sometimes we can talk more about but one thing you can say is that you're really very concerned about people think about you kind of prevents you from doing what you want to do and think about yourself. And that's really... the thing that is important, isn't it?	人々があなたのことをどう思うかについてはもっと話し合うことができます．まずここで言えることは，あなたは自分がどう思われるかを心配して，やりたいこと，考えたいことをできずにいるということです．それは重要なことだと思いませんか？	
C	What I think about myself?	私が自分のことをどう思うかですか？	
AB	Uh.	ええ．	
C	Yeah, I guess.	はい，そうですね．	
AB	And recently you've not been thinking too highly about yourself.	そして最近のあなたは，自分のことをあまり評価していない．	
C	No.		
AB	So maybe that's something you can do something about.	そのことを何とかできるかもしれませんね．	④ソクラテス的問答 ⑧-d 中核信念の修正
	Like, can you think of anything about the talk you had that's good about you?	自分について，いいことを考えられますか？	
C	Good about me?	私についてのいいことですか？	

Aaron T. Beck 1『絶望感―初回面接』

AB	Yeah.	はい．	
C	Er... what's good... I can think of nothing.	さあ…いいこと…何も考えつきません．	
AB	Can't you think of a single thing that's good about you?	自分についてのいいことを1つも考えつきませんか？	
C	My head feels clogged or something.	頭の中が詰まった感じです．	
AB	At the moment as soon as... Let's try the opposite. Can you think of anything bad about yourself? That shouldn't clog you.	今ここで…では，反対のことをしましょう．自分について悪いことを考えられますか？　それなら行き詰まらないでしょう．	④質問による発見
C	Oh, yeah.	もちろんです．	
AB	It's easy to think of bad?	悪いことを考えるのは簡単ですか？	
	Yeah.	はい．	
AB	OK. What's some of the bad things?	では，悪いことは何でしょう？	
	Some of the bad things? I waste too much time. I don't do any thing. I don't make first steps. I put myself down. I'm... I spend too much time doing nothing. I think that's the worst thing.	悪いことをいくつかね．私は時間を無駄にします．何もしません．第一歩を踏みだしません．自分を低く見ます．私は何もしない時間がとても長いです．それが一番悪いことだと思います．	
AB	Just gonna make some notes. You spend too much time doing nothing. Now, if you could spend less time doing nothing, do you think you'll feel better about yourself?	メモをとりましょう．あなたは何もしない時間が長い．では，何もしない時間が少なければ，自分のことをもっとよく感じると思いますか？	⑧-o 書き留める ④質問による発見
C	I guess so.	たぶん．	

33分

やはり認知の修正よりも，行動活性化を進めるほうにギアチェンジした．

AB	OK. Now, between now and Wednesday, what are some of the things you could do to fill in the time so that you would not be able to say you still spend much time doing nothing?	いいでしょう．では，何もしない時間が長いとは言えなくするために，今から水曜日までに，あなたにできることは何でしょう？	④質問による発見 ④協力的実証 主義 ⑧-h 行動活性化
C	What could I do... I could take my kids out.	私に何ができるか…．子どもたちを連れだしてやることです．	
AB	OK.	いいですね．	
C	I could... go visit somebody. I could go shopping.	私は…誰かのところに行くことができます．買い物に行けます．	
AB	OK.	はい．	

C	I don't know. I like to... I used to like to read a lot. I can't concentrate on reading any more.	以前は本を読むのが好きでした．でも今は本に集中できません．
AB	Between now and Wednesday, I was gonna say..	今から水曜日までに…．
C	Now and Wednesday. I don't have to take them out tomorrow afternoon.	今から水曜日までに．私は子どもたちを，今日の午後，どこかに連れていく必要はないですね．
AB	You can take them out tomorrow afternoon. Tuesday afternoon?	明日の午後か，火曜日の午後はどうですか？
C	Yeah.	はい．
AB	OK. Now, when could you go visit somebody?	では，いつ，誰かのところへ行くことができますか？
C	That's hard because when I go visit somebody, I have to take my kids usually. And then if I go with my mother, she already has two kids living with her, two of my sister's children. And like when they get together, it's like a lot of noise. I don't know. I don't know if I can do that.	難しいですね．誰かのところへ行く時は子どもたちをいっしょに連れて行かなくてはならないので．母には同居している子どもが2人いるし．姉の子どもたちです．子どもたちがいっしょになるととてもうるさくて．誰かのところへ行くことができるかどうか，わかりません．
AB	Uh. Why don't we just put a question mark and see how you're feeling. But you think you might possibly do it for five or ten minutes? Even with your kids?	"？"をつけておいて，あなたがどう感じるかをみてみましょう．5分か10分ならできると思いますか？ 子どもたちといっしょでも？ ⑧ - h 行動活性化 ⑧ - k 段階的課題設定
C	Yeah.	ええ．
AB	Twenty minutes? Then maybe your mother would feel good just to see them even if they stay for a short time.	20分では？ 短い時間でも顔を見ることができれば，お母さんもうれしいかもしれませんよ．
C	Right. Yeah.	そうですね．はい．
AB	So, I'll put a question mark. And if you do it, you could check it off. And you mentioned shopping.	"？"をつけておきます．もしできたら消してくださいね．それから，買い物ですね．
C	I've been thinking about buying myself some clothes. I haven't got around to doing it for a long time.	自分の洋服を買いたいと思っていました．もうずっと買いにいっていません．
AB	When do you think you can do that?	いつ，できると思いますか？ ⑧ - m 行動用語で記述
C	Well, I don't know. I don't know.	さあ，わかりません．
AB	Could you go shopping at night?	夜，買い物に行けますか？
C	If I had somebody watch my kids.	誰かに子どもたちを見ていてもらえれば．

Aaron T. Beck 1『絶望感—初回面接』

AB	Your husband?	ご主人は？
C	He doesn't.	だめです．
AB	You can't count on that.	ご主人は当てにならない？
C	No.	なりません．
AB	Can you leave your kids with your mother?	お母さんに預けることは？
C	No. Can't do that.	いいえ，それはできません．
AB	OK. So, we'll have to put it a big question mark about that right now, but we can talk about that in the future.	わかりました．では今のところは，大きな"？"をつけなくてはなりません．でも後日，これについては話をしましょう．
	What else do you think you could do between now and Wednesday? Is there anything else you might wanna read besides... you read the newspapers, right?	今から水曜日までの間に，ほかに何ができると思いますか？ 本以外に読みたいものはありますか？ 新聞はどうですか？
C	Uh.	ええ．
AB	That can help your concentration. You'd like to read something else?	集中力の助けになります．ほかに読みたいものはありますか？
C	Oh, I know what I wanted to read. I wanted to go buy myself a book on how to count cards to Black Jack it, you know, how they do it at a casino?	ええ，読みたいものがあります．ブラックジャックの時のカードの数え方について，カジノでどうやって数えるか，書いてある本を読みたいです．
AB	If you find out, let me know how they work it out. They have a whole book on that now.	わかったら私にも教えてください．それについて書かれた本もたくさんありますね． ⑧-e 行動実験
C	They have somebody wrote a book on it 'cause I've seen them on the same shelf.	ええ，書いた人がいます．棚に並んでいるのを見たことがあります．
AB	OK. So, you first have to buy the books. So go down buy the book, hook on Black Jack.	いいでしょう．まず本を買わなくてはなりませんね．本を買いに行って，ブラックジャックに夢中になる．
C	This is getting expensive.	お金がかかる話になっていますね．
AB	That's probably paperback, isn't it?	文庫本ですよね？
C	I don't know. Probably. No, I meant between the bowling, trying to go shopping, and then....	さあ，たぶん．そういう意味ではなくて，ボーリングに行って，買い物をして…．
AB	Well, all you have to do is find out about the bowling.	ボーリングについては，情報を得るだけでいいのですよ． ⑧-k 段階的課題設定
C	Right.	はい．

37分

ここまで37分．残り10分程度なので，セッションのまとめに入る．

AB	As far as the shopping is concerned, the main thing there would be to find out how you could get the kids taken care of. Remember the first step doesn't mean going out and doing it. The first step is the preparation. Like you prepare a garden before you plant the seed.	買い物については，重要なことは，子どもたちを見てくれる人を探すことです．第一歩は，出かけていって実行することではないのですよ．そのための準備が第一歩です．種を植える前に，まず土を整えるように．	
	Right. OK.	そうですね．はい．	
AB	You've got to prepare.	準備をしなくてはなりません．	
C	OK.	はい．	
AB	Coming here, you're preparing for your preparation. And then after next visit, we'll see about actually doing some of the things.	ここに来たことも，あなたの準備のためになります．次回は，その中のいくつかを実際にやってみることについて考えましょう．	⑧-e 行動実験 ⑧-h 行動活性化
C	OK.	はい．	
AB	Now, however, one of the things you can do right off is take your children out. So, I'm gonna give you this. You also have an activity schedule.	さて，あなたにすぐできることは，子どもたちを連れだすことです．これをあなたに差し上げます．活動スケジュールです．	⑧-g 活動モニタリング
C	Oh, yeah, there is.	はい，これですか．	
AB	Now what you could do is fill in how you actually spend your time to see we have you write down from 9:00 in the morning to 12:00 at night. You could fill in roughly for me how you spend your time starting, say, at 4 o'clock this afternoon. And bring that back in on Wednesday. And that would give me a better idea as to how you are spending your time and find little places to use your time in better ways. How does that feel to you?	午前9時から夜中の12時まで，あなたが実際にどのように時間をすごしたかを記入してください．あなたの時間のすごし方が私にわかるようなおおよその記入で構いません．今日の午後4時から始めましょう．それを水曜日に持ってきてください．それを見れば，あなたがどうすごしているのか，もう少し上手な時間のすごし方が私にわかります．どうですか？	
C	Well, I guess it's a start.	ええ，そこから始めるのですね．	
AB	Did you have a negative thought, then?	否定的な考えが浮かびましたか？	⑦セッションの中のホットな認知を見逃さないこと
C	Yeah. I thought that's not solving my big problems.	はい．そんなことで私の大きな問題が解決するとは思いませんでした．	

Aaron T. Beck 1『絶望感―初回面接』

AB	Right. And what's the answer to that?	そうですね．それに対する答えは？	④質問による発見：ホットな認知のあとなので、非常に効果的
C	Well, I've always felt like I've been impatient. That's my big problem. But I haven't really... 'cause they've been going on for a long time. But yet I've always wanted a solution with them all like, have it ten seconds.	私はいつも，自分は気が短いと感じていました．それが私の大きな問題です．それはずっと私の問題でした．私はいつも，どんなこともあっという間に解決したいと思います．	
AB	Well, you should know very well that they are real problems, not phony problems. So we can't really solve them but we can do is start getting ready to solve them.	あなたには，それは架空ではなく本物の問題だということがよくおわかりですよね．だから私たちにはそれを解決してしまうことはできませんが，解決するための準備はできます．	①問題解決モード
C	Right.	そうですね．	
AB	Before, you're feeling so hopeless that the problems had you completely overwhelmed.	これまでは，あなたはとても絶望的に感じていて問題に圧倒されていました．	
C	Uh.	ええ．	
AB	Now, do you still feel hopeless about your problems? Still feel hopeless about your future?	今もまだ，問題に対して絶望的だと感じていますか？自分の将来について絶望的だと感じますか？	⑦ホットな認知 ④質問による発見：セッションの始まりと終わりで感情の変化を自覚させる
C	Maybe not hopeless. Maybe just concerned.	絶望的ということではないです．心配しているだけです．	
AB	Uh. Well, that's an improvement. OK, now here's your... if you can read my writing. Those are the things to look at between now and Wednesday.	ええ，それはいい方向ですね． ではこれがあなたのリストです．私の手書きが読めますか．それらが，今日から水曜日までの間にチェックすべきことです．	②セッションの構造化：宿題設定
C	Uh.		
AB	And... do you have any questions about any of the things we went into today?	今日話し合ったことの中で，何か質問はありますか？	②セッションの構造化：まとめ

C	I don't think so.	ないと思います．	
AB	Do you have any reactions?	何かご意見は？	②セッションの構造化：まとめのフィードバック
C	I know I went through stages from happy to sad to happy to sad to happy to sad.	私は自分が，幸せから悲しみに変わり，それからまた幸せに，そして悲しみにと変わったことがわかりました．	
AB	Where are you at now?	今はどうですか？	⑦ホットな認知
C	Where am I at now? Well, half decent.	今どの状態にあるかですか？　半分まとも，ですね．	
AB	Half sad, half happy? Kind of...?	半分悲しくて，半分幸せということですか？	
C	A little more happier than I am sadder.	悲しいよりも幸せが少し多めです．	
AB	Maybe that when you leave, you'll be thinking well we haven't really worked on the big problems. And you have to have a way to answer that.	ここから帰る時には大きな問題について何もしなかったとあなたは考えるかもしれません．あなたにはそれに対する答えがわかりますね．	④質問による発見
C	Er... I guess I'll just say... it'll take a little more time.	えーと，つまり…もう少し時間が必要だということです．	
AB	Yeah. You have to.. it takes more time. So I don't wanna kid you and say they're small problems. They are big problems, but that doesn't mean they're not solvable.	はい．もっと時間がかかります．私はあなたに，それは小さな問題だと嘘をつくつもりはありません．大きな問題です．しかし，だからといって解決できないわけではありません．	
C	Uh.	ええ．	
AB	Just because it takes more time doesn't mean it's not solvable.	時間がかかるということは，解決不可能ということではありません．	⑧ - b 自動思考への反論
C	Uh. Right.	ええ，そうですね．	
AB	It's a bigger trip to go from here to New York than it does to go to North Philadelphia. But it doesn't mean you can't do it. Just takes longer.	ここフィラデルフィアから北フィラデルフィアに行くよりもニューヨークへ行くことのほうが大旅行です．でも行けないわけではありません．時間がかかるだけです．	
C	Right.	そうですね．	
AB	If it takes longer doesn't mean it can't be done.	時間がかかるということは，できないということではありません．	
C	Right.	はい．	
AB	Ah, it'd make you feel better if it could be done right away. I wish it could be done right away, then you'd feel better right away.	すぐにできてしまえば気分はいいでしょうが，すぐにできてしまえばいいのにと思いますよ．そうすればあなたもすぐに気持ちが楽になります．	

Aaron T. Beck 1『絶望感—初回面接』

AB	But just take the time and the big problems can be reduced to small problems and as you go along with the small problems you'll find that the big problems are already been taken care of.	しかし時間をかけてください。そうすれば大きな問題も小さくなり，小さくなった問題に取り組んでいるうちに，大きな問題もすでに解決しているということがわかるでしょう．	⑧-k 段階的課題設定
C	Uh. OK.	はい，わかりました．	
AB	Does that sound realistic to you?	現実的な話だと思いますか？	④ソクラテス的問答：患者の理解のフィードバックを求める
C	Yeah.	はい．	
AB	OK. So, I guess the thing to do now is to set our next appointment.	では，次回の予約をしましょう．	
C	Right.	はい．	
AB	How does 2 o'clock on Wednesday suit you?	水曜日の2時はどうですか？	
C	That's fine.	けっこうです．	
AB	OK.	はい．	
C	I'm very easy to get along all the time.	私はつきあいやすい人間ですよ．	
AB	Fine. That's wonderful. If you do, sometimes people have negative thoughts about the interview, a lot of things or negative thoughts about therapy. Now, if you do, that's really very important. So remember to write them down for me?	いいですね．すばらしい．面接について，さまざまなことについて，治療について，否定的な考えを持つ人もいます．もしあなたがそう感じたら，それはとても重要なことなので，書き留めておいてください．	⑧-o 書き留める
C	Write down any thoughts I have about the interview?	面接について思ったことを何でも書いておくのですか？	
AB	Yeah. And particularly the negative ones are the ones we really like.	はい．特に，否定的な考えです．	
C	Like the newspapers, right? OK. I'll probably have them, all of them.	新聞みたいに，ですね？ いっぱい書くと思いますよ．	
AB	Right, great. That'll get you a little confused. Point some out. OK. Well, I think we have to say good-by and get them to remove out mikes, or we won't be able to get out of here.	いいですが，いっぱい書くと混乱しますよ．いくつか選んでください．ではこれで終わりにしましょう．マイクを外してもらうことにしましょう．	

Aaron T. Beck 2『家族の問題—初回面接』(Disc 2)

登場人物　**Aaron T. Beck**(以下 **AB**)
　　　　　患者　　　(以下 **C**)

AB	Now, Marcia, I gather from my telephone conversation, the reason you're here is because you've been feeling low?	電話のお話では，あなたはこのところ落ちこんでいるのでここへいらっしゃったのですね．
C	Uh.	ええ．
AB	Can you tell me a little bit about it?	そのことについて少し話してもらえますか． ④ソクラテス的問答
C	…Yeah… it's hard to even talk. Um… I've been… I've been really depressed for… months.	…ええ，話をするのも大変で…．もうずっと…何か月もほんとに落ちこんでいます．
AB	Uh.	はい．
C	I think it must've been six months, or seven months, I don't know. Um… this is getting so bad that… I find it hard to get out of bed. All I wanna do is just sleep and sleep…. House is a mess. I don't have any energy to… do anything.	6か月か，もっとでしょうか．とても調子が悪くて…ベッドから出るのも大変だと感じます．ただもう寝ていたいだけです．家の中も散らかっています．何もしたくありません．
AB	What kind of feelings have you had, Marcia?	これまでどんな気持ちになりましたか．
C	I just… I feel like… like everything's closing in on me and… I just feel like life isn't worth living any more sometimes.	何もかもが私の周りに押し寄せてくるような感じで…．もう生きていく価値もないと感じる時もあります．
AB	Uh. You've been feeling pretty bad.	かなり調子が悪いのですね．
C	Yeah.	はい．
AB	Do you have any explanations to how this came about?	この状態がどうやって生じてきたか，何か説明のつくことがありますか． ④ソクラテス的問答
C	Yeah… well… my husband… let's see, we have two kids and we used to be a close family, you know. Anyway, my husband used to come home and fidget around, spend some time with the children, you know.	はい…えーと，夫が…あの，私たちには子どもが2人いて，仲のいい家族でした．以前は，夫は家に帰ってきていろいろなことをしていました．子どもたちともいっしょに過ごしていました．
AB	Uh.	

C	Anyway, he doesn't do that any more. He tells me that he has to work. He's a lawyer and er... he just doesn't come home any more.	でも彼はもう、そういうことをしません．仕事があると言います．夫は弁護士なんですが…とにかくもう家に帰ってこないのです．
AB	Uh. He doesn't come home for supper?	夕食にも家に帰ってきませんか．
C	Well, sometimes he doesn't come home till 11 o'clock at night.	11時まで帰ってこないこともあります．
AB	I see. Does he let you know when he's gonna be late?	なるほど．遅くなる時は連絡してくれますか．
C	Yeah, usually, but er... he... see... I don't know if I really believe him. That's... see, I think that he might be having an affair with somebody. And er... that's got me really worried.	はい，だいたいは．でも，あの…私は…夫の言うことを信じていいのかどうかわかりません．つまり…彼は誰かと浮気しているかもしれないと思うので．それで…とても心配です．
AB	Uh.	はい．
C	'Cause he just... he just doesn't come home, and he's not acting the same. We haven't had any sex for months and... just... it seems like there's no more communication between us and I'm so scared to ask him. I don't know. I'm just afraid to ask him.	だって彼は…とにかく家に帰ってこないから，これまでと様子が違うのです．私たち，何か月もセックスしていないし…コミュニケーションもうまくいっていない感じだし．でも尋ねるのがとても怖くて．よくわからないけど，とにかく尋ねるのが怖いのです．
AB	You're afraid to discuss the subject with him.	そのことをご主人と話し合うことが怖いのですね．
C	Uh.	ええ．
AB	So, one of your problems then is not knowing what's going on with your husband. Is that the main thing that's troubling you now?	つまり，問題の1つは，ご主人が何をしているのかわからない，ということですね．それはあなたが今一番困っていることですか． ④ソクラテス的問答
C	Well, it's that I gained weight, I don't know, I'm having problems with my son. Um... the teacher keeps calling and telling me that he's been stealing pencils at school.... It's just... everything is going wrong. I don't know. I can't handle that kid. He was so... I don't know, he's just... going bad. I don't know what to do. So, she keeps phoning, and my husband doesn't know about that. I tried to tell him once, and he told me it was my fault. I don't know. I just feel like I'm failing in every way as a wife and as a mother and as a human being. I just... I don't know. Sometimes it just doesn't seem like it's worth it to go on, you know.	ええ，そのことと，それから私は太ったし，息子の問題も．学校の先生が電話してきて，息子が学校で鉛筆を盗むと言うのです．私は…とにかく何もかもうまくいっていないのです．よくわからないけど．私は息子を扱いきれません．あの子は…よくわからないけど，あの子はとにかく悪いことをするようになっているのです．どうしたらいいのか私にはわかりません．先生は電話ばかりかけてくるし，夫はそのことを知らないし．一度話そうとしたのですが，夫は私のせいだと言いました．よくわかりません．私はとにかく…妻としても母親としても人間としてもダメなのです．なんとなくもうやっていく意味がないように思えて．

AB	Have you thought of killing yourself?	自殺しようと思ったことはありますか？
C	Well... yeah... I... I sometimes... yeah... I haven't told anybody about that but sometimes I... I think that when it gets so bad I just can't stand it any more and at least I can do that.	ええ…時々…．誰にも言ったことはありませんが，あまりにも悪くなると，もうこれ以上がまんできない，でも死ぬことならできると思います．
AB	Uh.	
C	I'll probably even mess that up.	私はきっと，自殺さえちゃんとできないでしょうね．
AB	You feel that bad.	それほどに調子が悪く感じるのですね．
	And do these problems seem to be just insolvable to you?	そういった問題は，解決できないと思いますか？
C	I don't know what to do.	どうしたらいいのかわかりません．
AB	Well, perhaps we can discuss some of these problems and sort them out. What would you like to talk about first? It seems that there's a problem with your husband, there's a problem with your child and there's a kind of general problem of managing at home. And there's also the weight problem.	たぶんいっしょにこれらの問題を話し合って整理することができると思いますよ．最初にどのことを話したいですか．ご主人との間の問題，子どものこと，家庭生活全般，それから体重の問題があるようですね． ②セッションの構造化:アジェンダの設定
C	I don't know... I don't know... Do you think it's gonna help to talk about it in any way?	よくわかりません…話したら何かの役に立つと思いますか？
AB	Well, what do you think?	あなたはどう思いますか．
C	I don't know.	わかりません．
AB	Do you think it's not gonna help?	役に立たないと思いますか？ ⑦ホットな認知
	Well, if I gather your mood correctly while you're sitting there is that you think it's probably hopeless and that talking won't do any good and you feel it might make it worse?	そこに座っているあなたの気分を私が正しく理解できているとしたら，あなたは問題は絶望的で，話をしても役に立たない，かえって悪化させるかもしれないと思っていますね．
C	Well, I'm feeling worse now.	今はもっとひどい気分です．
AB	You're feeling worse than when you came in?	ここに来た時よりもひどい気持ちですか？
C	Yeah.	
AB	And so you're concerned that maybe it'll feel even worse by the time you leave?	そして，帰る時までにもっとひどい気分になるのじゃないかと心配している？ ⑦ホットな認知

Aaron T. Beck 2 『家族の問題―初回面接』

C	I just wish that you could make everything better.	先生がすべてをよくしてくれればいいのに．	
AB	Uh.		
C	I just hope you can do that.	そうしてくれたらいいのに．	
AB	Well, let's see what we can do and perhaps you yourself can take the lead in solving some of these problems. Now, would you like to talk about your husband, or your son, or...	ではいっしょに，何ができるか考えてみましょう．あなた自身が問題解決に向かうことができるのではないでしょうか．では，ご主人の話をしますか．それとも息子さんの話がいいですか．	①破局化モードの患者を問題解決モードへ

6分

ここまで6分経過．これでアジェンダを設定し，導入部を終え，本題に入る．

C	Well... let's start with my son 'cause he's worried. I don't... I think he's gonna get kicked out of school. I guess we could start.... It doesn't matter.	じゃあ息子の話から…．心配だから，あの子は学校を辞めさせられるだろうと思います．その話か…別に何でもいいですけど．
AB	You think he's going to get kicked out of school and why is that?	あなたは，息子さんが学校を辞めさせられるだろうと思うのですね．それはなぜですか？
C	'Cause he's been stealing like... I don't know. I don't know a seven-year-old did stuff like that. Anyway, he's been stealing pencils and.... The teacher says that he's been cheating on tests.	盗みをしているから…よくわかりませんけど．7歳の子がそんなことをするとは知りませんでした．とにかく，あの子はずっと鉛筆を盗んでいるらしくて．先生はテストでカンニングもしていると言っています．
AB	Uh.	はい．
C	She keeps calling me, but what am I supposed to do? I don't know what to do.	先生は電話してきますけど，でも私にどうしろというの？ 私はどうしたらいいのかわからないのに．
AB	What does the teacher say to you when she calls you?	先生は電話で何と言うのですか．
C	She says.... "Mrs. B, I wanna tell you that your son stole again. We had to keep him from recess and things like that. And we expect you to do something about it." She even had me come in one time. That... I never got along so well with teachers myself so I couldn't... I don't know... I don't know what to do.	先生は，「お母さん，あなたの息子さんはまた盗みました，罰として休み時間を与えませんでした」と言います．「親として何とかしてください」と．学校に呼びだされたことも一度あります．私自身，学校の先生は苦手だから…．どうしたらいいのかわかりません．
AB	So you're having some problem actually handling the teacher.	つまりあなたには，先生をどう扱うかという問題もあるのですね．

C	Teacher and I can't seem, I mean I don't know what to do with my son	先生と，それから私は…つまり私は息子をどうしたらいいのかわからないのです．
AB	Uh, well, that...	
C	And that's...	それは…．
AB	Yes, well, that's a good question. When you know the teacher says all these things about your son, how does it make you feel?	ええ，それはいい疑問です ③認知行動モデル よ．先生があなたの息子さんについてそういったいろいろなことを言ってくる時，あなたはどんな気持ちになりますか．
C	It makes me feel like I'm a failure, like I'm a rotten mother, you know.	自分は落ちこぼれだと…ダメな母親だと感じさせられます．
AB	And you feel you're a rotten mother because?	なぜあなたはダメな母親なのですか？
C	'Cause my son is bad, and I don't know what to do to make him better.	息子が悪いし，私はそれをどうやってよくすればいいのかわからないからです．
AB	You're saying he's a bad kid?	あなたは彼が悪い子だというのですか．
C	Uh.	ええ．
AB	Bad through and through?	どんな時でも悪い？　⑧-b 自動思考への反論
C	Well, you put it that way... he's pretty bad these days, but I don't know if he's bad through and through. That's harsh.	そういうふうに言われると…．あの子は最近かなり悪いことをしますが，どんな時でも悪いかどうかは…．その言い方はきついです．
AB	So, he's pretty bad and because he's bad, you're a bad mother.	彼はかなり悪いことをする，そして彼が悪いことをするからあなたは悪い母親だ，と．
C	Yeah.	はい．
AB	So, you hold yourself responsible for his badness.	つまり，あなたは彼の悪さについて自分に責任があるというのですね．
C	Oh, yes.	はい，もちろん．
AB	Uh.	
C	So does my husband. So does the school.	夫もそう言います．学校も．
AB	Uh. So, because your husband and school imply that he's bad, and that means you are bad, too.	つまり，あなたのご主人も学校も，彼が悪いことをするのはあなたも悪いという意味だ，とほのめかすのですね．
C	Yeah. Sure, I'm the one who raised him.	はい，もちろん．彼を育てたのは私だから．
AB	Now, when you look at it, is the problem that the child is bad or is it because you have certain types of conducts at school that don't fit in with what's expected?	では，そのことを考える時，問題は，子どもが悪いことをするということなのですか？それともあなたの何らかの行為が，学校側の期待するものではないからということなのですか？

Aaron T. Beck 2 『家族の問題—初回面接』

C	Isn't that the same thing?	同じことじゃないのですか？	
AB	Well, the way you're talking about it is in a very global sense you're making an enormous value judgment, moralistic judgment that you're saying he's a bad kid. When you say he's a bad kid, that doesn't communicate anything to me. And what seems to come across to me is that this big bad problem, that's so overwhelming and so pervasive that there's nothing anybody can do about it. And I wonder if you've really tried to break the problem down into its little components and try to see exactly what the problem is.	あなたは子どもが悪い子だと話す時、広い意味でとても大きな価値判断、道徳的判断をしています。あなたが彼は悪い子だと言っても、私には何も伝わってきません。私に伝わってくるのは、これがとても悪い大問題で、あまりにも圧倒的で広範囲すぎて、誰にも何もできないということです。あなたは、この問題を細かい要素に砕いて、問題が何なのかを正確に見ようとしたことはあるのでしょうか。	⑧-j 問題解決技法
C	I see what you mean. Well, then I guess it's... I guess it's his behavior or his misconduct.	そういうことですか。ええ、それなら…彼の行動と非行だと思います。	
AB	It's behavior rather than there's just a big hunk of badness, floating around?	問題は、単なる大きな悪いことのかたまりなのではなく、行動なのですね？	
C	I guess so. But why is he doing all this bad stuff? I mean...	そうでしょうね。でもあの子はなぜこういう悪いことをしているのでしょう？　だって…。	
AB	You seem to think he's doing it because you're bad and we can come to that in a minute. But one of the things that I'd like to point out to you is that as soon as you put a label on him as bad, it kind of obscures the whole problem. Now there's no question that there's a problem there. The teachers are on him, he's probably feeling bad himself, and he's got you and your husband all upset. So the problem exists. What we wanna do first of all is to define specifically what the problem is.	あなたは、自分が悪いから彼がそういうことをしていると考えているようですね。後でその話をしましょう。でもその前にあなたに指摘しておきたいのは、子どもに悪いというレッテルを貼ったとたんに、問題全体が曖昧になるということです。問題があることは疑問の余地がありません。先生たちも彼に目をつけているし、彼自身もたぶん悪いと感じているだろうし、あなたもご主人も動揺しています。確かに問題は存在します。そこでまず最初に、何が問題なのかを具体的に見てみましょう。	①問題解決モード
C	OK.	はい。	

AB	So first, before we can even get to the problem, you'll have to suspend judgment as far as the morality of the child. Now, specifically, what does he do at school? When does he steal?	まず，問題の話をする前に，子どもの品行に関する限り，良し悪しの判断をしないようにしてください．では，具体的に彼は学校で何をするのですか？ いつ盗みをしますか？
C	Er... you mean what time, what day?	えーと…何曜日にとか，何時に，ということですか？
AB	What situations bring that about?	どのような状況でそうなるのでしょうか？
C	I don't know. I've never observed it, but... I think it's probably closer to the beginning of the week than the end of the week.	わかりません．私は見たことがないし．でも…たぶん週末というよりは週の初めでしょう．
AB	Is he upset just before he steals?	盗みをする前は，お子さんは動揺している様子ですか？
C	I don't know. The teacher didn't tell me.	わかりません．先生は何も言わなかったし．
AB	The teacher didn't tell you. Well, what did your son say?	先生はあなたに何も言わなかった．あなたのお子さんは何と言いましたか？
C	Well, see, I didn't talk to my son. I don't know what...	あの，私は息子と話していません．私にはわかりません．
AB	You mean he's so bad you won't even talk to him?	彼がとても悪いことをするので，あなたは彼に話もしないということですか？
C	I don't know. I just didn't know how to handle it... I was afraid of talking to him, too, I guess.	わかりません．とにかく，どう扱っていいのかわからなかったのです．たぶん私は，あの子に話をすることも怖かったのだと思います．
AB	Oh, I see. You're afraid to talk to him. So you really don't know yet what the problem is.	ああ，なるほど．あなたは ①問題解決モード 息子さんに話をすることが怖い．つまりあなたは，何が問題なのかを本当はよく知らないのですね．
C	I just know what the teacher's saying...	先生が言うことを知っているだけで…．
AB	Sure. I suppose the teacher is upset because she likes to have a well-disciplined household, well, classroom. From the standpoint of your son, what's going on?	そうですね．先生は自分の学級をきちんとしておきたいから，怒っているのでしょうね．あなたの息子さんの立場から見て，どうなっているのでしょうか？
C	I guess I don't know.	私にはわかりません．
AB	Right. Now, perhaps he has a problem. Did that ever occur to you? Rather just being a big, amorphous blob of badness, perhaps he's trouble himself.	そうです．たぶん彼は問題を抱えているのでしょう．そう考えたことはありますか？ 非常に大きな悪い問題というよりむしろ，彼自身，困っている，と？
C	I guess that's possible.	その可能性はあるでしょうね．

AB	And if... What do you think you could do to find out about this?	では，それについて知るためには，あなたに何ができると思いますか？ ④質問による発見
C	I guess I could start finding out some of the answers to the questions you just asked me, because I really don't know... I don't know when it is, or I don't really know how he's feeling. I don't even know, come to think of it, I don't even know if it's true. I guess I've just been believing what the teacher says.	今のお話に出た質問の答えを探すことから始められると思います．だって，私には本当にわからないから…問題が何なのかも，あの子がどう感じているかもわかりません．そういえば，本当のことなのかどうかも私にはわかりません．私はただ先生の言うことを信じていただけなのですね．
AB	That's right. Maybe it's some game that's going on for all you know.	そうです．もしかすると，何かの遊びなのかもしれません．
C	Yeah, I guess so.	はい，そうですね．
AB	So, you really could talk to him about it.	ですから，あなたは息子さんと話をするといいですね．
C	Yeah.	はい．
AB	And see just what it is.	そして何が問題なのかを知る．
C	Maybe I could go to the school.	学校にも話ができるかもしれません．
AB	Uh.	ええ．
C	Yeah. You're right.	はい，おっしゃるとおりですね．
AB	Now, what about the self-blame and the blaming him? Do you think you're going to be able to do your job, choosing problem-solving, if you go in with a critical attitude towards him?	では，自分を責めていることや，彼を非難していることはどうでしょうか？　あなたは彼に対して批判的な態度で向き合ったら，問題解決を選ぶことができると思いますか？ ①問題解決モード ④質問による発見
C	Mmm... that blaming...	えーと…非難していること…．
AB	Well, for instance, if you think that he's such a bad kid, you're likely to say "Why did you steal?" And I agree that he may take the defensive because I don't know him, but I know a lot of kids are. He may feel so guilty, or so afraid of punishment from you that he may cover up. So, if you go in with the attitude that he's a bad kid, it's bound to transmit itself to him, isn't it?	たとえば，あなたが彼のことをそんなにも悪い子だと思っているとしたら，「なぜ盗んだのか」と言いたくなるかもしれません．すると彼は自分を防御しようとするかもしれません．もちろん言い切れませんが，多くの子どもたちがそうであることを私は知っています．彼は罪悪感から，あるいはあなたからの罰を恐れるあまり，ごまかそうとするかもしれません．つまり，彼は悪い子だという態度で向き合えば，それは彼にも伝わりますね？
C	Uh.	ええ．
AB	How are you gonna get rid of that attitude that he's a bad kid?	彼は悪い子だという態度で向き合うことをどうやって避けますか？ ④質問による発見

C	I guess I could... well, love him.	彼のことを愛していれば何とか….
AB	How are you going to love him if you consider him a bad kid?	悪い子だと思っていたら，どうやって彼を愛していけますか？
C	...I don't know.	…わかりません.
AB	OK. Now, let's see. If he's just bad all the way through or whether he has any redeeming qualities, perhaps the label bad doesn't even apply in the usual sense. Does he have any redeeming qualities at all?	いいでしょう．では，もし ④質問による発見 彼がずっと悪いことをし続けたら？ あるいは彼には何か取り柄がありますか？ 悪いというレッテルも，通常の意味で当てはまらないのかもしれませんよ．彼には何かいいところがありますか？
	Or, does he brush his teeth in the morning?	朝は歯を磨きますか？
C	Well.... If I tell him to, he does.	ええ…磨きなさいと言えばしますけど.
AB	Uh. Is there anything else that he does that's positive?	ほかに何か，彼はいいことをしますか？
C	Yes, well, he gets on pretty well with his sister. And he's affectionate.	はい，あの子は妹と仲良しです．それに優しいです.
AB	He's affectionate? To whom?	優しい．誰に対して？
C	To his sister, to his father when his father's there... I don't know. His friends. He helps around the house 'cause our house is such a mess... I don't know, he's good to have, but not any more. I remember back before this started he used to be pretty helpful, kept his room clean. Our rooms are a mess, too. I can't really expect the kids to tidy up if their mother doesn't...	妹や，家にいる時の父親に．たぶん友達に対しても．あの子は家のことを手伝ってくれます．家は片付いていないので，昔はあの子がいてくれると助かりました．今は違うけど．こうなる前は，よく手伝ってくれたし，自分の部屋もきれいにしていました．うちはどの部屋も片付いていないから，母親がそうなのに，あの子に整理整頓することは期待できません.
AB	So you seem to be telling me so far is that at home he gets along well with his sister, he's affectionate towards you, when he's given some directions he tidies up at home, and in general seems to fit in the whole family constellation.	つまり，家では息子さんは妹と仲がよく，あなたに対しても優しくて，言われれば片付けるし，全体としては家族の中に居場所がある，とおっしゃるのですね.
C	Uh.	ええ.
AB	How do you reconcile that with the idea that he's a bad kid?	そのことと，彼が悪い子だ ④質問による発見 という考えとを，どう折り合いをつけますか.
C	Doesn't fit, does it?	合わないですね.

AB	No. Now maybe you could be a little more specific then instead of describing him in terms of some moral code, if you could just describe him in terms of what the specific problem that needs solving is.	ええ．では，不道徳な子という言い方をする代わりに，もう少し具体的に表現できるかもしれませんね．解決が必要な具体的な問題という観点から息子さんのことを整理できますか？
C	Well, right now, the one I know about is... the stealing and cheating in school.	えーと，今，私にわかっているのは…あの子は学校でものを盗み，カンニングをするということです．
AB	OK. Can you be problem-oriented then, and see that it isn't a question of a good kid or a bad kid. But the real problem is that the school has certain standards and expectations. And that when a child does not live up to those specific expectations, then they apply sanctions and one of the sanctions that's applied is to imply to the parents or to the kid himself that there is badness there rather than there is a specific behavior that could be modified.	いいでしょう．良い子か悪い子かということではなく，問題に向き合っていますね．しかし本当の問題は，学校にはそれなりの基準や期待があり，子どもがそれらの具体的な期待にそわない場合，学校は制裁を加えるということです．制裁の1つは，保護者や子ども本人に対して，直すべき具体的な行動があるということよりも，子どもに悪いところがあると示唆することです．	①問題解決モード ⑧-m 行動用語で記述
C	Uh.	ええ．
AB	Now if you go in with that attitude that there is a behavior which is not adaptive for him at the present time, you are less likely to feel angry at him or guilt-ridden of, and you're more likely to be helpful.	現在の息子さんには不適応行動があるという態度で臨めば，彼に対してそれほど怒りを覚えず，罪悪感も少なく，あなたはもっと助けになるでしょう．
C	How can I help him?	どうすれば私があの子の役に立てますか？
AB	First you have to see what the problem is.	まず，何が問題なのかを知る必要があります．
C	Yeah.	
AB	It may very well be that he feels that he's not getting enough attention at home, just use a very simple type of thing he may feel that...	息子さんは，家で十分手をかけてもらっていないと感じているのかもしれません．そういう非常に単純なことかもしれないのです．
C	Well, that's not...	
AB	...You're not loving him. All right, if that's what he feels as it's important for him to say, it isn't. Don't you sometimes feel better after you've said something like that?	あなたに愛されていないと感じているのかもしれません．もし息子さんがそういうふうに感じているとしたら，それを伝えてもらうことは大切ですね．あなたは，思っていることを伝えてよかった，と感じることはありませんか？	⑧-i アサーション訓練

C	Yeah.	あります.	
AB	And then you could be honest with him. If he says, "I just feel as though you don't love me, there's no love at home," you could say, Tony, or whatever his name is, "I've been depressed lately and one of the things about depression is that people cannot express their inner feelings very well." Can you see that he might feel better if he knew that?	それならば，息子さんに対して正直になることです．もし彼が，「お母さんはぼくを愛してくれていない，家では愛されていない」と言うなら，あなたは，「お母さんはこのところずっと落ちこんでいて，うつ病の人は気持ちをうまく表現できないの」と言えばいいのです．それがわかれば，彼は気持ちが楽になると思いませんか？	⑧-i アサーション訓練
C	Yeah.	そうですね．	
AB	All right. Now, I can't tell you where to carry it from there because first we have to define the problem, but I'm just saying that whatever the problem is, that will then lead to a solution.	問題が明確ではないので，私にはそれ以上のことは言えません．しかし問題が何であれ，そのようにすれば解決に向かいます．	
C	OK. Well, maybe I can let you know.	はい．どうなったか，今度お話しできるかもしれません．	⑧-e 行動実験
AB	Yes, next visit I'd like you to do is to come in and give me as detailed description of what's going on inside of him as you can.	そうです．次回は，息子さんの気持ちをできるだけ詳しく私に説明してください．	
C	OK.	わかりました．	
AB	And take the role of an investigator or an explorer who's trying to find out something rather than a policeman.	警察官ではなく，どうなっているのかを知りたいという調査官，探検家の役割でいることです．	

17分

時間があるので，2つめのアジェンダにも取り組む．

AB	Now you also mentioned that what's got you down is the problem about your husband that he comes home late and then you say you feel rotten. What feeling do you get?	さて，あなたが落ちこむのには，ご主人の帰宅が遅くみじめな気持ちになるという問題があるということもおっしゃいました．どんな気持ちがするのですか？	⑦ホットな認知：感情の重視
C	I get really scared.	怖くなります．	
AB	You get scared. And anything else?	怖くなる．ほかには？	

Aaron T. Beck 2 『家族の問題—初回面接』

C	Jealous 'cause I feel he's having an affair. I feel like he doesn't... he doesn't love me any more. I don't know...	嫉妬です．夫は浮気していると思うから．彼は…もう私のことを愛していないのでしょう．
AB	Now, this feeling that he doesn't love you any more, what's bringing that about?	彼があなたのことをもう愛していないという気持ちはなぜ生じるのですか？
C	He doesn't come home.	彼は家に帰ってきません．
AB	Uh. So we have a fact that he doesn't come home. And then when he doesn't come home, what do you feel?	つまり，彼が家に帰ってこないという事実があるわけですね．ご主人が家に帰ってこないと，あなたはどんな気持ちになりますか？
C	I feel so... I feel scared and I feel sad.	私は…怖くなって悲しくなります．
AB	Uh. Now, what's making you feel sad and scared?	では，なぜ悲しく，怖くなるのですか？
C	That he isn't coming home, he doesn't love me.	彼が家に帰ってこなくて，私を愛していないから．
AB	So the fact is he's not coming home and he doesn't love you is what's making you feel scared and bad.	つまり事実はご主人が家に帰らないことで，あなたを愛していないからあなたは怖くて悲しくなるのですね．
AB	Now, I suspect that there's something missing from that, which you are not aware of.	しかし私は，あなたが気づいていない何かがそこには欠けていると思いますよ． ③認知行動モデル ⑤心理教育
C	Yeah, him.	彼のことでしょ．
AB	He's the one who's missing.	彼がいない．
C	Yeah, he...	彼は…．
AB	Well, let's go over a typical situation and see what it is. In a typical situation, I gather that's dinner time comes, he doesn't show up. Then he calls, doesn't he, and says I'm gonna be, late, don't wait for dinner or something like that? And then you feel sad, or bad, or scared.	では，よくある状況で何が起こっているのか見てみましょう．典型的な状況というのは，夕食の時間になってもご主人が現れないことですね．すると彼は電話をかけてきて，遅くなる，夕食は先にすませてくれと言う．そうですね？ そしてあなたは悲しくなる，嫌な気持ちになる，怖くなる．
C	Yeah.	はい．
AB	Now, what is it that made you sad, scared, bad then?	あなたを悲しませたり，嫌な気持ちにさせたり，悲しくさせたものは何ですか？
C	Well, he called up and say he's not...	彼が電話してきて遅くなる，と…．
AB	Was it the phone call that made you feel bad?	その電話で嫌な気持ちになったのですか？
C	Well...	えーと…．

AB	I think the missing link is something like this. It's something that you think that you might say to yourself when the telephone rings. And it's THAT that makes you feel bad.	欠けているのは，電話が鳴った時にあなたが自分で自分に言っていることではないかと思いますよ．そしてそのことがあなたを嫌な気持ちにさせているのです．
C	Yeah. He's making me feel bad.	そう，彼が私を嫌な気持ちにさせます．
AB	I know. This sounds you're confused. I'm sure that it's confusing to yourself. Let me explain what I mean. I say the telephone rings and you answer it. You see that it's he. And then you get some kind of a thought. And it's not the phone itself that makes you feel bad, or his voice, but it's the thought that you get that makes you feel bad.	混乱するのももっともです．わかりにくいことですからね．どういうことか説明させてください．電話が鳴り，あなたは電話に出ます．かけてきたのはご主人です．するとあなたにはある考えが浮かびます．あなたを嫌な気持ちにさせたのは，電話そのものではなく，ご主人の声でもありません．あなたは自分の考えたことで嫌な気持ちになったのです．
C	I don't know. It's the thought I get…? You mean like he doesn't love me?	わかりません．私の考えたこと…？ 彼は私を愛していないということですか？
AB	Well, I don't know. It might be a thought like that. I don't know that it would follow.	さあ，それはわかりません．そういう考えかもしれません．私にはわかりません．
C	That's what I think.	それが私の考えたことです．
AB	That's the thought that comes to your mind?	それが頭に浮かぶ考えですか？
C	Well, that comes to my mind right now.	今も頭に浮かびますよ．
AB	Let's try to put ourselves in the situation and see if we can capture the thought and see if there is a negative thought that goes through your head. So, let's just imagine. I'd like you to try to picture yourself at home. Can you do that?	その状況にいっしょに身をおいて，あなたの考えを捕まえることができるかどうか，あなたの頭の中に否定的な考えが浮かぶかどうか見てみましょう．では想像してみましょう．自分が家にいる様子を思い浮かべてください．できますか？ ⑧-a 自動思考の同定
C	Yeah.	はい．
AB	You're sitting at the dinner table. What I want you to do is, go through in your own mind, kind of rehearse your own fantasy or imagery the scene of the phone ringing, you're answering it and the husband, your husband saying, "I can't come home for dinner tonight, I won't be home till 11 o'clock." And after you've gone through this image, you tell me what went through your mind, while you were having the image. Is it clear to you what I'd like you to do?	あなたは食卓に座っています．自分の心の中で想像してください．電話が鳴り，あなたは受話器を取り上げ，ご主人が，「今夜は夕食には帰れない，11時まで帰れない」と言います．ここまで想像したら，どんな考えが浮かんだか，どんなことを想像しているか，私に話してください．何をすればいいのかわかりますか？

Aaron T. Beck 2 『家族の問題―初回面接』

C	Uh. ...Oh... I guess a lot of things go through my mind.	ええ．あの…いろいろなことが頭に浮かびます．
AB	Tell me what image went through your head.	どんな想像が浮かんだか話してください．
C	Well, see, he calls up and he's really abrupt, like he doesn't have any time.... He's gonna tell me I'm not coming home and (click). And I sometimes say, but then, can we... and he would just hung up.	電話があって，彼は時間がないみたいに無愛想です．帰らないと言ってガチャンと切ります．私が何か言いかけることがあっても，彼はただ電話を切ります．
AB	Is that what he did in this image?	今の想像の中で，彼はそうしましたか？
C	Yeah.	はい．
AB	So, what feeling did you have after he hung up?	彼が電話を切った後，あなたはどんな気持ちになりましたか？
C	Here we go again, here comes again, he's not coming home.	またдわ，また帰ってこないんだわ．
AB	That's the feeling you had?	そういう気持ちがしたのですね？
C	Er...	
AB	What I meant by feeling, did you feel sad or happy?	悲しい気持ちですか，嬉しい気持ちですか？
C	Oh, very sad, I mean... sad and hopeless.	とても悲しかったです．悲しくて，絶望的…．
AB	Uh. And then you indicated that there's some thought that went through your head.	そしてその後も，何らかの考えが頭に浮かんだとおっしゃいましたね？
C	Uh.	
AB	What thoughts did you have?	どんな考えでしたか？ ⑧-a 自動思考の同定
C	I thought... he doesn't love me. I guess I'm not a very good wife. Who would wanna come home to somebody who's this fat? That's probably why he's with somebody else. I bet she's... size 10 or something. Then I think he loves someone, he loves me, and one of these days he's just gonna come home and say, "Marcia, I'm leaving you, I've met somebody else. I don't know I wanna be with you or the children any more" then it's...	私は…彼が私を愛していないと思いました．私はあまりいい奥さんではないと思うから．こんなに太った奥さんのところへ帰ってきたい人なんていないでしょ．だから彼は誰かほかの女性といるのよ．その人はきっと10号サイズを着る．彼はほかの女性を愛している．近いうちに彼は，「ほかに好きな女性ができた．家を出ていく」と言うでしょう．もう私や子どもたちといっしょにいたくない，と．

AB	So, what you do is you're getting up a whole scenario, aren't you? When the phone rings and your husband doesn't come home, you have a whole story cooked up in your head, which is that he has another woman and so on, that he doesn't care for you. Then you carry that on to a self-caricature, say, well, I'm big and fat and sloppy, why should he wanna come home to me, and a bad mother and a bad housewife and so on. Now the question is what is it that made you feel bad. Was it the ringing of the telephone and the vibrations from his voice? Or was it your own thoughts?	あなたは筋書きを全部作っていますね。電話が鳴ってご主人が帰ってこないとなった時、あなたは頭の中でストーリーを全部作り上げています。彼には別の女性がいて，もうあなたのことを想っていない。それからあなたはその話をどんどん進めています。自分は太くてだらしがない，そんな自分のところに帰ってきたいはずがない，悪い母親で悪い妻だ。さて、問題は，あなたを嫌な気持ちにさせたのは何ですか？ 電話の鳴る音でしたか？ 電話から伝わるご主人の声でしたか？ それとも，あなた自身の考えでしたか？	③認知行動モデル
C	Well, I guess... some of it... really true? I never thought of things that way. So, even I thought I'm no good?	えーと…いくぶんかは…本当にそうですか？ そういうふうに考えたことはありませんでした。だから私は自分がダメだとまで思ったのですが。	
AB	You could say you're no good because your thoughts are no good. Or, it could be that you perceive only the most negative aspects in any particular situation. Maybe they just put the most extreme, negative construction on it. And why do you suppose you do that?	自分の考えがダメだから自分はダメだ，と言うことはできるでしょう。あるいは，あなたはどんな状況でも，もっとも否定的な側面だけを見るからかもしれません。きわめて極端な，否定的な解釈を積み上げているのかもしれません。あなたはなぜそういうことをするのだと思いますか？	③認知行動モデル ④質問による発見
C	I don't know.	わかりません。	

AB You could say because you're a rotten person and you don't think straight, or you could say 'cause you're depressed. And one of the common features of depression is that the person tends to see things in the most negative light possible. Now this is indeed possible, I don't have all the information that your husband might have another woman, but that in itself does not need to make you feel bad. What's making you feel bad is the construction you're putting on that.

To start with, first of all, all that we know for a fact is that he doesn't come home. You then put a very bad construction on that, namely, he has another woman. You then put a very bad construction on that, which is that he doesn't love you. You then put a very bad construction on that. And that is the reason he doesn't love you is because you're not good and sloppy, fat and ugly and so on. You see the way your mind goes?

自分はダメな人間だからだ，ちゃんと考えられないからだ，と言うこともできます．あるいは，あなたは落ちこんでいるから，なのかもしれません．うつ病によくある特徴の1つは，ものごとを可能な限りもっとも否定的な観点から見ようとすることです．それは実際に可能なのですよ．
あなたのご主人には他に好きな女性がいるかもしれないということについて，私には情報が不十分でわかりませんが，そのこと自体があなたを嫌な気持ちにさせているのではありません．あなたを嫌な気持ちにさせているのは，あなたがそこに積み上げている解釈です．
そもそも私たちにわかっているのは，ご主人が帰宅しないという事実です．あなたはそこへ非常に悪い解釈を加えています．彼にはほかに好きな女性がいる，ということです．そしてさらに，彼はあなたを愛していないという解釈を加えます．さらには，彼があなたを愛していないのは，あなたがだめでだらしがなく，太くて醜くて，などという悪い解釈を積み上げます．自分の心がやっていることがわかりますか？

⑤心理教育：疾患と認知行動モデル

AB	I'm willing to grab the worst possible construction which is that he has another woman and he doesn't love you any more. All right? Just for the sake of argument, why don't we go along with that?	あなたは可能な限り最悪な解釈に飛びついてしまう．彼にはほかに好きな女性がいて，私のことをもう愛していない．わかりますか？議論のために，その考えで進んでみましょうか？	
	You seem to think that's a very terrible thing. I can tell by the expression on your face. That's pretty bad. Now, why is it bad that he doesn't love you any more?	あなたは，それはとてもひどいことだと思っているようですね．あなたの表情からわかります．表情がよくないですから．では，彼があなたをもう愛していないということは，なぜ悪いことなのですか？	⑧-b 自動思考への反論
C	Because I need him. I need him.	私には彼が必要だから．彼が必要です．	
AB	You need him? What do you mean you need him?	あなたには彼が必要？　彼が必要というのは，どういう意味ですか？	④質問による発見：患者の独特の言い回しを早わかりしない
C	I can't imagine being without him.	彼なしでいることは想像できません．	
AB	You say you can't imagine being without him.	彼なしでいることは想像できない．	
	Well, why don't we try, for the sake of the therapy, why don't you imagine what the situation would be like if he wasn't there? You say you can't imagine you being without him.	では，治療のために，もし彼がいなかったらどんな状況になるか，想像してみてください．あなたは彼なしでいることは想像できないとおっしゃいますが．	
C	That's when I started feeling like life isn't worth living.	そう考えた時，生きている価値がないと思い始めたのですから．	
AB	Because?	なぜ？	
C	Because I wouldn't have David.	デビッドを失うと思ったから．	
AB	You wouldn't have David. Now you make it sound as though David is essential for life itself.	デビッドを失う．まるでデビッドがあなたの人生そのものに不可欠であるかのように聞こえますが．	
C	I don't know.	わかりません．	
AB	How long have you known David?	デビッドと知り合ってどのくらいになりますか？	
C	Well, been married for 8 years. I guess 10 years.	結婚して8年ですから，10年です．	
AB	So you've known him for 10 years all told. How old are you now?	10年間，彼を知っている．あなたは今おいくつですか？	
C	Thirty-two.	32歳です．	

Aaron T. Beck 2　『家族の問題―初回面接』

AB	Thirty-two. So, you first met David when you were 22. Now, since the age of 22, then, your life has revolved around David, is that right?	32歳．あなたは22歳の時にデビッドに出会ったのですね．22歳の時から，あなたの人生はデビッドを中心に回ってきたのですね？
	I understand you correctly in saying that you simply cannot exist without David. Is that right that you'd sooner die if you face life without David?	あなたはデビッドなしでは存在すらできない，と言っていいのでしょうか？ デビッドなしの人生に直面することになったらあなたは死んでしまう，ということは正しいですか？
C	Oh, he's so...	だって，彼は…．
AB	Well, I don't mean to ridicule that, I'm just trying to see if there's some error in your thinking here, if you're not creating a problem that's worse than the problem that exists. There is no question there is some problem. He doesn't come home in time. But it seems to me that that problem carried to its ultimate conclusion, leads you to believe that you can't exist without him and that you'd be better off dead.	からかっているのではありませんよ．あなたの考えの中に間違いはないのか，実際の問題以上に悪い問題をあなたが創ってしまっているのではないか，見ようとしているだけです．何らかの問題があることは確かです．彼は夕食の時間に帰ってこない．しかし私には，その問題は究極の結論にまで至り，あなたは彼なしでは存在できない，死んだほうがまし，と信じてしまっているように思えます．	③認知行動モデル ⑧-b 自動思考への反論
AB	Now, at the age of 21, did you know David?	21歳の時，あなたはデビッドを知っていましたか？	④質問による発見
C	No.	いいえ．	

AB	Did you feel then that life was not worth living?	ではその時，あなたは人生は生きている価値がないと感じていましたか？
C	Oh, no. Then I felt that life was ... just more open.	いいえ，違います．その頃私は，人生はもっとオープンだと感じていました．
AB	Well, it's kind of a contradiction there, isn't it? Because at the point when you were without David, you found life was indeed worth living. Now that you're with David, even though in a partial way, you find that life isn't worth living. How can you explain that contradiction?	そうすると矛盾しますね？ ④**ソクラテス的問答** デビッドがいなかったその時点で，あなたは人生には生きる価値があると思っていた．今のあなたは完璧ではなくてもデビッドといっしょにいるのに，生きる価値がないと思っている．この矛盾をどうやって説明しますか？
C	I can't explain.	説明できません．
AB	See, it seems to me you have this very strong belief. I cannot be happy unless I have David. I cannot function unless I have David. Indeed, I cannot even exist unless I have David. And yet when we go back to the period of time before you knew David, you existed, you functioned, and you were happy. So perhaps you're operating off of a false premise.	あなたは非常に強く信じているように思えます．デビッドなしでは幸せになれない．デビッドなしでは何もできない．デビッドなしでは生きてさえいけない．しかし，デビッドと知り合う前までさかのぼって考えると，あなたは生きていたし，うまくやっていたし，幸せだった．すなわち，あなたは間違った前提から出発しているのかもしれません．
C	I haven't really thought of the time before I was married for a long time.	もう長い間，結婚する前のことを考えたことはありませんでした．

Aaron T. Beck 2　『家族の問題―初回面接』

AB	Uh. Well, that's a good way to test out some of these beliefs.	それはあなたが信じていることを試してみるいい方法ですね. ⑧-e 行動実験
AB	Now, this is an example of where an erroneous belief can really get you into trouble and can make you feel so terrible that the only solution seems to be to end life itself. And yet when you really start to examine your underlying premise, your basic belief, you find that it is not true. Now, how you got that belief is highly speculative but a lot of women in our culture have it, even with the feminist movement, we've had one woman after another come in to our clinic and say I cannot live without a man. And yet they all have functioned at some period within their life very well without a man. In fact, in almost all these cases they functioned better when they weren't married than when they were married.	これは,間違って信じていることが,どのようにあなたを困らせ,人生を終わりにすることでしか解決できないほどひどい気持ちにさせるかという例です. 心の底にある前提,自分の信念を確かめてみると,本当のことではないとわかります. あなたがどのようにしてその信念を得たかは推測しかできませんが,私たちの文化では,フェミニスト運動が起こっても,多くの女性たちがそのように信じています. このクリニックにもそういう女性たちがやってきて,男性なしでは生きていけないと言います. しかし彼女たちはみんな,過去の人生では男性がいなくてもきちんと生きていました. 実際,結婚してからよりも,結婚する前のほうがうまくできていた女性がほとんどです. ③認知行動モデル
AB	Now, the solution to the problem about David is exactly the same thing as the solution about your son. As you have to follow the same pattern in solving the problem. Now, what is the pattern that you have to follow in order to solve the problem about David?	デビッドについての問題を解決するのも,息子さんの問題とまったく同じことです. 問題解決のためには同じやり方が必要です. では,デビッドの問題を解決するためには,あなたはどんなやり方をしなくてはならないでしょうか? ④質問による発見

C	Well, with my son, you said I had to... not blame him and to be an investigator and get all the facts, right?	息子のことでは，あなたに言われたのは…あの子を責めないこと，調査官でいること，事実を全部知ること，ですね？	
AB	Uh.	ええ．	
C	But... see, what I'm afraid is David.	でも…私が怖いのはデビッドです．	
AB	All right. So, let's imagine that you do ask David. What are you afraid happens then? Let's just say that you ask David. What happens then? Let's start your mind going as you tend to put the worst construction anyhow. What's the worst thing that might be?	わかりました．では，あなたがデビッドに質問するところを想像してみましょう．どうなることを怖れているのですか？　あなたはデビッドに尋ねたとしましょう．するとどうなりますか？　あなたは心の中で最悪の解釈をする傾向がありますよね．起こりうる最悪のことは何ですか？	⑧-b 認知再構成
C	Well, see, I did try to ask him a couple of times and he got really angry and he told me I, real soon... nagging at him. So then I never asked him any more because if I nag at him, then I'll give more reason to leave me. So, it's better not to say.	私は何度か，夫に尋ねようとしたことがあります．彼はすごく怒って…うるさいと言いました．だから私はもう聞かないのです．うるさいと思われたら，それもまた出ていく理由になるから．だから何も言わないほうがいいのです．	
AB	Perhaps later on, we could role-play how you could ask him without nagging him. Just in a straight forward way such as.... What would be a straight forward, non-nagging way to bring up the subject	うるさいと思われずに質問する方法を，後日，ロールプレイしましょう．率直に，です．率直に，しつこくしないで，話題を持ちだすにはどうしたらよいですかね	⑧-i アサーション訓練 ⑧-l ロールプレイ
C	Tell me why don't you come home?	どうして家に帰ってこないの？	

Aaron T. Beck 2 『家族の問題―初回面接』

AB	Well, the why-don't-you is always has accusatory tone to it and most people in our culture use that instead of saying, I noticed that you come home late and I was wondering what the reason for that is. The why-don't you always has accusatory like parents say to their children, why don't you come in out of doors, instead of I'd like you to come in out of doors. But for some reason you don't do it. I'd like to know what's behind it. So, the thing to do is just state a fact, David, you've been coming home late for a long time, and I really would like to know what it's all about. I think it would help to clear the air if we just could have a talk. Do you think then he would think you're nagging him?	「どうして何々しないのか」という言い方には，相手を非難する雰囲気があります．私たちの文化では多くの人が，「あなたの帰りが遅いようだが，なぜなのかなと思っている」の代わりにそう言います．「どうして何々しないのか」は親が子どもに対して，「家の中に帰ってきなさい」と言う代わりに，「どうして家の中に帰ってこないのか」と言うような批判的な表現です．でも人々はその表現を使います．私はその表現の背景を知りたいと思います．言うべきは，事実だけを述べることです．「デビッド，このところずっと帰宅が遅いけど，何があるのか私は知りたいの．話し合うことができればすっきりすると思うわ」そういうふうに言った場合，彼はあなたがうるさくしていると思うでしょうか？	⑧-ⅰ アサーション訓練
	Right. Now, that doesn't solve the problem, does it? 'Cause you don't know what he's gonna say. He might say something real bad. Now, what's the worst thing that you imagine he'd say?	そうですね．でもそれでは問題は解決しませんね？あなたには彼が何と言うかわからないからです．彼は本当に悪いことを言うかもしれません．あなたに想像できる，最悪のことは何ですか？	
C	What I was telling you.	さっきも話したことです．	
AB	Namely what?	つまり？	
C	Tell me that he might be having an affair. That's... I'm not sure he's telling me... believe what he tells me.	浮気をしているということ．私は彼が本当のことを言っているのかどうか…彼の言うことを信じていいのかどうかわかりません．	
AB	Well, let's just say, since it's the worst thing that could happen, he says, yes, I am having an affair.	それが最悪のことならば，彼がそう言ったとしましょう．自分は浮気をしている，と．	

C	OK.	ええ.
AB	Then what?	するとどうなりますか？
C	Then I'll probably start to cry.	私はきっと泣きだします.
AB	OK. Then after you finish crying, what happens after that?	いいでしょう．では泣いた後は，どうなりますか？
C	Then he says, well, ...so I'll leave you.	彼は…家を出ていくと言います.
AB	So, then, it ends up that once he's told you and it's all out in the open there's no reason for him to stay, out of guilt, or trying to conceal, so he leaves you. All right, now he's left you. Now, is that pretty bad? Then what happens after he leaves you?	つまり，彼はいったんあなたに話せば明らかになるので，あなたといっしょにいる理由もなくなり，罪悪感もなく，隠す必要もなく，彼は家を出ていくのですね．わかりました．さあ，彼は出ていきました．それはかなり悪い状況ですね？　では，彼が出ていった後はどうなりますか？
C	I don't know how.	わかりません.
AB	Well, we're running out of time, so I don't like to put words in your mouth but I'd like you to think about this possible formulation, which is that you've made up in your own head that it'll be a very terrible thing if he left, if you split up, that somehow you yourself are not strong enough to function. But my own sense without having to take the detailed history is that you functioned very well before him. You were happy before you met him. You were able to do things and so on, so forth. It seems to me that same person who was able to function at the age of 22, and was able to be happy at the age of 22, can still be happy and function at the age of 32, and that somehow you're terribly underestimating your own ability to cope with the situation and to function and to be happy.	あなたに考えてもらいたいことを私が言葉にしてしまいたくはありませんが，そろそろ時間がなくなってきましたので，この可能性を考えてみてください．あなたは自分の頭の中で，ご主人が出ていってしまったらとても大変なことになる，もし別れることになったら生きていけない，と思っています． しかし，詳しい事情はわかりませんが私には，あなたは彼と出会う前にはちゃんと生きていたと思えます．彼と知り合う前には幸せだった．いろいろなことができた．22歳の時にちゃんとしていて幸せだった人は，32歳でも幸せにやっていけると私は思います．それなのにあなたは，状況に対処し，ちゃんと生きて幸せになるという自分の能力を，なぜかひどく過小評価しています．	②セッションの構造化 ④ソクラテス的問答

AB	Now, if you can now approach David with the idea that you are able to cope with the worst possible thing that can happen, if you can take that attitude that confident attitude that no matter what the problem is you're gonna find some mechanism for dealing with it, then you're gonna be able to get the information that you need. Now, there's a tendency to globalize now even if David is having an affair it does not mean that it has to be decisive in terms of splitting up the marriage. It maybe that there's a kind of vicious cycle that he's withdrawing love from you, you get depressed, he then transfers the love to somebody else and get involved in this whole vicious cycle. So the first thing to do is to try to find out what the problem is. And after you've found out the problem then you can start working on solutions. For instance, David could come in here and three of us could talk to have some marriage counseling. There are numerous solutions if you know what the problem is.	起こりうる最悪のことにも自分は対処できる，と考えてデビッドに向かえば，問題が何であれ自分には対処法が見い出せるという自信のある態度でいれば，あなたは求める情報を得ることができるでしょう．あなたはものごとをすべてに当てはめる傾向があります．デビッドが浮気していたとしても，それが離婚を決定的にするというわけではありません．彼があなたへの愛情を控えるようになり，あなたが落ちこみ，それが彼の愛情をほかの人に向かわせる，という悪循環があるのかもしれません． ですから最初にすべきことは，何が問題なのかを知ることです．問題がわかったら，解決を考えます．たとえば，ご主人にもここへ来てもらっていっしょに話し合い，結婚カウンセリングを受けることもできます．何が問題なのかがわかれば，解決法はたくさんあります．	①問題解決モード
C	That makes sense. I guess I've been doing an awful lot of stuff in my head but not even knowing what's really going on.	それならわかります．何がどうなっているのかさえわからないまま，私は頭の中でものすごくたくさんのことを考えていたのですね．	
AB	Right. You've not really been problem-oriented. You've been catastrophe-oriented.	そうです．あなたは問題に向かわず，破局に向いていたのです．	①破局化モードと問題解決モード
C	You're right.	そうですね．	

36分

36分が経過し，残り10分ほどとなったので，まとめに入る．

AB	OK. Now, our time is running out so I'd like to just make sure that we understand each other. Could you just kind of play back to me what I... what you feel has been the main point of today's talk?	時間がないので，お互いに理解できていることを確かめましょう．今日の話し合いの中で重要だと感じたことをもう一度話してもらえますか？	②セッションの構造化：まとめ
C	Well, repeat what I said that I've been making things really terrible in my mind without even knowing what to say, so I don't really know what's going on at school with my son and I was making him bad, making me a bad mother, and I don't for all I know. As you said, it could be some kind of game and perhaps a lot of other kids and not just mine and I guess I've been blaming him without even giving him the benefit of knowing his side of the story. Same thing with my husband. I don't even know what's going on. I've just been turmoil all inside my head making it the worst possible thing. And blaming myself gets all muddled up in that. Then I even forgot where I used to be.	繰り返すと，私は何もわかっていないのに心の中でものごとをひどくしてしまってきたということです．だから私は息子が学校で実はどうなのか知らないのに悪い子に，自分を悪い母親にしていました．言われたように，何かの遊びかもしれないし，あの子だけじゃなくてほかの子たちもそういうことをするかもしれないのに，私は彼の話を聞きもせずに彼を責めていました． 夫のことも同じです．どうなっているのか，実は私は知りません．私は頭の中が混乱し，最悪のことを考え，自分を責めていました．そして昔はどうだったかさえ忘れていました．	

Aaron T. Beck 2 『家族の問題─初回面接』

AB	Yeah. Well, that's really a very good capsule summary of what went on. Now, there are a couple of things that you might be able to do in addition to what we just talked about that could help out. But you don't have to do this. This is something purely optional. We've already agreed that you're gonna do what you can in order to get the true facts regarding David, regarding your son and if you're up to it then you'll do it, if you're not when you come in the next time we'll talk about it some more. But what I'd like to get at are the thoughts that you have in your self statements that tear you down. I wonder if it'd be asking you too much, if you could just write down the negative thoughts that you get. And write them down with the idea that you bring them in next time and we go over them and see whether they're valid or not.	はい．すばらしいまとめですね．話し合ったことに加え，役に立つことであなたにできることがまだいくつかあります．やらなくても構いませんよ．あくまでも任意ですから．私たちが同意したのは，デビッドについても息子さんについても，事実を知るためにできることがあればする，ということと，それについて次回また話し合うということですね． しかし私は，あなたを傷つけている，あなた自身の言葉の中にあるあなたの考えを知りたいと思います．思いついた否定的な考えを書き留めてもらいたいのですが，できますか？書き留めて，次回持ってきてもらえれば，それらが根拠のあることかどうか，いっしょに話し合いましょう．	②セッションの構造化：宿題の設定 ⑧-o 書き留める
C	OK.	はい．	
AB	'Cause as you could see today a lot of the thoughts that you had do not really seem to be accurate. And maybe most of these negative thoughts aren't accurate and it so you should feel better if you can correct them.	今日おわかりのように，あなたの考えの多くは，実は正確ではないように思えるからです．そういう否定的な考えのほとんどは正確ではなく，間違っているところを正すことができれば，あなたはもっと楽になるはずです．	⑧-a 自動思考の同定
C	OK.	はい．	
AB	All right. Now just before we leave I want to make sure, was there anything that I said today or anything that happened today that rubbed you the wrong way?	いいでしょう．ではセッションを終える前に確認させてください．今日私が言ったこと，ここで起こったことで，あなたが嫌だったことはありますか？	②セッションの構造化：患者からのフィードバック

C	No.	いいえ.
AB	Was there anything about my manner that bothered you?	私の態度で，気に入らなかったところはありましたか？
C	I just don't like men who wear a bow tie.	蝶ネクタイの男性は好きじゃないけど.
AB	Well, that's a cross you'll have to bear.	えーと，それは我慢していただかないと.
C	No, you were fine.	大丈夫です.
AB	It's better that we're able to get a laugh out of you. It's always a good sign. There's a little man outside there with a movie camera and he's photographing people. Someday he's gonna try to find somebody who look worse after they've been practicing. All right.	こうして笑うことができるのはいいことです．いい兆候です．さて，外ではカメラを持って待っている人がいます．セッションが終わった後の表情が悪くなっている人を探していますからね.
AB	Well, then why don't we plan to meet again the same time next Wednesday? Is that all right?	では，次回は来週の水曜日，同じ時間でいかがでしょう？　いいですか？
C	OK.	はい.

Aaron T. Beck 2 『家族の問題―初回面接』

付録

1. 認知療法尺度
Cognitive Therapy Rating Scale（CTRS）
2. 認知行動療法についてよくある質問

認知療法尺度

Cognitive Therapy Rating Scale(CTRS)

　Beck らは認知療法のトレーニングにおいても，臨床研究においても，水準以上の認知療法が行われているかどうかを評価するのに CTRS を 1980 年代からずっと使用している．例えば，Beck Institute で行われるトレーニングコースを成功裏に終了するためには，3 つのセッションでこの CTRS の合格点(66 点中 40 点以上)に達しなくてはならない．CTRS に従って自分のセッションを評価することはなかなか難しいが，項目を見ると，有効な認知療法には何が重要かが明らかになるので，認知療法の習得の途上で CTRS の細目を見てみることは非常に有用なことであろう．実は，本解説で挙げた認知行動療法の大原則もこの CTRS に上手にカバーされている．『認知行動療法トレーニングブック』(大野裕訳, 医学書院, 2007)から許可を得て転載する．

(Young JE, Beck AT: Cognitive Therapy Scale. Philadelphia, University of Pennsylvania, 1980.)

認知療法尺度

治療者名：＿＿＿＿＿＿＿＿＿＿＿　　患者名：＿＿＿＿＿＿＿＿＿＿＿
セッション日：＿＿＿＿＿＿＿　　セッション番号：＿＿＿＿＿＿

実施方法：パフォーマンスを0～6の尺度で評価し，項目番号横の線上に評点を記録する．定義説明は尺度の偶数ポイントについて提供されている．評定が2つの説明文の中間にあたると考えられる場合は，その中間の奇数(1，3，5)を選択する．

　ある項目の説明文が評価対象のセッションには該当しないと考えられる場合は，説明文を無視し，以下の一般的尺度を使用して構わない：

0	1	2	3	4	5	6
劣悪	不十分	並み	妥当	よい	非常によい	素晴らしい

パートⅠ．基本的な治療スキル

____**1．アジェンダ**

0　治療者はアジェンダを設定しなかった．

2　治療者はアジェンダを設定したが，そのアジェンダは不明確または不完全であった．

4　治療者は患者とともに，標的となる具体的な問題(例：職場での不安，結婚生活への不満)を含む，双方にとって満足のいくアジェンダを設定した．

6　治療者は患者とともに，標的となる問題に関し，使用可能な時間に合った適切なアジェンダを設定した．その後優先順位を決定し，アジェンダに沿って進行した．

____2. フィードバック

0 治療者は,セッションに対する患者の理解度や反応を判断するためのフィードバックを求めなかった.

2 治療者は患者から若干のフィードバックを引き出したものの,セッションにおける治療者の議論の筋道を患者が理解していることを確認する,または患者がセッションに満足しているかを確かめるのに十分な質問を行わなかった.

4 治療者はセッション中終始,患者が治療者の議論の筋道を理解していることを確認し,患者のセッションに対する反応を判断するのに十分な質問を行った.治療者はフィードバックに基づき,必要に応じて自分の行動を修正した.

6 治療者はセッション中終始,言語的および非言語的フィードバックを引き出すことにきわめて長けていた(例:セッションに対する反応を聞き出した,定期的に患者の理解度をチェックした,セッションの終わりに主要点をまとめる手助けをした).

____3. 理解力

0 治療者は,患者がはっきりと口に出して言ったことを理解できないことが度々あり,そのため常に要点をはずしていた.患者に共感するスキルが不十分である.

2 治療者は,たいてい患者がはっきりと口に出して言ったことを繰り返したり言い換えたりすることができたが,より微妙な意思表示には対応できないことが度々あった.聴く能力や共感する能力が限定的である.

4 治療者は,患者がはっきりと口に出して言ったことや,より微妙なとらえにくい表現に反映された患者の「内的現実」を概ねとらえていたと考えられる.聴く能力や共感する能力が十分に

ある．

6 治療者は患者の「内的現実」を完全に理解できていたと考えられ，またこの知識を適切な言語的および非言語的反応によって患者へ伝達することに長けていた(例：治療者の返答の調子は，患者の「メッセージ」に対する同情的理解を伝えるものであった)．聴く能力や共感する能力がきわめて優れている．

＿＿＿4．対人能力

0 治療者は対人スキルに乏しく，反友好的，侮辱的など患者にとって有害な態度がみられた．

2 治療者は有害ではないが，対人能力に重大な問題があった．ときに，治療者は不必要に性急，冷淡，不誠実にみえることがあり，または信頼感やコンピテンシーを十分に示すことができていなかった．

4 治療者は十分なレベルの思いやり，気遣い，信頼感，誠実さおよびプロフェッショナリズムを示した．対人能力に特に問題はない．

6 治療者は，この特定の患者に対するこのセッションに最適なレベルの思いやり，気遣い，信頼感，誠実さおよびプロフェッショナリズムを示した．

＿＿＿5．協同作業

0 治療者は患者と協同関係を築く努力を行わなかった．

2 治療者は患者との協同作業を試みたが，患者が重要と考えている問題の特定や信頼関係の構築が十分にできなかった．

4 治療者は，患者と協同作業を行い，患者・治療者の双方が重要と考える問題に焦点を当て，信頼関係を築くことができた．

6 素晴らしい協同作業ができたと考えられる：治療者は，治療者と患者が一つのチームとして機能できるよう，セッション中患者が積極的な役割を担うことをできるだけ促した（例：選択肢の提示）．

____6．ペース調整および時間の有効使用

0 治療者は治療時間の構成・調整を全く試みなかった．セッションは目的のない漠然としたものに感じられた．

2 セッションにある程度の方向性はあったが，セッションの構成や時間配分に重大な問題があった（例：構成が不十分，時間配分に柔軟性がない，ペースが遅すぎる，または速すぎる）．

4 治療者はそれなりに時間を有効に使用することができた．治療者は話の流れや速さに対して適度な統制力を維持していた．

6 治療者は，核心からはずれた非生産的な話をうまく制限し，セッションの進行を患者に適した速さに調整することによって，時間を有効に使用した．

パートⅡ．概念化，方略および技術

____7．誘導による発見

0 治療者は主に議論や説得，または「講義」を行っていた．治療者は患者を尋問している，患者を防衛的にする，または自分の視点を患者に押し付けようとしているように見受けられた．

2 治療者は誘導による発見ではなく説得や議論に頼りすぎていた．しかし，治療者の姿勢は十分に支援的であり，患者は攻撃されたと感じたり防衛的になる必要を感じたりはしなかったと考えられる．

4 治療者は，全体的に議論ではなく誘導による発見（例：根拠の

検証，別の解釈の検討，長所と短所の比較評価）を通して，患者が新しい観点を見出す手助けを行った．質問法を適切に活用した．
6 治療者はセッション中，誘導による発見の手法を用いて問題を追求し，患者が自分自身で結論を出す手助けをすることにきわめて長けていた．巧みな質問とそのほかの介入法とのバランスが非常によくとれていた．

____8．重要な認知または行動への集中

0 治療者は，具体的な思考，思い込み，イメージ，意味，または行動を聞き出す努力を行わなかった．
2 治療者は認知または行動を聞き出すために適切な技法を用いた．しかし，焦点を見つけることに支障があった，あるいは患者の主要問題とは関連のない見当違いの認知や行動に焦点を当てていた．
4 治療者は，標的となる問題に関連した具体的な認知または行動に焦点を当てた．しかし，より前進につながる可能性の高い中心的な認知や行動に焦点を当てることも可能だった．
6 治療者は，問題領域に最も関連が深く，前進につながる可能性がきわめて高い，重要な思考，思い込み，行動などへ巧みに焦点を当てていた．

____9．変更へ向けた方略

（注：この項目については，方略がいかに効果的に実施されたか，または変更が実現できたか否かではなく，治療者の変更へ向けた方略の質に焦点を当てて評価すること．）
0 治療者は認知行動的技法を選択しなかった．

2 治療者は認知行動的技法を選択したが，変更を成し遂げるための全体的な戦略は漠然としていた，または患者を手助けする方法としてあまり見込みがなさそうであった．
4 治療者には，全体的に変更に向けた首尾一貫した方略があると見受けられ，その方略にはある程度の見込みがあり，認知行動的技法が取り入れられていた．
6 治療者は，変更に向けて非常に見込みがあると考えられる首尾一貫した方略にしたがって治療を進行し，最も適した認知行動的技法を取り入れていた．

____10．認知行動的技法の実施
（注：この項目については，標的となる問題に対して技法がいかに適切か，または変更が実現できたか否かではなく，技法の実施技術に焦点を当てて評価すること．）
0 治療者は認知行動的技法を一つも使用しなかった．
2 治療者は認知行動的技法を使用したが，その適用方法に重大な不備があった．
4 治療者は，認知行動的技法をある程度のスキルをもって使用した．
6 治療者は，巧みかつ機知に富んだやり方で認知行動的技法を使用した．

____11．ホームワーク
0 治療者は認知療法に関連したホームワークを治療に組み入れようとしなかった．
2 治療者にはホームワークの組み入れに重大な問題があった（例：前回のホームワークの見直しを行わなかった，ホームワークに

ついて詳細を十分に説明しなかった，不適切なホームワークを課した）．
4 治療者は前回のホームワークを見直し，基本的にセッションで取り扱った事項に関連した「標準的な」認知療法のホームワークを出した．またホームワークについて十分に詳細を説明した．
6 治療者は前回のホームワークを見直し，次の1週間用に認知療法を用いたホームワークを慎重に課した．その課題は，患者が新しい観点を受け入れ，仮説を検証し，セッション中に話し合った新しい行動を試すことなどの手助けとなるよう，患者に合わせて設定したものと考えられる．

____**合計点**

認知行動療法についてよくある質問

Q.
認知行動療法とはどのような治療法でしょうか

　人間は状況,状況に応じて,反応をします．人間の反応は,気持ち,体,考え,行動の4つの側面に分けることができます．特定の状況に応じて,特定の気持ちを抱き,体が特定の反応を起こし,ある考えを持ち,ある行動を起こすわけです．これらの4つの側面は互いが互いに影響を及ぼし合って,状況に対する反応を形成しています．

　あなたは認知行動療法を受けたいとお考えですから,ある悩ましい気持ちもしくは体の反応を示しがちでいらっしゃるのでしょう．例えば,ついつい不安になって,心臓がどきどきしやすい．あるいは,しばしば憂うつになって,体が重いし食欲もない,など．しかし,残念なことに,どのような感情を抱き,どのような体の反応が起こるかは,人間が自分で意識的に変えることはできません．

　しかし,幸いなことに,どのように考え,どのように行動するかは,ある程度,人間の意識の支配下にあります．そして,これら4つの側面は互いに密接に影響し合っていますから,考え(認知)や行動を変えるこ

とによって，感情や身体反応を変えてゆくことができます．これが認知行動療法です．

Q.
認知行動療法を受ける前に何を準備しておくとよいでしょうか

　重要な第一歩は，目標を立てることです．「この治療を終えた段階で，何ができるようになっていたいか」「何ができるようになれば，あなたは病気を克服したと言えるか」を考えてください．職場で，家庭で，友人関係で，夫婦関係で，家族関係で，あるいは趣味や余暇の領域で，何ができるようになりたいか，できるだけ具体的に考えてください．また，どのような症状がつらいか，どのような症状をなくす，あるいは減らしたいかをできるだけ具体的に考えてください．治療者はあなたと一緒にこれらの目標を検討し，あなた自身で働きかけることができるであろう目標や，治療の課題として取り組むとよいであろう目標が何になるかをあなた自身が判断されるお手伝いをします．

Q.
認知行動療法のセッションでは何をしますか

　認知行動療法では，1回1回の治療時間を**セッション**と呼びます．まずこれを覚えてください．

　認知行動療法ではしばしばセッションが始まる前に，質問用紙などへの記入をしていただきます．これはあなたの状態や，治療の進展の具合をあなたと治療者がより客観的にかつ詳しく知るために重要な情報を提供してくれます．

　セッションの最初に，治療者はこれらの質問用紙も参考にしながら，

前回から今日までのおおよその状態をお聞きします．前回のセッションで何が重要だったか何が難しかったか，家ではどの宿題ができてどの宿題が難しかったか，も確認します．そして，今日のセッションであなたが主に何を検討したいか，どの問題を話し合いたいかをお聞きします．このようにその日のセッションで主に扱う話題を**アジェンダ**といいます．これも聞き慣れない言葉ですね．話題とかテーマという意味です．このようにして，あなたは治療者と一緒にその日のアジェンダを決めます．

アジェンダはあなたが決めるのですよと言われて，あせらなくてもけっこうです．治療の最初の間は治療者のほうから提案させていただくことが多いでしょう．しかし，治療が進み，何をするのが自分のためになるかがわかるにつれて，あなたのほうでアジェンダを持ちだすようにされるとよいでしょう．

セッションの中心は，アジェンダに沿って，あなたにとって大切な課題を検討してゆくことです．その課題を解決するには，どのような考え方をして，どのような行動をすればよさそうか，一緒に検討してゆきます．新しい考え方，新しい行動の仕方をするためのスキルの習得に重点が置かれます．認知行動療法で扱うスキルはいろいろとあります．あなたの抱えておられる問題と病気の種類に応じて，治療者から順次提案してゆきますので，一緒に学んでゆきましょう．

セッションの最後には必ずまとめの時間をお取りします．まずそのセッションで何を発見したか，何を学んだか，あるいは何が難しかったか，何が役に立ちそうか，何か不快なことはなかったかなどのフィードバックをお願いします．次に，セッション中に学んだ新しいスキルを身につけるために，次回のセッションまでにどんな練習をすると良いかを一緒に考えます．これを宿題と言います．ちょっと嫌な言葉ですね．「課題」「家庭学習」「セルフヘルプ練習」などと呼ぶ人もいます．

このように認知行動療法の治療では，患者さん自身も治療者も積極的

に参加することが大切です．

Q.
認知行動療法はどれくらい続きますか

　セッションの回数は患者さんと治療者の話し合いで決めます．実際に治療セッションそのものを開始する前に，あなたが抱えていらっしゃる問題や症状について評価をしておりますので，治療者のほうはおおよその回数の目安を持っています．10回から20回の間で，患者さんのニーズと治療の進展具合で決めてゆくのが通常です．治療者との話し合い次第で，10回未満で終える人もいますし，慢性の問題に取り組むために20回以上を必要とする方もあります．

　認知行動療法による治療の全体の流れは，原則，以下のようになります．

1. 診断と評価
2. 問題の同定
3. 認知行動療法における目標の設定
4. 具体的な手段・技法の選択
5. 具体的な手段・技法の実践
6. 効果の検証
7. 4-5-6の反復
8. 再発予防の計画，終結
9. フォローアップ

　治療が進展すると，頻度を週に1回から，2週間に1回，さらには月に1回というように，間隔をあけることもよいでしょう．このようにして，あなた自身で，新しく学んだ考え方や行動の仕方のスキルを実践できる自信を付けていってください．

Q.
お薬はどうしたらいいでしょうか

　認知行動療法に薬物を併用した方がよいかどうかは，病気が何であるか，またどのタイプの薬であるかによって，変わってきます．医師とよく相談しましょう．

Q.
治療効果を最大にするには私は何をしたらよいでしょうか

　第一は，セッションの最後に治療者と一緒に設定した宿題に積極的に取り組むことです．「取り組む」とは実施するということとまったく同じではありません．実施できればそれに超したことはありませんが，実施できなかったとしても，それはそれで非常に重要な情報です．やろうとしたらどうなったか，何が難しかったかを治療者に教えてください．宿題にどのくらい熱心に取り組めるかが治療の効果を決める最大の要因であることを研究は示しています．

　第二は，第一を含むと言えますが，セッションを日常生活へ持ち込むことです．そのためにはセッションのまとめをノートに取るとよいでしょう．あるいはセッションを録音して家でもう一度聞くという方もいます．

　第三は，これまた第一とも絡んできますが，次のセッションに対してよく準備をすることです．次のセッションでは何を相談したいか，宿題のどういう点をもう一度治療者と一緒に検討したいかを考えておきましょう．また前回のセッションでわかりにくかったところ，もう一度教えて欲しい点はないかなどを「ふりかえりシート」に記入しながら反省することも，よいでしょう．

　第四は，認知行動療法のマニュアルや本を読むことです．どのようなマニュアルや本があなたの問題に役立ちそうかは治療者におたずねください．

終わりに

認知療法の2人の大家の初回セッションを題材に，認知行動療法の大原則を勉強してきました．認知行動療法を習得するには詳しい学習と実習が必要でしょうが，それらを貫く「精神」に触れていただければ，日本語版 監修・解説者として本望です．

最後に，私がBeck Instituteの精神科レジデンシー指導者用プログラムでスーパービジョンを受けていた時に，スーパーバイザーのCory F. Newman博士が教えてくれた一言で本書を締めくくりたいと思います．「認知療法のセッションにおける認知行動療法技法は，空気と酸素の関係です．認知行動療法セッションのすべてが認知行動療法なわけではないのです」．そして，特に患者が困難な問題を呈した時，自分のスタイルを持っていることが重要です，と続きます．
「フランス人も，フランス料理の教科書的マナー通りに食事しているわけではない．しかし，原則を知って外しているのと，原則を知らずに外れているとは，本質的に違う」というたとえ話を聞いたことがあります．あくまでも認知行動療法の大原則に則りながら，各臨床家が自分のスタイルを生かしていかれることを期待しています．

なお，認知療法家の認証を行っている，国際的な非営利団体のAcademy of Cognitive Therapyという団体があります（http://www.academyofct.org）．Aaron T. Beckを名誉会長とし，Judith Beckは前会長です．ここで認証を受けるには，メンタルヘルス関連の分野で修士または博士または同等の資格を持っていること，臨床資格を

持っていること，認知療法のトレーニングを40時間以上受けていること(大学院での講義，学会，ワークショップなどを含む．うち10時間以上はスーパービジョンを受けていることが望ましい)，認知モデルに従って10人以上の患者を治療していることなどの要件を満たしている上に，実際の症例のフォーミュレーションと，実際のセッションの録音を提出して，審査を受けなくてはなりません．私も録音ファイルを提出し，その逐語英訳を添えて審査してもらいました．その際の審査基準の1つが，本書付録に収載した認知療法尺度です．客観的基準で臨床力のある認知療法家を認証している世界で唯一の機関ですので，このDVDに触発された読者諸兄姉の中から，ここにチャレンジされる方が出てくれば，望外の幸せです．

古川壽亮

索引

欧文

- activity monitoring 40
- assertion training 41
- automatic thought 16
- Beck Depression Inventory 9
- behavioral activation 40
- behavioral experiment 39
- behavioral terms 44
- catastrophizing mode 6
- cognitive-behavioral case formulation 16
- cognitive-behavioral conceptualization 16
- cognitive restructuring 37
- Cognitive Therapy Rating Scale
  (CTRS) 176
- collaborative empiricism 22
- compensatory behavior 18
- conditional belief 18
- core belief 18
- graded task assignment 43
- guided discovery 23
- homework 31
- hot cognition 33
- imagery rescripting 38
- merits - demerits analysis 39
- mood check 9
- open question 23
- problem-solving mode 6
- problem-solving technique 41
- psychoeducation 28
- role play 43
- schema work 38
- Socratic questioning 22
- structuring of session 9
- structuring of treatment 14
- subjective units of distress (SUD) 45

あ

- アサーション訓練 41
- アジェンダ 188
  - ── の設定 10

い・お

- イメージ書き換え（イメージ再構成）.... 38
- 教える代わりの質問 25

か・き

- カードの利用 45
- 課題 31
- 活動モニタリング 40
- 患者の固有の言い回し 23
- 協力的実証主義 22

こ

- 構造化
  - ──, セッションの 9
  - ──, 治療全体の 14
- 行動活性化 40
- 行動実験 38
- 行動用語 44
- 困りごとリスト 14

し

- 自記式調査票 9
- 自己主張訓練 41
- 疾病そのものの心理教育 28
- 質問
  - ──, 教える代わりの 25
  - ──, 適度に制約された 23
- 質問による発見 22

自動思考 16
　―― の同定 35
　―― への反論 37
宿題 **31**, 188
　―― の復習 10
症状チェック 9
条件信念 18
心理教育 14, **28**
　――, 疾病についての 28
　――, 認知行動療法についての 29

す
数量化 45
スキーマ 19, 38

せ
セッション 187
　―― の回数 189
　―― の構造化 9
　―― のまとめ **12**, 188

そ
相対化 45
ソクラテス的問答 22

た
代償行動 18
段階的課題設定 43

ち
中核信念 18
　―― の修正 38
治療全体の構造化 14
治療全体のまとめ 15
治療同盟 22

て
適度に制約された質問 23

な・に・の
なげき破局化モード 6
認知行動的概念化 16
認知行動モデル 14, **15**
　―― による症例の
　　フォーミュレーション 15
認知行動療法 3
　―― における治療者患者関係 .. 22
　―― についての心理教育 29
　―― についてよくある質問 186
認知再構成 7, **37**
認知的概念図 20
認知療法 3
認知療法尺度 178
ノートの利用 45

は
破局化モード 6
橋渡し 9
橋渡しワークシート 10
発見的質問 23

ひ・ふ・へ
開かれた質問 23
フィードバック **12**, 188
ベック抑うつ質問票 9

ほ
ホームワーク 31
ホットな認知 33

ま
まとめ
——, セッションの **12**, 188
——, 治療全体の 15

め
命名 45
メリット・デメリット分析 39

も
問題解決技法 6, **41**
問題解決モード 6
問題リスト 14

ろ
ロールプレイ 43